THE BURLESQUE NAPOLEON:

BEING THE STORY OF THE LIFE AND
THE KINGSHIP OF JEROME NAPOLEON
BONAPARTE, YOUNGEST BROTHER OF
NAPOLEON THE GREAT

BY PHILIP W.
SERGEANT, B.A.
AUTHOR OF "THE COURT-
SHIPS OF CATHERINE THE
GREAT"

FULLY ILLUSTRATED

T. WERNER LAURIE
CLIFFORD'S INN, LONDON

1905

Jerome Napoleon

CONTENTS

		PAGE
Preface	. . . .	ix
Chapter I.	From Ajaccio to Paris . . .	3
Chapter II.	Jerome at Sea	31
Chapter III.	The Bonaparte-Patterson Marriage	55
Chapter IV.	Napoleon 'Conquers . . .	83
Chapter V.	The Way to a Throne . . .	115
Chapter VI.	Jerome Napoleon, King of Westphalia	143
Chapter VII.	The Art of Bankruptcy . .	175
Chapter VIII.	The King in Court and Camp .	215
Chapter IX.	Palace Life at Cassel . . .	249
Chapter X.	The Volcano's Edge . . .	281
Chapter XI.	The End of Westphalia . .	311
Chapter XII.	1814 and Waterloo . . .	333
Chapter XIII.	Exile, Restoration, and Death .	355
Index .	. . . .	381

LIST OF ILLUSTRATIONS

	PAGE
JEROME NAPOLEON BONAPARTE	*Frontispiece*
GENERAL LECLERC	36
ELIZABETH PATTERSON BONAPARTE. From unfinished Painting by GILBERT STUART	55
THE MARRIAGE OF JEROME BONAPARTE AND CATHERINE OF WÜRTEMBERG. In Versailles Museum	143
JEROME BONAPARTE IN MIDDLE AGE	333
PRINCE JEROME, PRINCE NAPOLEON. From Photographs	355

PREFACE

ALTHOUGH the study of a libertine's career could never in itself be particularly edifying, such a study, perhaps, need not be dismissed as entirely valueless when the libertine has played a distinct part, if a small one, in an important period of the world's history. This may be said to have been the case with Jerome Bonaparte. His chief claim to notoriety, indeed, lies in the fact that, among all princely followers of Don Juan, he distinguished himself by the pertinacity of his gallantry, from the days of his precocious exploits as a schoolboy of thirteen to those of the courtly, almost dignified, dissoluteness of an Imperial Prince of seventy. But, apart from being a monumental rake, Jerome had a career of wonderful variety and interest. If he was so entirely light in character as he seemed to be it was with the lightness of a cork in a Niagara of waters. Amid the tremendous movements of the Napoleonic period in Europe, Jerome was always to be found floating gaily on the top. When the terrific downfall of 1815 appeared to swallow up for ever all connected with the name

Preface

of Bonaparte, then, indeed, Jerome seemed to go under—only to emerge again, however, in the time of the Second Empire, volatile as before, rising always to the highest point attainable. No man, probably, ever won his way to honours as airily. Yet to the brother who so early forced him up to the ranks of Admiral, General, Prince, and King, Jerome was as serious an obstacle as any of his family. One of those who contribute noteworthy details to the biography of Jerome, de Norvins, remarks that "one thing was wanting to the good fortune of Napoleon—to have been alone in the Bonaparte family as he was in the human family." Fate having given him, on the contrary, a large circle of brothers and sisters, Napoleon endeavoured to mould them. But never was a family less easy to mould. As another writer of the period, the Chancelier Pasquier, says, the Bonapartes must be admitted to have been of uncommon stamp. "Their qualities and defects, their virtues and vices, had no ordinary proportions. What above all distinguished them was obstinacy of will, inflexibility of resolution." Jerome possessed this inflexibility in a high degree, perhaps more than any except Lucien. This may seem a strange statement to make about the man who

Preface

so basely deserted Elizabeth Patterson. But the pressure then brought to bear upon him was enormous; and, miserable as was his failure in honour, it was at least intelligible. For the most part, it is the persistence of his pursuit of the aims which he proposed to himself that renders the youngest of the Bonaparte brothers interesting. His dealings with Napoleon, as revealed in their correspondence, and in the abundant documents of the time, furnish a study of the conflict of two wills, one of a great man, the other of a little man, in which conflict the lesser knew how to resist and to gain his ends, in spite of all the power of the greater.

The circumstances of French history in the nineteenth century secured that Jerome Bonaparte should have a wondrous diversity of biographers, especially of French biographers. A remarkable point was that impartial writers were almost entirely lacking. A wide choice for the reader lay between the adulation, on the one hand, of Baron du Casse, when he edited Jerome's " Memoirs and Correspondence," under the Second Empire, or of M. Martinet, who dedicated his book to the ex-King's daughter; and, on the other hand, the malice of anti-Bonapartist writers from the time of the

Preface

"Témoin Oculaire," who revealed, soon after Waterloo, the secret history of Westphalia to that of M. Joseph Turquan, the modern author of "Le Roi Jérôme." Baron du Casse, in his later work, "Les Rois Frères de Napoléon Ier," no longer trammelled by dynastic considerations, presented some twenty years ago a more dispassionate picture, and proved its accuracy by the publication for the first time of the most valuable and interesting documents of Napoleon's agents in Westphalia. Of the memoirists who were actually contemporary with Jerome, the Duchess of Abrantès and M. J. de Norvins appear to give us the most lifelike glimpses of the boy and the young man. In their accounts is neither adulation nor bitterness. In such an indifferent spirit the life of Jerome must be considered. Certainly there is no room for eulogy of one who seemed so consistently to avoid acts which might merit praise. But to add to the list of his vices those which in reality he had not is to deprive the portrait of all significance. The present writer has attempted only to paint Jerome as he was, undisguised by the gilding touch of Bonapartists or by the blackening brush of Bourbon or Republican partisans. There is no excessive dwelling on

Preface

his intrigues, it is hoped; but, of course, without attention to them it would be impossible to represent him. His follies went most of the way to making the man. It was Jerome the rake, Jerome the spendthrift, Jerome the designer of Court costumes, Jerome the inventor of baths of Bordeaux (or of rum, one lady of the period avers), who ruled Westphalia for his brother. Jerome the wise statesman we must dismiss as the agreeable fiction of M. Martinet.

Such must be the writer's excuse for confining himself nearly to the frivolous side of Westphalian history. The more serious, the political side, belongs rather to the story of Napoleon, the maker of Westphalia, than to that of Jerome, its mal-administrator. Moreover, the political history has been dealt with admirably, only two years ago, by Mr. H. A. L. Fisher in his "Studies in Napoleonic Statesmanship: Germany." That work, with its researches into the German contemporary writings, has been consulted on several points by the author of the following pages. With the French authorities on Jerome's life he may claim, perhaps, a fair acquaintance. Jerome's character and adventures have interested his countrymen. Possibly there is enough to interest others also in the

Preface

curious doubly meteoric career, from street urchin to King, and again from ruined exile to Prince Imperial and Marshal of France, of one whom his celebrated brother once summed up as a *polisson*, but who in his own eyes was every inch a King.

PHILIP WALSINGHAM SERGEANT.

FROM AJACCIO
TO PARIS

CHAPTER I

FROM AJACCIO TO PARIS

BORN in the family house of the Bonapartes, in what is now the Place Letizia, Ajaccio, on the 15th November 1784, Jerome[1] was the youngest of the eight children surviving out of thirteen borne to Charles Bonaparte (or rather Carlo Maria di Buonaparte) by Maria Letizia Ramolino. At the time of the child's birth the father was in France, having gone to Montpellier to consult a doctor about the cancer of the stomach which killed him four months later. His eldest son, Joseph, was with him, while Napoleon had just left the school at Brienne for the military college at Paris. Jerome never saw his father, who died before he could return home, at the house of the Permons, close friends of the Bonapartes. There seems to have been no little resemblance between the characters of Charles and his youngest

[1] The name Jerome is of old standing in the Bonaparte family, for we find mention of a Jerome or Hieronimus de Buonaparte in the middle of the seventeenth century.

The Burlesque Napoleon

son, for the former's reputation was that of a vain and ostentatious man, prodigal with his money. His expenditure of 6000 livres, about double his annual income at the time, on a banquet to celebrate the passing of his final law examination, was an act akin to many of Jerome's. Of the mother's characteristics it is hard to find a single one in Jerome, though he remained far longer under her care than did any of his brothers. Next to Napoleon he was the object of her special love; perhaps because of the greater resemblance to his father.

The death of Charles Bonaparte left his family very poor. His estates in the interior of Corsica had long been mortgaged. Two houses remained to the widow—the one in Ajaccio, the other a country mansion, the Villa Milelli—but of money on which to keep these up there was little. The French Government allowed Madame Bonaparte a pension, just sufficient on which to bring up her young family, and with the aid of this she lived in very economical retirement. Her husband's uncle, Lucien Bonaparte, Archdeacon of Ajaccio, the spiritual adviser of the family, helped her with counsel on other matters also. Of the sons, Joseph had returned to Corsica with the news of his

From Ajaccio to Paris

father's end, and remained to study law; Lucien had followed Napoleon to France. The five younger children shared the home life of their mother. Exceedingly little is known of these early years of Jerome. The fragment of "Souvenirs," which Madame Bonaparte began to dictate in later life to Rosa Mellini, gives no information beyond the fact that in the large playroom of the Ajaccio house Jerome and the three children nearest to him in age amused themselves by "jumping about, and by drawing comic figures on the walls"; whereas Napoleon had shown a martial preference for a drum and wooden sword, and had painted nothing but soldiers. Of education they had but what their mother could give them herself, and that was little indeed. This most remarkable woman, to the end of her life, could not write readily, and, fluent in Italian, always found great difficulties in the French language. During the visits of Napoleon to Corsica on military leave she was glad to hand over to him the instruction of his juniors; and we are told[1] how the interior of the Bonaparte home resembled a school or a convent, where "prayer, sleep, meals,

[1] By Nasica, who says that the Bonaparte family was "the model of the town" ("Mémoires," chap. ii.).

The Burlesque Napoleon

study, amusements, and walks were all measured out." But Jerome was only a baby at the time of Napoleon's stay at Ajaccio in 1786; and even at the beginning of the long visit of 1789-1791, being barely five, he can hardly have had much share in the studies.

It was when Jerome was a little over five and a half that the change occurred in Corsica which was to have so great a significance for his family. On the 14th July 1790 Pascal Paoli landed once more on the island, having been recalled by the French to be the first Governor of Corsica, now declared an integral part of the French monarchy. At this time the Bonaparte household included regularly, beside the mother and the four youngest children —Louis, Pauline, Caroline, and Jerome—Joseph, now twenty-two years old, who in his inadequate way filled the place of father to the four; and Lucien, who had returned to Ajaccio after his education in France, and was already beginning to make a local name as a politician. Further, Napoleon in the September of the previous year had obtained a year's furlough on account of illness; so that only Eliza, who was at school at Saint-Cyr, was missing from the circle. If Jerome derived any benefit from his brother's

From Ajaccio to Paris

instruction it must have been at this period, when Napoleon overstayed his leave in Corsica by six months. Political matters, however, left the future leader of France less leisure than during 1786. The history of events in the island during these years has very frequently been told, and, as we are concerned only with Jerome, may be passed over rapidly here. The child can have seen very little of the circumstances which divided his family from the Paolists. He knew nothing outside his home probably, except through the coming and going of his brothers and sisters. Louis, the one of whom Jerome saw most during their boyhood, and towards whom he always retained much affection, was taken to France by Napoleon in the spring of 1791, to be educated at his expense. Both returned in the autumn of the same year. Again, in 1792, Napoleon had gone, to reappear bringing Eliza home for safety after the terrible events of September in France. Now it was that the breach between the Bonapartes and the party of Paoli became open; and the whole family was soon to feel the effects.

It is well known that the Bonapartes were ardent Corsican patriots previous to the Re-

The Burlesque Napoleon

volutionary era. Letizia Bonaparte, who might almost be said to have served with her husband in the Corsican struggles for independence, retained the genuine esteem of Paoli. Napoleon had been an indiscriminating admirer of his countryman. But a coldness grew between the young man and the old as the former became imbued with the new ideas of the period in France. This feeling communicated itself to such of his brothers as were of the age to think about politics, and after Napoleon's arrival in Ajaccio in 1792 there was no question of reconciliation. Paoli detested the Revolution, and determined to sever Corsica from France. Napoleon, on the contrary, had now almost sunk the Corsican in the Frenchman, and, though not a "Septembrist," had accepted the Revolution. Corsica could not hold them both for long. Napoleon joined Salicetti, another Corsican, who had been prominent in Paris, and who arrived in his native island early in 1793. Following Salicetti came a summons to Paoli to appear before the Convention. Not being ready to sacrifice his head, Paoli proclaimed a revolt, and was acclaimed president of the insurrectionary assembly at Corte and head of the patriotic forces. Napoleon, planning

From Ajaccio to Paris

to seize Ajaccio for France, narrowly escaped ruin, being actually imprisoned by the Paolists on his way to Bastia early in May, and only rescued by some friendly peasants. He returned to Ajaccio to find himself proscribed and the confiscation of the family property ordered. The sentence was not carried out at once. Friends of the family stood on guard outside the house, which Madame Bonaparte firmly refused to quit. Napoleon, Joseph, and Lucien left, in order not to imperil the remainder—the first to renew his plans against Ajaccio at Bastia, and the last to sail for France. Only the two youngest boys and the three girls stayed with their mother and her half-brother, the Abbé Fesch, the religious guardian of the family since the Archdeacon Lucien's death in 1792. For their own greater security it was decided to send the eight-year-old Jerome and Caroline, aged eleven, to their grandmother, Signora di Pietra-Santa. The others waited in Ajaccio, ready to fly at once. Thus it happened that Jerome was not present on the dramatic night of the 24th May, when Letizia Bonaparte, sleeping half dressed, awoke to find her bedroom full of armed mountaineers. They were friends, however, who had come to warn her that the

The Burlesque Napoleon

Paolists were at hand. In spite of great difficulty and hardship the fugitives made their way on foot to the Villa Milelli, watching, as they went, the flames of their home lighted by the infuriated Paolists; and, still guided by friends, all reached the coast. Here, by a curious and lucky coincidence, they found Napoleon also a fugitive on the shore, with a boat and a few friends, expecting to see, not his family, but a party of armed enemies. He had shared in the ill-success of the French. The failure of the Saint-Florent expedition, which reached Ajaccio on the 29th May to discover the whole town in revolt, decided the victory of the insurgents throughout the island. Only Bastia, Saint-Florent, and Calvi remained in French hands. To the last-named place Napoleon returned at the beginning of June, having sent his family thither before him. On the 11th he and Joseph embarked with the rest, except Lucien, who had reached France in May, and set sail for Toulon. The passage was accomplished in safety, in spite of there being a British fleet in the neighbourhood; and the history of the Bonapartes as a Corsican family came to an end.

The refugees had escaped destruction, but not

From Ajaccio to Paris

destitution. After brief stops at La Valette and Bandol, the mother, with Louis, Jerome, and the girls, settled down in Marseilles to a hard struggle with poverty. Napoleon said at Saint Helena that his mother had expected to find at Marseilles the welcome which her sacrifices merited, but barely found safety. As having lost everything in Corsica because of their attachment to the French cause, the fugitives met, of course, with sympathy of a kind. A shelter was found for them, first on the fourth floor of a poor house; then in a ruined *mairie*, monument of the Reign of Terror; and finally in a better house in the Rue du Faubourg de Rome. A pittance was allowed them by the Convention,[1] and this was supplemented by the kindness of a Corsican friend. Nor were the prospects of speedy relief bright. Napoleon, after vainly applying to be transferred to the army of the Rhine, rejoined his regiment in Provence. Joseph and Lucien were just able to maintain

[1] Mr W. M. Sloane ("Life of Napoleon Bonaparte") says that, with the allowance from the Convention, the Bonapartes were better off in Marseilles than in Corsica. It is, of course, known that their circumstances were very bad in Ajaccio; but the evidence of their contemporaries as to the extreme poverty of the family in the early days at Marseilles is incontestable.

The Burlesque Napoleon

themselves. For the others, their daily life was very simple. Madame Bonaparte is described as rising early every morning and apportioning the work of the day which her daughters were to do; while towards evening all sewed, and either Louis read aloud from a paper or a letter, or the mother related stories of Corsica and the War of Independence. Lastly, she said evening prayer in their midst. Jerome seems hardly accounted for in this scheme. He was but a listener or a spectator, or he played about the streets. If we are to believe some of the writers of the period, he was allowed to run completely wild—a statement which is, perhaps, borne out by that early development which made him consider himself a full man at fifteen. His mother's vigilance over him was certainly impaired by the excessive indulgence which she always showed towards him.

The rise of the Bonapartes from their uncomfortable circumstances at Marseilles was not so rapid as suggested by the fact that Napoleon made himself first famous at Toulon at the end of 1793, six months after he left Corsica. Nevertheless, the siege of Toulon marked a turning-point, if the turn was slow. Never were the devotion of his family to Napoleon

From Ajaccio to Paris

and their dependence on him more shown than when, in the September of 1793, he obtained, by the influence of Salicetti, the command of the artillery in the siege of Toulon. Madame Bonaparte, taking Louis, Jerome, and their sisters with her, actually went to the neighbourhood of the town to be near the soldier at this time of anxiety. It was at the inn where they had established themselves at Mionnac that the new Brigadier-General came in triumph to greet his mother; and she returned to Marseilles with the promise of better times in store. Joseph and Lucien benefited at once by their brother's success to get more lucrative appointments. Joseph, moreover, now a commissary-general, was enabled to do his family a good turn when he married Marie Clary, daughter of a rich Marseilles merchant, who gave two queens to Europe—the other marrying Bernadotte, and so being the ancestress of the Swedish royal line.

The family was at last well housed, but there was no great abundance of money. General de Ricard in his memoirs speaks of them living very simply, of the austere, almost hard, appearance of Madame Bonaparte, and of her great desire to marry her daughters as well

The Burlesque Napoleon

as Joseph had married. Ricard, whose aunt had married a brother of Joseph Bonaparte's wife, was on intimate terms with the Bonaparte children, being two or three years younger than Jerome. He has told one story of his playmate which deserves quotation; it is the most creditable to Jerome of the few tales about his childhood. At this time everyone was supposed to wear the tricolour cockade. Jerome, Ricard, and the latter's two cousins were out in the streets of Marseilles together when a sentry, catching sight of them, said: "Little citizens, why aren't you showing cockades?" "Because we wear them in our hearts," Jerome replied.

Before the fortunes of Napoleon's family were definitely assured they were still doomed to pass through a painful period. Part of Napoleon's success hitherto had been due to his connection with the Robespierres and their party. Now, in *thermidor an II* (July 1794) the Robespierres fell, and Napoleon nearly followed them to the scaffold. Only with difficulty, and perhaps by the aid of Salicetti again, was he released from imprisonment and restored to his rank of general in August. After a term as inspector of the Mediterranean coast artillery, and a share in an unsuccessful descent on Corsica, he had been

From Ajaccio to Paris

transferred to the army in the Vendée, a prospect which he loathed. In the May of 1795, taking his fortunes in his own hand, he started for Paris, with Louis in his charge, and in the capital met the events which finally decided that he was to mount and not to fall.

The day of the *13 vendèmiaire*, so important to his brother, decided also for Jerome the question whether he should have a high career or not; for when Napoleon had established himself in Paris, a man of mark at last, he sent for the spoilt child of the family, already eleven years old, that he might begin to receive some training. The school which he had selected for him was the Collége Irlandais at Saint-Germain-en-Laye, outside Paris. This had just been started by an Irishman, Patrick MacDermot, tutor to Henri, son of the celebrated Madame Campan, whose pride it was afterwards that she had been the teacher of so many queens and princesses. MacDermot's school was housed in an old Ursuline convent, close by the Institution National de Saint-Germain, as Madame Campan called her own school in the Hôtel de Rohan. Napoleon's primary reason for sending Jerome to the Collége Irlandais was, no doubt, to be found in his infatuation for the widow,

The Burlesque Napoleon

Josephine Beauharnais, whom he was already courting rather more than warmly, and whom he married in the following March. In September 1795, Josephine's son Eugène, then fourteen, had been sent to MacDermot, while Hortense had been entrusted to Madame Campan's care. To Saint-Germain now Jerome followed Eugène. About this same time Caroline went to Madame Campan, whither a little later Pauline was also sent, though only for a few months. Apart from the advantage which he saw in the connection with the Beauharnais children, Napoleon may have thought it well to have the boys and girls close together. But he assuredly did not approve of anything approaching co-education; and when, twelve years later, he appointed Madame Campan head of the Maison Impériale d'Ecouen, he prescribed "rigorous seclusion, gratings, and towers, and no male visitors on any account." But at Saint-Germain there was a certain amount of contact between the two establishments, for on such days as Shrove Tuesday Madame Campan used to give dances, to which MacDermot's boys were invited, the results of which were "more than one little romance," according to Madame d'Arjuzon, the biographer of the early years of Hortense

From Ajaccio to Paris

Beauharnais. There is extant still a letter from Hortense to a girl friend, in which she laments the departure of M. MacDermot for Paris and the closing of his school, and anticipates a *Mardi-Gras fort triste*.

MacDermot did, in fact, give up his school near the end of 1797; but a M. Mestro rented the Ursuline convent after him, and carried on the establishment with the former pupils. Hardly anything has been recorded about Jerome's schooldays under Mestro. In 1798 he won a prize for geography, and we are assured by M. Martinet that his reports were *sublimes*, and that masters and pupils alike were proud of having among them the brother of Napoleon. From the mere hints one can gather, it was certainly Napoleon's brother, and not Jerome Bonaparte, of whom they were proud. But it was rather in holiday time that Jerome chose to exhibit his developing characteristics. His vacations were divided between the house of his brother Joseph, after he had settled in Paris, and the hotel in the Rue Chantereine, where Madame Josephine Bonaparte now lived. Apart from this, Jerome and his sisters and the Beauharnais appear to have had occasional leave to visit Paris in term time;

The Burlesque Napoleon

for Madame Campan speaks of them setting out on an excursion one day in charge of Madame Voisin, and being so hard up (though one should not attribute such a phrase, of course, to the excellent Madame Campan) as to be obliged to content themselves with seats in the gallery of a theatre. After the first victories of Napoleon in Italy his whole family was better off, and Jerome was now allowed more pocket-money than was good for him. Though he was only thirteen he thought himself a man, and, as Madame Junot expresses it, "*faisait des sottises*" whenever he came to Paris. Laure Permon, afterwards Madame Junot and Duchesse d'Abrantès, was from the earliest days very intimate with the Bonapartes, and her sketches of the various members of the family are certainly not actuated by bias against them. Her mother, the beautiful Madame Permon, friend of Letizia Bonaparte, and at one time, in spite of the difference in their ages, wooed by Letizia's son Napoleon, joined in the conspiracy to spoil Jerome—a conspiracy which included every Bonaparte and every marriage connection of the Bonapartes. Naturally, however, his adorers could not see with pleasure a child of thirteen displaying a taste for dissipation, and Joseph,

From Ajaccio to Paris

Lucien, and Eliza all lectured him in turn, without effect. Madame Junot thinks that her mother's lectures did more good, for the others made the mistake of holding up Eugène Beauharnais before his eyes as a model boy: "they could not tolerate him themselves, but they made him a perfect bugbear to Jerome, who made not the slightest effort to contest his title to perfection."

After his campaign in Italy, and shortly before his departure for Egypt, Napoleon withdrew Jerome from Saint-Germain and sent him to the Collége de Juilly, founded by the Oratorians in the seventeenth century, and the most famous of their establishments. There is no proof that Jerome ever learnt much there; but he continued on the career which appealed to him. His elders frequently came to visit him, and still more often he came up to Paris. He was always welcome at the house of Josephine, and seems to have engaged in small flirtations with Josephine's daughter and niece, especially with Hortense, the pretty "half-sister" whose blue eyes and fair hair easily turned a little head so ready to go round, says Madame Junot. It has been maintained by some, without any valid evidence, that Josephine was thinking of a

The Burlesque Napoleon

match for her daughter when she encouraged Jerome to run about the house and garden of the Rue Chantereine. She was, at least, generous to him from her purse, and this kept him for a time from joining in the undisguised hostility of Napoleon's brothers against her. As long as he remained a boy, and while he lived at the Tuileries, he continued on good terms with his sister-in-law. Later, his brothers found means to bring him over to their side against Napoleon's wife, never to be reconciled with her again.[1]

After the return of the hero of Egypt in the October of 1799 Jerome's shortcomings in the matter of education were obvious to him, as appears later, but for the present he had matters of greater importance to think about. So until after the *18 brumaire* Jerome stayed on at Juilly. When the First Consul, however, was settled in the Tuileries in the following February Jerome left his unprofitable studies at the

[1] What Josephine thought of Jerome in later years may be gathered from an exclamation in conversation with Madame Junot on the succession to the Imperial Throne: "Ah! do not wrong the French by thinking them so indifferent about themselves as to accept a prince like Jerome Bonaparte for their sovereign." There was more than contempt for his gallantries in that remark.

From Ajaccio to Paris

college, and was now given rooms under those of his brother in the Pavillon de Flore. He was also given what was little to his taste: a number of private tutors to repair the deficiencies of his previous training, But as compensations he had his handsome allowance and the unlimited indulgence from all about him. The life at the Tuileries was to him his introduction to the world—or to the polite world, at least. Here was beginning the Court of Napoleon; or if it was not yet a Court, it was said, it was no longer the camp of the revolutionary days. In this circle, according to Baron du Casse, Jerome received the imprint which he kept all his life, and learnt the secret of that charming affability and politeness of which, in his old age, he was a model to a careless generation — that of the Second Empire, to wit. The unfortunate part, on which du Casse does not care to dwell,[1] was that the foundation on which this pleasing veneer was laid was not quite worthy of it Laure Permon's portrait seems to be just when,

[1] Du Casse, however, thus sums up the prominent characteristics of Jerome during his life at the Tuileries in 1800: "Sound sense, solid judgment, great personal bravery, true nobility, a vivacity changing sometimes to mere giddiness, a certain levity which paralysed at times all his good qualities, and a love of pomp and show."

The Burlesque Napoleon

describing Jerome at this time, she sees in him all the levity, giddiness, and frivolity of his family combined, and more of them than any of his brothers showed; in fact, a companion picture to his sister Pauline.[1]

Nevertheless, at the Tuileries, and under his brother's eye for a brief while, Jerome, no doubt, made better progress than hitherto. At least he was inspired with a strong desire for some of the glory with which his elder was covered. When Napoleon was about to start for Italy on the campaign of 1800 Jerome begged him again and again to take him with him. But Napoleon was obdurate in his refusal, considering the boy of fifteen too young to go to the front. Jerome, therefore, stayed behind, in great discontent, while the other members of his family served their country with honour and profit. There only remained the solace of abundant pocket-money and a capacity for pleasure and extravagance, which it is not sur-

[1] The Chancelier Pasquier, in his "Histoire de Mon Temps," advances the most reasonable excuse for Jerome at this period—that the rise of Napoleon towards supreme power had already accustomed Jerome to look on himself as on the steps of the throne, and that "the illusion sufficed to produce in him the faults which too often result from the education of princes."

From Ajaccio to Paris

prising that he indulged fully. He found it hard to forgive Napoleon. On the latter's return in July after Marengo, amid the frantic enthusiasm of the people and the joy of his own family, there was one cold face to greet him. Jerome had no word for the conqueror, and made no answer to a caress. "Let us make peace," said Napoleon; "I will give you whatever you want." Impetuously throwing himself on his brother's neck, Jerome asked for the sword which he carried at Marengo. His wish was granted, the sword was his, and he kept it to his death, when he left it to his son, Prince Napoleon.

The wound being healed, Jerome took his share in the gaieties of the Napoleonic circle, naturally increased in extent and importance since Marengo, and enjoyed himself therein.[1] He found no encouragement to restrain himself; for Napoleon, while well aware of his defects, unhappily continued to look on his caprices with a lenient eye. The story is well authenticated of the curious debt incurred by

[1] We find a mention of his taking part in theatricals at Malmaison in the Correspondence of Madame Campan. An old friend of her and her school writes to her that he has found "*Hortense delicieuse! M. Bourrienne parfait! Jerome unique! . . .*"

The Burlesque Napoleon

Jerome at the sign of the Singe-Violet, Rue Saint-Honoré. Soon after Napoleon's return to Paris from Italy, his secretary, Bourienne, was given a pile of bills whose payment was pressing. Running through them, he found one for as much as 8000 or 10,000 francs. Naturally, there was an immediate enquiry how the First Consul came to owe M. Biennais, dealer in objects of art, so large a sum. The charge was for a travelling-case, with silver fittings, mother-of-pearl and ivory articles, razors and everything connected with shaving— all, in fact, which any young man of fifteen could want in this way except a moustache. Biennais, interviewed, described the young man who had ordered the goods, and who had said: "Send them to the Tuileries, the First Consul's aide-de-camp will pay!" Napoleon waited until dinner-time, and then said to Jerome: "So it is you, sir, who indulge in travelling-cases costing 10,000 francs." "Oh," replied Jerome, unembarrassed, "I am like that: I only care for beautiful things." Napoleon told the little story afterwards, "in a very pleasant manner," to Madame Permon, according to her daughter. But he was, nevertheless, concerned about the extent to which Jerome's character had been

From Ajaccio to Paris

spoilt for many years; he had a conversation on the subject with Madame Permon on the same day. Jerome's name being mentioned, Napoleon remarked: "Well, you have brought our gallant little citizen up nicely for me while I was away! I find him self-willed, and obstinately set on bad objects. The Signora Letizia spoils him so much that I doubt whether he can pull up at the point he has now reached." Madame Permon, whose heart was still tender for Jerome, declared that the boy was full of good feeling, and warm-hearted, a true sailor, who only needed to get tanned by the sea-breeze to develop into a naval hero.

The recorder of this conversation says that Napoleon was perfectly right in saying that he found Jerome very strangely brought up. And it was beyond the power of his elder brother to do much to correct his training. He did not abate his extravagances even now, with Napoleon in Paris, if another tale be true which is told in the memoirs of Mademoiselle Cochelet, a school-fellow of Caroline and Hortense under Madame Campan. Jerome one day, having spent all his quarter's pocket-money in advance, and urgently requiring twenty-five louis, did not know where to get them. All

The Burlesque Napoleon

his brothers were away except the First Consul, whom he dared not ask; and his mother, fond as she was of him, was readier with good advice than with money. An inspiration came. He went to his uncle Fesch. The future cardinal had a large dinner-party that night, and asked Jerome to stop. He accepted. After dinner a move was made to the *salon* for coffee. Seeing his uncle enter an adjoining room, Jerome followed, and, drawing him into the window recess, asked for a loan. The abbé did not see his way to granting the request, and was turning to rejoin his guests, when the boy suddenly drew a sword he was wearing. Fesch was an enthusiastic collector of pictures, and had already began to form a gallery, which later became celebrated. Pointing to a Van Dyck, Jerome remarked that the rascal in the picture looked as if he were laughing at the insult to him, and that he must avenge himself. The agitated priest caught at his arm, beseeching him to stop. Jerome mentioned again the twenty-five louis, the uncle gave way, the sword was sheathed, and an embrace followed the bargain. A few days later the First Consul was told of the affair, and was much amused.

Nevertheless, with a view to making him some-

From Ajaccio to Paris

thing more than a spoilt child, however amusing, Jerome had been put into the Chasseurs de la Garde Consulaire, a duty which kept him near the First Consul, while giving him the benefit of military discipline. With the attraction which glory had for him he, perhaps, did not find this altogether distasteful. But an unfortunate incident occurred to put an end, for the time, to his career as soldier. Among the other young men in the Consular Guard was a Davoust, brother of the General. Between him and Jerome there was a strong antipathy from the beginning, and they early found an opportunity of fighting a duel. The conditions, which they settled themselves, were sufficiently bloodthirsty to suggest the earnestness of the combatants. No seconds or witnesses were present, each had a horse-pistol and a pocketful of cartridges, and separated by twenty-five paces, they started to fire until their ammunition should be exhausted. The result of the affair was that Jerome was hit in the breast, the ball being flattened against the bone, and remaining there till his death, when it was discovered as his body was being embalmed, sixty years later. The duellists won for themselves some celebrity; but Napoleon on this occasion failed to

The Burlesque Napoleon

be amused at Jerome. On the contrary, he decided at once to try the effect of the sea-air which Madame Permon had advised. No doubt it would have been most beneficial, had the elder brother only maintained a consistent attitude towards the younger, and insisted on the carrying out of the orders which he was so careful to give. But, as in nearly all his subsequent dealings with Jerome, Napoleon first laid down the correct course to be pursued, and then suffered it to be abandoned.

JEROME AT SEA

CHAPTER II

JEROME AT SEA

It is a fact familiar to students of Napoleonic history that for several years previous to this period Napoleon had been cherishing the idea of improving the French navy, in order to meet the perpetual menace of England. Even during his first Italian campaign he had sent to the Directory 2,000,000 francs for naval purposes; but the Directors had used the money otherwise. His experiences in Egypt served to strengthen his views. It was not until the year following that in which he put Jerome into the navy that he wrote to Lucien: " Whatever the cost, we must become masters of the Mediterranean, or force the English to efforts which they will be unable to sustain long." The words, however, serve to show what his desire was years before. When, therefore, the First Consul started out to make a sailor of his youngest brother he offered him a career in which he hoped that the rewards would be

The Burlesque Napoleon

of the highest; and had Jerome been what Napoleon wanted him to be his entrance into the navy should have meant not a little for France and for himself. The scheme was, nevertheless, most unpalatable to Jerome, who made vigorous protests, and, according to some accounts, took care to fail in his preliminary examination. But he only found, as he was destined often to find later, that protests had no strength against his brother's will. Scouting the idea that a post of aide-de-camp, such as Louis had filled in Italy, would be suitable for Jerome, Napoleon sent him as a mere midshipman, an *aspirant de seconde classe*, to Rear-Admiral Ganteaume's flagship *Indivisible* at Brest. Ganteaume, who had succeeded in bringing Napoleon safely home from Egypt, was entrusted now with a mission dangerous enough to make it sure that those under him would see real service. The Mediterranean had been under the domination of the British fleet since Aboukir, and the duty of Ganteaume's squadron was to cross over to Egypt, in spite of the British, and to revictual Menou's army. The First Consul made it clear to the Admiral that his brother was to get no special consideration. "I send you, citizen general," he wrote

Jerome at Sea

on the 22nd November, "citizen Jerome Bonaparte to serve his apprenticeship in the navy. You know that he needs to be treated strictly, and to make up for lost time. Insist on his carrying out exactly all the duties of his profession."

With a prospect of hard work before him, and with his hopes of military advancement and glory shattered, Jerome joined Admiral Ganteaume at Brest. The perils of the voyage to the Mediterranean were soon apparent. The port of Brest was watched by the enemy; and though Ganteaume was able to put out with his seven line-of-battle and three smaller ships on the 7th January, he had to return, and it was not until the 23rd that he got away, with the aid of a strong wind. This turned into a tempest, which scattered the squadron. The Admiral's ship, on which Jerome suffered so rude an introduction to the sea, with one frigate arrived off Cape St Vincent before the rest, and had the fortune to capture an English corvette. The squadron managed to reassemble by the end of the month, and passed Gibraltar, and into the Mediterranean, on the 7th February. Another small English vessel was picked up six days later; and it was thought

The Burlesque Napoleon

at the time that Ganteaume might have reached Egypt successfully had he made an immediate dash. An unsigned letter has been found among Jerome's papers criticising Ganteaume's constant delays, and expressing doubts as to his anxiety to get to Egypt. This may be a proof of discernment on the part of the young midshipman, as it is in his writing; his admirers later interpreted it as such. Ganteaume now, instead of continuing his voyage towards his goal, sailed north in the direction of Toulon, escorting one of his ships which was crippled, when the appearance of the British compelled him to put into Toulon himself. He left again in March, returned in April, and in May made an unsuccessful demonstration against Elba, then held by an Anglo-Tuscan garrison. It was not till June that part of the squadron reached a distant point of the Egyptian coast. Then, a landing being declared impossible, it was decided to return, leaving Menou to his fate. A small success was obtained as the only compensation for the failure of the mission, for on the 24th June the French battleships *Indivisible* and *Dix-Août* met the English 74-gun ship *Swiftsure*, on her way from Aboukir

Jerome at Sea

to Malta, and compelled her to surrender. Ganteaume singled out Jerome Bonaparte to send on board the *Swiftsure* to receive the captain's sword—a choice which hardly seems consistent with Napoleon's instructions when he sent Jerome to Ganteaume.

Napoleon, however, expressed himself as delighted with the reports he had of his brother. "I learn with pleasure that you are getting on at sea; it is there only that great glory is to be won to-day," he wrote. He added the advice to climb the masts, and study the different parts of the ship. "Let me be told that you are as active as a very cabin-boy. Don't allow anyone to do your work for you. Seek every chance of distinguishing yourself. Make up your mind that the navy is to be your profession." When Jerome himself arrived in Paris on the 26th August, after nearly nine months' service, he was received with open arms. He lodged, as before, in the Tuileries, and saw Paris at her gayest, in the midst of the rejoicings over the peace at last reigning throughout Europe. But, not being seventeen years old yet, he was not a very important member of his family circle, and practically no record exists of his three months'

The Burlesque Napoleon

holiday in France beyond the remark found in a letter of his old school-fellow, Henri Campan, that he had "altered considerably for the better." Napoleon had no idea of letting Jerome remain in Paris to undo the good which naval life might be doing for him; and while giving him a step in the service, he ordered him, in a letter of the 29th November, to present himself at Rochefort to join the fleet about to start for the West Indies, under the command of his brother-in-law, Leclerc.

Towards the end of his life Napoleon admitted the unwisdom of the expedition to San Domingo. To Barry O'Meara at Saint Helena he declared it one of the greatest follies of which he was ever guilty. He ought, according to his later ideas, to have declared San Domingo free, acknowledged the black government, and before the Peace of Amiens to have sent out French officers to help the rebels; in that case, he thought Jamaica and the other British colonies in the neighbourhood would have risen against their rulers in sympathy with revolutionary ideas in San Domingo. His excuse at Saint Helena was that he was beset with applications from proprietors of estates, merchants, and others, and yielded to the popular desire

GENERAL LECLERC.

Jerome at Sea

to regain the island. Josephine appears to have dreaded the result of the expedition, and to have suspected that the military commander chosen by Napoleon lacked the necessary combination of tact and vigour for his task. Victor-Emmanuel Leclerc, who won Napoleon's regard at Toulon, where both seized their first chance of glory, had also gained by Napoleon's aid the hand of Pauline, the most beautiful and most frivolous of the Bonapartes. He had fought in Italy and in Egypt, and had succeeded in impressing others besides Napoleon. A very favourable picture of him is drawn by de Norvins, who accompanied him to the West Indies as private secretary, attracted alike by the General's character and by Pauline's charm. De Norvins speaks of Leclerc as the Bonaparte of San Domingo; and the part was one which Leclerc made great efforts to sustain. Unfortunately for himself, though he copied Napoleon's mannerisms, and is alleged to have gone so far as to speak of himself as "*le Bonaparte blond*," he absolutely failed to reproduce the essential qualities of a Napoleon. His death, by yellow fever, however, may have done him an injustice in cutting his career so short. He showed at least discretion, and

The Burlesque Napoleon

perhaps also humanity, in not applying to San Domingo the secret decree of Napoleon in May 1802, re-establishing slavery in the West Indian possessions of France. As soon as the decree became known the doom of the expedition was sealed, as Leclerc's successor found very soon.

Napoleon resolved that Pauline should accompany her husband to the West Indies. *La belle des belles*, who had no great attachment to the husband whom her brother had given her, protested and wept. "*Mon Dieu, comme je vais m'ennuyer!*" she cried, and was inconsolable until she was persuaded that the Creole costume would become her well. So, at least, declares Madame Junot, whose view of Pauline is that she was "one of those characters remarkable for their childishness, and interesting to study because of their very nullity." Pauline yielded to compulsion, and went to San Domingo with her three-year-old child. She returned in a year, bringing back the embalmed body of her husband, and with her hair cut off in sign of mourning. It seems uncharitable to say that strong proofs of mourning were required from her. But it is evident that even the admiring de Norvins found much amiss in her attitude

Jerome at Sea

towards Leclerc; and she married again within less than a year of her first husband's death.

The fleet which Admiral Villaret-Joyeuse had under his command appeared ample for the purpose to which it was destined, for it numbered over fifty sail, and there were 20,000 troops on the transports. Of the three divisions, which started respectively from Brest, Rochefort, and Lorient, Jerome was with the second, led by Admiral Latouche-Tréville, reputed the most daring officer in the French navy. He was attached to the flagship *Foudroyant*, which left Rochefort with thirteen other vessels on the 14th December 1801. Owing to Latouche-Tréville not following his instructions as to the place of meeting, this section of the expedition reached San Domingo first, and was obliged to cruise off the island in bad weather awaiting the rest, which arrived on the 29th January. Jerome had as yet had no opportunity of distinguishing himself save by endurance of bad weather, but he experienced once more the benevolence of an admiral entrusted with the duty of training up the brother of the head of the State. One of Villaret-Joyeuse's first acts on arriving at his destination was to appoint the young midshipman provisionally *enseigne*

The Burlesque Napoleon

de vaisseau. Jerome entered on his duties with a high idea, perhaps, of the importance of his rank, but certainly with small regard to what was suitable to that rank. A scene described by de Norvins reads like comic opera, and might be taken for fiction but for the sobriety of the narrator. Leclerc had established his headquarters at Cap Haitien on his arrival in San Domingo, and it was here that the General and his secretary were seated at breakfast one morning, when a salute announced the arrival of a warship, soon followed by the appearance of Jerome in the uniform of a captain in the Berchiny Hussars. He had no claims to that dress, of course, and he was only an *enseigne* of seventeen. But he "only cared for beautiful things," and, no doubt, the Berchiny Hussars' uniform was such in his eyes. Leclerc expressed his disapproval of the freak; but Jerome bore pleasing recollections of the costume, for he recalled it afterwards to de Norvins in Westphalia.

Annoyed though he might be at Jerome's ideas of how to dress as an *enseigne de vaisseau*, Leclerc was at this very time writing to the First Consul that he was "very pleased with Jerome, who has all the essentials for an

Jerome at Sea

excellent officer." (De Norvins might have remembered this phrase, as he probably wrote the letter for Leclerc, but he does not mention it.) He kept his brother-in-law with him, moreover, during the early fighting round the coast towns, and when the time arrived to send off another report to Napoleon it was Jerome who was chosen for the task of conveying the despatch. Leclerc asked Villaret-Joyeuse for an active, intelligent officer; and whom could the Admiral suggest better than Jerome? Accordingly, early in March, Jerome started for France on the *Cisalpin*, the fastest sailer in the fleet, commanded by a Lieutenant Halgan, with whom Jerome at once struck up a warm friendship. They arrived at Brest on the 11th April, and started for Paris at once. The journey was marked by an incident which impresses some of Jerome's biographers with the idea of his determined character, and remained, it was said, the delight and wonder of Nantes for years to come. When the carriage conveying Jerome and Halgan was still some miles from that town the postillion, a Breton, got down, and refused to go any farther. Alternate coaxing and threatening proved no good. Jerome pushed the lieu-

The Burlesque Napoleon

tenant into the coach, asked the postillion once more if he would proceed, and, being again refused, sprang into the saddle himself, and rode triumphantly into Nantes—a postillion in knee-breeches and silk stockings, bare-headed, and flourishing a whip.

This exhibition of his capacity as "handy man," no doubt, did not prejudice him when he arrived in Paris. His news from Leclerc was good, and France was rejoicing over the signature of the Peace of Amiens, foreshadowed when Jerome left Paris in the previous year. Moreover, the preparations for declaring Napoleon First Consul for life were being made, and the circle which surrounded his family was growing rapidly more imperial. In this society Jerome was made much of, as might have been expected. But Napoleon, as at all periods in his life, had the power of attending to the concerns of all his family when his own might have seemed most engrossing. So, after Jerome had been little more than a month at the Tuileries, he was told that the brig *Epervier* would start from Brest for the Antilles, and that he was to join her, his appointment as *enseigne* being confirmed. Napoleon yielded to Jerome's request to give

Jerome at Sea

the command of the brig to Halgan, and then sent them both off early in June to join her. To their delight, no doubt, they found she had still to complete her armament, which gave them the opportunity of spending some weeks very agreeably at Nantes, a favourite resort for young naval officers of the period. All that Jerome wanted was money, for which he wrote to Paris frequently. One of Napoleon's replies survives, written on the 27th June, in which he addresses the spendthrift as *monsieur l'enseigne de vaisseau*, and says: "Die young, and I shall be consoled for it; but not if you live sixty years without glory, without use to your country, without leaving behind a trace of your existence. It would be better not to have existed at all."

The bills, however, seem to have been paid. That was the chief thing—and the *Epervier* did not leave for another two months. Even then a storm arose—Jerome was always meeting storms—and drove the brig back on the 6th September for repairs. Jerome was thus able to spend nearly another fortnight at Nantes, in a manner which may be presumed but has not been handed down. So much did his time in Nantes give him a preference for land

The Burlesque Napoleon

that, when the *Epervier* finally left France, he tried to persuade Halgan to put into Lisbon on the way to the West Indies. But Halgan declined to take this risk for the sake of his gay young companion; and so, near the end of October, the brig appeared off Martinique, where Admiral Villaret-Joyeuse was acting as Captain-General. The Admiral was delighted to see him, and lost no time in appointing him a lieutenant. Jerome had, it seems, brought a letter of instructions to Villaret-Joyeuse from Napoleon, in accordance with which his brother was to make a cruising tour of the French colonies in the Antilles, to complete his naval education. This would be best carried out, the Admiral considered, if Jerome were lieutenant. The next step was for Halgan to fall ill, which he did with alacrity. It was thus as Lieutenant Bonaparte, commander of the *Epervier*, that Jerome, just eighteen years of age, sailed for Saint Lucia. The other Admiral, Villeneuve, was equally devoted to him, finding him "penetrated with the noble ambition of making his name as famous in the navy as it is already in the annals of war and politics." All he could wish was to find him a little more assiduous in his attendance on board his

Jerome at Sea

ship! As Jerome was at this time writing home to Bourrienne (whose charge over Napoleon's purse seems to have been a godsend to him) for 20,000 francs, it may be imagined that he saw more scope on land for living in the style proper to a naval lieutenant.

Apart from this attraction towards the pleasures of Martinique, Jerome had conceived a dislike for his ship. His visit to Saint Lucia brought on fever, through his visiting a crater in the middle of the day; while his crew melted rapidly through desertions and yellow fever. "All Europeans, my dear Bourrienne," he wrote home, "die in this country." The exaggeration was not so great. At the beginning of November, Leclerc had died in the Tortugas of the disease which killed 4500 of the men lost by the French under his command. Toussaint Louverture, the black general, was alleged, truly or not, to have said, after his surrender to the French in May: "*Moi compter sur la Providence!*" La Providence was the name of the chief hospital at Cap Haitien, and it was within its walls that so many Frenchmen succumbed on this fatal expedition. Jerome fully appreciated the horror of the situation, and wished to resign the command of the *Epervier*.

The Burlesque Napoleon

This, however, Villeneuve could not consent to; and as soon as he could fill up the ship's crew again he sent Jerome to visit Guadeloupe, and to pay a call on the British Governor of Dominica. On his return to Saint-Pierre, in March 1803, Jerome rather ingeniously secured a respite by having the whole of the *Epervier's* interior painted with oil, which dried very slowly. He further excused himself from a proposed visit to San Domingo on account of the painful associations of Leclerc's recent death. The completion of his education designed by Napoleon was sadly interfered with by Jerome's prejudices. He had not much longer to wait, however, for at the end of April, Villeneuve, probably by order from France, directed the *Epervier* to return home. This she prepared to do, after the deficiencies of her crew had once more been made up, and after Jerome had got over another attack of fever. But now an incident occurred which nearly changed the whole course of her young commander's life.

The *Epervier* left Saint-Pierre on the last day of May, to the relief, no doubt, of the two Admirals, for whom the responsibility of Jerome's education was proving too great. The very next day, however, she returned, and

Jerome at Sea

Jerome sent off to Villaret-Joyeuse a letter of explanation. He had the honour to inform him that, on his return voyage to France, in accordance with orders, he had the previous evening sighted a large merchantman in the Dominica channel. Judging from the vessel's position and course that she was French he lay to, and declared his colours. The merchantman took no notice; whereon he signalled to her to stop and send a boat alongside. As she still held on, he crossed her bows and sent a shot among her rigging, to show his desire to communicate with her. She then lay to, and revealed her British nationality. Annoyed at the mistake, continued Jerome, he despatched an officer on board the merchantman to express his regrets, and at the same time to ask for the political news when the ship left Europe. The reply was that all had been peaceful when she sailed, and he thereon decided to return to Martinique to tell the Admiral the good news.

The receipt of this message did not produce on Villaret-Joyeuse the effect which Jerome had apparently expected. Although intelligence of the rupture of the peace of Amiens had not yet reached the West Indies, it was

The Burlesque Napoleon

known that affairs were very critical, and Villaret-Joyeuse was not at all anxious that anything done by his fleet should precipitate matters. Accordingly, in reply to the "good news," he could only send a reprimand to his lieutenant, whom, however, he addressed as "my dear Jerome." For him to sanction such proceedings as Jerome's, he pointed out, would be equivalent to a declaration of war against England. Jerome must get away, and must by no means be found at Martinique when complaints were made. He should proceed to France to inform the First Consul of the affair. "Nothing must stop you; and if my request to you is insufficient, I shall send you to-morrow a positive order." Jerome's answer to this was written on the 15th of the month, and was of a nature to astonish most admirals. " I have received your letter, my dear Admiral," it began; " our opinions differ, but I gladly submit my views to yours." He proceeded to explain a plan by which he might reach France more certainly than by sailing on the *Epervier*; for, in spite of the good news which he had gathered from the English merchantman, he evidently suspected that war had broken out in Europe. His idea was to procure Danish

Jerome at Sea

papers for a French merchant vessel, and to embark on her as a passenger. He announced, however, his readiness to sail the next day on the *Epervier*, and concluded with the words: "If ill-fate wills that I am to be captured off the coast of France, this letter will show you, my dear Admiral, that I foresaw it."

Villaret-Joyeuse, when he read this letter, appears actually to have modified his views concerning the manner of Jerome's departure. It would seem as though he agreed that a passage on a neutral vessel would be better. The *Epervier* did not leave Martinique at once, but stayed there for more than another month. On the 20th July she sailed, after Jerome had resigned his command and another officer had been appointed in his place. Suspicions concerning the sharp look-out kept for him by the British were verified almost immediately, for on the 27th the *Epervier* was made prisoner by the British, and the captors were strongly under the impression that they had taken the First Consul's brother.

Writing to Jerome on the 25th July 1809, in perhaps the bitterest letter he ever addressed to the scapegrace, Napoleon speaks of him as

The Burlesque Napoleon

having deserted the sea, and left his Admiral without orders. The reference there is evidently to Jerome's conduct in the summer of 1803.[1] This cannot, however, be taken as conclusive evidence of Jerome having left the *Epervier* without Villaret-Joyeuse's knowledge or consent. Napoleon in a rage was apt to be as inaccurate as most other men in a rage. Jerome appears to have regarded himself as having some sort of mission from his Admiral to Napoleon. The only mission of which we know was to tell the First Consul what happened on the 31st May. To get to France, obviously the least likely way would be to sail as commander of his ship, now only too well known to the British in consequence of the affair in the Dominica channel. Even had he started from Martinique, as intended, at the beginning of June, he would have escaped capture in West Indian waters, but would have reached France in July only to find the British fleets blockading the coast. Still, whatever excuse he may have had, in his "mission," for not proceeding in the

[1] That the reference was to 1803, not to 1806, seems proved by the statement that "one warship more or less was a trifling matter." The *Epervier* in 1803 was lost; the *Vétéran* in 1806 was not. For the letter, *vide* Chap. VIII.

Jerome at Sea

Epervier he could find none in it for spending a year and a half in the United States after quitting Martinique. Jerome very soon ceased to look for an excuse: he had found an infatuation.

THE BONAPARTE-
PATTERSON MARRIAGE

ELIZABETH PATTERSON BONAPARTE.

CHAPTER III

THE BONAPARTE-PATTERSON MARRIAGE

HAVING left Martinique on an American vessel, Jerome reached Norfolk, Virginia, on the 20th July 1803. He was accompanied by a suite of four, which might have been remarkable in any other naval lieutenant of eighteen. Meyronnet was, like his patron, from the *Épervier*, and was also a lieutenant. Alexandre Le Camus was a young Creole, whom Jerome had made his private secretary; he was destined to play a considerable part in Jerome's history a few years later. The third, Rewbell, whose father was prominent enough in the early years of the Revolution to become one of the Directors, was also to follow Jerome to Westphalia. Lastly, there was a doctor from the *Épervier*. Possibly Jerome's poor health in the West Indies had convinced him that he still needed medical care. The other three provided him at once with companionship and dignity; it is difficult to find other grounds for their attendance on Jerome.

The Burlesque Napoleon

The connection, however, was very advantageous to them, and seems to prove them men of foresight.

On landing in the United States, Jerome apparently was sincere in his intention of proceeding at once to France in a neutral vessel. To arrange about the chartering of such, Meyronnet was sent to Philadelphia; while the rest of the party went on to Washington to find the French Consul-General. Pichon, who held the post at this period, was one of the many people whom Napoleon in his conversations at Saint Helena stigmatised as a *coquin*; and he was condemned for embezzlement on his return to France from America. If we judge him, however, by his correspondence over Jerome's affairs he appears rather in the light of a worthy, well-meaning, but very harassed official. He was at his residence in Georgetown when Le Camus presented himself to him, and announced Jerome's arrival. Pichon hastened to see him, found him a better inn than that to which he had gone, and listened to his ideas as to reaching France. Jerome told him what Meyronnet was doing at Philadelphia, but also suggested that the United States Government might be willing to send him across the Atlantic in one

The Bonaparte-Patterson Marriage

of their own warships. Pichon was afraid that this would be thought a breach of neutrality, and could not be entertained by the United States; but he approved of the scheme to charter a vessel at Philadelphia, and sent word to his agent there to co-operate with Meyronnet. At the cost of 10,000 dollars it was arranged that the *Clothier* should convey Jerome and his party to Europe, starting on the 3rd August. This was made known to Jerome at once; and when he dined with Pichon the day after his arrival in Washington he said he had abandoned the other idea of applying to the United States Government, and would go to Philadelphia. Pichon impressed on him the necessity of preserving a strict incognito, as the English were still keenly on the look-out for the First-Consul's brother. He now, doubtless, congratulated himself on having managed what might have been a difficult affair very expeditiously. He little knew Jerome yet.

Instead of going to Philadelphia on the 24th July, Jerome went to Baltimore. The reason for his change of plan was this: serving with the French fleet in the West Indies there had been an adventurous American called Joshua Barney, with whom Jerome had become closely

The Burlesque Napoleon

acquainted. Barney had heard of his arrival in Washington, and wrote to invite him to Baltimore, where he had a hotel. Jerome accepted at once, and scarcely four days had passed before he was writing to Pichon that his name was no longer a mystery in Baltimore. He added, consolingly: "This has not caused me to alter my plans nor my manner of life." As a matter of fact, it made a very considerable change in both. Jerome refused to leave America by the *Clothier*, although her departure was delayed until the 11th August in hopes of his consenting to embark. He now said that he thought it advisable to await the First Consul's orders as to the mode of his journey to France: these Meyronnet must be sent to France to inquire. Already Jerome's mission from his Admiral had begun to lose its importance! The revelation of his identity, which was, no doubt, due to Commodore Barney, probably had much to do with his determination to spend some time in Baltimore. As soon as it became known that the young lieutenant was no less than brother of the famous First Consul of France, Jerome Bonaparte became the centre of attraction. Every door was open to him in Baltimore; and, as the town was a great

The Bonaparte-Patterson Marriage

social centre, it is not to be wondered at that he enjoyed the situation. He seems to have landed in the States with a considerable sum of money, drawn presumably from France, through Bourrienne; and he was, for his age, exceedingly well trained in the spending of money. Moreover, this was the first time in his life that he was absolutely his own master, and he had the opportunity of putting into practice his theories as to the life of a prince. It is very curious that he should have managed to anticipate his future rank so successfully. But his good manners, and his at least moderately good looks, combined with his perfect assurance, completed the work which his name began, and he had no difficulty in getting himself taken at his own valuation among the honest Republicans of Baltimore.

Pichon, as might be supposed, was not at all pleased at Jerome's countermanding of the *Clothier*, the expense of chartering which fell on him; and he had already had a difficulty with Meyronnet over the opening by the lieutenant of a consular packet because it included a letter to Jerome. He now wrote to the latter, earnestly recommending him to leave "the very unhealthy town of Baltimore," and

The Burlesque Napoleon

recommending a tour in the Western States. As this produced no effect, Pichon wrote again on the 16th August, objecting to the friendship with Barney, whose bad reputation, he said, would cast a reflection on Jerome. He suggested that he should leave Baltimore, and join himself and Madame Pichon on a holiday tour. The answer which this inspired was not encouraging. Thanking Pichon for the interest which he took in him, particularly in the choice of suitable society for him, Jerome said that his principle was to judge men by their conduct, and that as long as Citizen Barney acted towards him as he had in the past he should not change his opinion of him. "I have sufficient discernment, I think, to choose the society which is fitting for me." Barney had won. Pichon afterwards complained in a letter to Talleyrand that the American was inciting Jerome to send denunciations of him to France. He could hardly expect Barney to be delighted with his view of his character, which Jerome, of course, showed to his friend. As to the Commodore, who was a son-in-law of Samuel Chase of Baltimore, one of those who signed the Declaration of Independence on behalf of the State of Maryland, his reputation certainly did not

The Bonaparte-Patterson Marriage

appear to injure Jerome in the society of the town.

The unhappy Pichon was soon to have a stronger influence than Barney's with which to contend. He was badly served by his agent in Baltimore, for he did not discover the facts until too late, and then from Jerome's own admission. Some rumours, indeed, had reached Pichon, but he had seen no importance in them. Important official business, in connection with the Louisiana purchase by the United States, kept him in Washington constantly; and so Jerome, while awaiting the First Consul's instructions, had no critical eye to spoil his enjoyment of liberty. Everyone in Baltimore was amiable to the brother of the greatest man in Europe, especially as he had all the superficial qualities required to keep up the part. A slight acquaintance with Jerome's life will persuade anyone that he did not avoid ladies' society during his stay in America. It is to his credit that his only known love affair was as honourable as it was in its beginning. Unfortunately, the romance had not long developed into marriage before it assumed an aspect entirely disgraceful to Jerome. That he suffered before consenting to his own dishonour is the only mitigation which can be

The Burlesque Napoleon

found in judging him, and his suffering was small beside that of his partner in the romance.

Elizabeth Patterson was eighteen years of age when she met Jerome Bonaparte. She was the eldest daughter in a family of thirteen born to William Patterson, a Donegal farmer's son, who had come to Philadelphia at the age of fourteen, and had risen from a shipping merchant's counting-house to a position second to none in his adopted country. His President, Thomas Jefferson, writing to the United States Minister in Paris at the time of Elizabeth's marriage to Jerome, described him as "a man of great worth and of great respectability," and the family's social standing as "the first in the United States." He had given large sums of money in support of the War of Independence, and was a friend of all the American leaders in that struggle. The esteem in which he was held, and his wealth, united to make his eldest daughter prominent in Baltimore, apart from her looks; and she was, in addition, the belle of the town. She is described as having possessed "the pure Grecian contour." "Her head was exquisitely formed, her forehead fair and shapely, her eyes large and dark, with an expression of tenderness which did not belong

The Bonaparte-Patterson Marriage

to her character; and the delicate loveliness of her mouth and chin, together with her beautifully-rounded shoulders and tapering arms, combined to form one of the loveliest of women."[1] The American verdict on her beauty was endorsed by Europe afterwards. Curiously, she had a distinct resemblance in appearance to the Bonapartes, particularly to Pauline, as we shall find mentioned by Madame Junot later. With regard to her mental accomplishments, Elizabeth Patterson has been variously described —according to the bias of the writers—as well educated and as quite ignorant. The sneer of Pichon, in his letter to Talleyrand on the 20th February 1804, has been accepted as true by most of the French biographers of Jerome. Now, Pichon was hardly in a good temper when he wrote that Elizabeth, " like all young persons in this country, has had an education limited to very little." Nor, on the other hand, had she any exceptional training, save in so far as a familiarity with Young's "Night Thoughts," and the "Maxims" of Rochefoucauld—her principal reading in childhood, it is told—should be considered such. When she married Jerome her prominent characteristics were ambition, love

[1] E. L. Didier, " Life and Letters of Madame Bonaparte."

The Burlesque Napoleon

of pleasure, and self-will. Under the influence of the cruel fate which the Bonaparte family brought upon her, she developed an admirable courage and a less admirable but surely pardonable hardness. Her native wit, encouraged perhaps by her early reading, was trained by undeserved humiliation into a bitterness which caused it to be said of her afterwards that she charmed with her eyes while she slew with her tongue. She has suffered in reputation from the vindictive remarks in her father's will. One might appreciate these remarks, however, at a truer valuation if one knew how far Mr Patterson's conscience was clean in the matter of his daughter's marriage. Many alleged that he secretly promoted it; but evidence is lacking. The daughter's pleading of her side of the case, if it exists, has never been put before the public.[1]

Circumstances combined to make Jerome

[1] *Vide* p. 68. The passage in William Patterson's will runs as follows:—" The conduct of my daughter Betsey has through life been so disobedient that in no instance has she ever consulted my opinions or feelings; indeed, she has caused me more anxiety and trouble than all my other children put together, and her folly and misconduct have occasioned me a train of expense that, first and last, has cost me much money." In accordance with these sentiments, he left Elizabeth less than any of the other children.

The Bonaparte-Patterson Marriage

Bonaparte and Elizabeth Patterson take notice of each other when they met in Baltimore. It is not easy, however, to judge how far all tales of the circumstances conducing to their intimacy are to be accepted. One story represents Elizabeth, at their first encounter, becoming somehow caught by a gold chain which formed part of the magnificent attire of Lieutenant Bonaparte, and being thereby reminded, as he disentangled her, of a prophecy made to her as a child, that she would be a great lady in France one day. As for Jerome, two American ladies are said already to have spoken enthusiastically to him of Elizabeth—one of them being Henrietta Pascault, whom Rewbell married soon after his arrival in Baltimore. Jerome had remarked that he could never marry an American. "Don't be so sure," said Madame Rewbell; "Miss Patterson is so beautiful that to see her *is* to marry her." After this Jerome, in jest, used to speak of Miss Patterson as *ma belle femme* before he had ever seen her. These may be fables. It is agreed that it was in September that the two first set eyes on each other; and the earliest meeting is usually placed in the house of Samuel Chase, where Jerome was a visitor through the introduction of his

The Burlesque Napoleon

friend Barney. But one writer, stating that Jerome and Elizabeth were first face to face at the Baltimore races, gives a strong verisimilitude to the story by describing the lady's costume on the occasion. Elizabeth wore a buff silk dress, a lace fichu, and a leghorn hat with pink tulle trimmings and black plumes.[1] Wherever it was that they were first introduced, Elizabeth's reception of the French lieutenant was cold, for she had heard of his presumptuous reference to his *belle femme*. This state of affairs did not last long, Jerome being piqued by the show of resistance, and determined to overcome it. The society which surrounded the two fostered the growth of their acquaintance, and soon their mutual attraction was evident to all.

Baltimore looked very benevolently on the infatuated young couple, some at least of Elizabeth's relatives encouraged them, and Jerome met with assistance from a curious source. The Spanish representative in the United States, the Marquis d'Yrujo, lent warm support to him in his suit. His intervention has been regarded as mysterious, and has been

[1] Virginia Tatnall Peacock on "Elizabeth Patterson," in *Lippincott's Magazine*, 1900.

The Bonaparte-Patterson Marriage

explained as prompted by hatred for France, and a desire to embarrass Napoleon by this marriage of his brother. It seems quite possible, nevertheless, that the Marquis acted as he did through liking for Jerome, rather than with the very Machiavellian designs attributed to him by French writers. D'Yrujo was finally deputed by Jerome to make, on his behalf, a formal demand from Mr Patterson for the hand of Elizabeth. The young lady herself had so much made up her mind that she assured her father that she "would rather be wife of Jerome Bonaparte for one hour than wife of any other man for life." Certain of her mother's relatives, particularly General Smith, a distinguished officer in the old Maryland Line, who was husband of a sister of Mrs Patterson, thought the marriage desirable from the point of view of the family's political advancement. He was anxious, it is alleged, to receive the appointment of Minister at Paris. William Patterson made a considerable show of opposition, although, as has been mentioned, he has been accused of secretly promoting the match. Writing in the following February to the United States Minister in Paris, he declared that he had never encouraged Jerome, but had

The Burlesque Napoleon

resisted his pretensions by every means in his power consistent with discretion; but, finding nothing short of force or violence could prevent the union, he had, with much reluctance, consented. Some unpublished papers of Elizabeth are said to be in the possession of her descendants, including a "Dialogue of the Dead" between William Patterson and Jerome. Possibly this, if it exists in reality, might throw some light on the father's attitude. It must be confessed that the spirit shown in his will, where it refers to his daughter, does not incline one to form as high an estimate of William Patterson as his contemporaries formed. There is a sort of posthumous brutality in his reflections on Elizabeth which can but revolt the reader.

Pichon, though not entirely without rumours about Jerome, did not credit them, and he was pleased when, on the 23rd October, his troublesome charge arrived in Washington to pay his respects, rather long after his arrival in the States, to President Jefferson. Jerome's behaviour and conversation, both at his first reception, and at a dinner with the President on the 26th, were all that could be desired, and Jefferson, as appeared later, was favourably

The Bonaparte-Patterson Marriage

impressed. But on the night before the dinner Jerome gave a great shock to his Consul-General by announcing to him that he was about to marry. The wedding would take place in nine days. Pichon was invited; and Jerome added that, as he could not stop the affair, propriety suggested his presence. Pichon in vain made every possible protest. The matter was concluded, Jerome said; and, as for his being under age, would not his lieutenancy prove that he was more than twenty-one years old? When the would-be bridegroom left for Baltimore after the President's dinner he had almost extracted a promise from Pichon to come to the wedding; but the Consul immediately set himself to hunt up his country's laws on the subject, and found that a Frenchman must be over twenty-five in order to marry without consent of father or mother. Jerome's premature lieutenancy could hardly prove him to be twenty-five! He wrote off at once to Jerome; to d'Hébécourt, representing France at Baltimore; and to William Patterson, whom he told that, Madame Bonaparte being still alive, the marriage could not be valid without her consent. He further went to call on the Marquis d'Yrujo, with whom he had a violent scene, finally making the

The Burlesque Napoleon

Spaniard promise not to attend the wedding. Pichon received an angry complaint from Jerome for writing to Patterson; and as the Consul also heard that the latter declared that he could not consent to the marriage, owing to Jerome not having reached the necessary age, he felt that he had at least administered a check. He posted off to France on the 3rd November, the day originally appointed for the marriage, the statement that he had full confidence that Patterson, warned as he had been, would not let things go any further. He knew that Jerome had a licence; but he attached no importance to this in face of the official disapproval of France, in his own person.

Jerome, indeed, had proceeded to get a licence at the Baltimore court-house on the 29th October; but not only could he not satisfy Elizabeth's father on the point of age, but he was also hampered by lack of money. He had spent 16,000 dollars in the United States; he saw no means of getting any more save through Pichon, and Pichon would only consent to furnish money in return for deference to his views. Nevertheless, Jerome sent to Washington on the 5th November an invitation to the wedding two days later. The invitation was naturally

The Bonaparte-Patterson Marriage

refused by Pichon, as also, through Pichon's influence, was one sent to d'Yrujo; but the refusals were unnecessary, for other circumstances had intervened.

It is not clear what exactly occasioned the breaking off of the engagement at this point. On the 5th November, the day that Jerome's message reached Pichon, Mr Patterson received an anonymous letter warning him against "the destroyer of others' happiness," "without exception the most profligate young man of the age." This may have helped the father in his decision. At any rate, the following day Pichon received another letter from Jerome, delivered by the hand of Le Camus, which stated that, after mature reflection, he had broken off the match, the affair having concluded honourably for him. Mr Patterson, he said, had sent Elizabeth away to the south. He asked Pichon to return to him his letters on the subject, and to say no more about it. To this Pichon agreed. He merely wrote to Talleyrand to tell him that the engagement was decidedly at an end—news which reached France about the middle of January. Jerome was going to New York, he added; and Le Camus had brought word that Mr Patterson had determined to send his daughter

The Burlesque Napoleon

to Virginia. Pichon could not refrain from showing his satisfaction over his supposed success; for he considered that his own conduct in very embarrassing circumstances, and the isolation in which he had managed to place Jerome, had prevented a catastrophe. But he was anxious to follow up his victory, and to remove Jerome permanently from danger, by getting him out of the United States. The French frigate *Poursuivante* had opportunely arrived in Baltimore harbour under the command of Willaumez, afterwards Admiral. Pichon pointed out the advisability of a return to duty and to France on the frigate. Jerome took the advice ill. When Willaumez added his recommendation to Pichon's, Jerome replied that he had no orders to take from anyone, and that he was on a mission. Having disposed of his unwelcome mentors he announced his intention of going to New York. To this there seemed no objection, and in the middle of November he proceeded north. His reception in New York now was as cordial and as flattering as that at Baltimore in July. A succession of festivities awaited him, and when he returned to Baltimore on the 1st December he was apparently very well satisfied.

The Bonaparte-Patterson Marriage

His Consul-General, looking on this as a good sign, augured the best, and sent, in reply to a request from Jerome, 1000 dollars from an advance of 10,000 of which he had held out hopes in event of good conduct. He did not know the truth, it need hardly be said, which was that Jerome had been in constant communication by letter with Elizabeth, exiled though the latter had been to a Virginian estate of her family. Morever, her bitter disappointment over her loss of the season's amusements at Baltimore had ended by softening her mother's heart, and she was soon allowed to come back. Her return almost coincided with that of her lover. If the Pattersons really intended to prevent the marriage this step of allowing Elizabeth to meet Jerome again was fatal. The temporary separation had merely made the two determined to have their own way. They were again constantly meeting in local society as in September and October; and finally William Patterson's opposition broke down. No invitation was sent this time to Pichon. The unsuspecting Consul-General, on the night of the 24th December, sent off to Jerome another 4000 dollars out of the advance which was expected from him. Next

The Burlesque Napoleon

day he received a letter written by Le Camus, which had crossed his, to the following effect:—
"Sir, I have the honour to inform you, on behalf of M. Jerome Bonaparte, that his marriage with Miss Patterson was celebrated yesterday evening. He charges me also to tell you that he is awaiting with impatience the 4000 dollars which you are sending him. His engagements are becoming pressing, and his household will soon be in need. He begs you, therefore, to be so good as to despatch this sum to him as soon as possible."

Le Camus's announcement was perfectly true. On Christmas Eve, less than four months after their first meeting, Jerome Bonaparte and Elizabeth Patterson were married, at the Patterson's house in Baltimore, by the Right Rev. John Carroll, Roman Catholic Bishop of that city, and afterwards Primate of the American Catholic Church. The Mayor and many prominent townspeople were present besides the bride's family; and France was represented by Le Camus, and Sottin, who had succeeded d'Hébécourt at Baltimore, and who had easily been persuaded by Jerome that he ought to be present at the ceremony. Descriptions of the costumes of the contracting parties were carefully preserved—indeed, the bridegroom's clothes

The Bonaparte-Patterson Marriage

may be in existence now, for they were kept by his wife to the day of her death. Jerome's coat was of purple satin, laced and embroidered, the white satin-lined skirts reaching to his heels. He wore knee-breeches, his shoes had diamond buckles, and his hair was powdered. The bride wore considerably less: as she remarked herself, dress at that time was chiefly an aid to setting off beauty to advantage. One of the wedding guests is reported to have said that he could have put all the bride's clothes in his pocket, and another witness relates in horror that she only wore a single garment underneath! To the world, however, her toilet was an Indian muslin gown embellished with old lace and with pearls. The wedding over, Monsieur and Madame Jerome proceeded to the Patterson's estate, "Homestead," outside Baltimore, for their honeymoon.

Pichon was powerless in the face of accomplished facts. He had already unsuspectingly sent the money which Jerome required for his expenses. There was no one on whom to vent his feelings except Sottin, who had written to him an amiable and ingenuous letter, in which he expressed the hopes that the young couple would be happy, and that the storm (which

The Burlesque Napoleon

they must expect) would be short. He also informed his chief that the lady was really pretty, and was said to have brains and to have been well brought up. The Consul, while crushing Sottin, could not see how to be otherwise than polite to Jerome, whom, with his wife and some of her relatives, he entertained to dinner at Georgetown on the 3rd January. On the next day he sent off to Talleyrand his first intimation of the fatal news. His chief anxiety, naturally, was to clear himself of all complicity in the affair. He made, however, this much excuse for the Pattersons, that he mentioned the general impression that the " young person had been as determined on her part as Jerome was on his, and that consent had to be given to the marriage to avoid a scandal." Having despatched his news, Pichon resigned himself to awaiting the effect. Mr Patterson also thought it wise to have his version of the affair conveyed to France promptly. He entrusted the mission to his son Robert, writing at the same time to Chancellor Livingston, the American representative in Paris, and enclosing letters to Napoleon from the United States President and Secretary of State. It seems probable that Jerome and his

The Bonaparte-Patterson Marriage

father-in-law had already written to Livingston, seeing that he knew all about the affair when Elizabeth's brother presented himself to him; but if so, the letters are lost.

On his arrival in Paris on the 11th March 1804 Robert Patterson called at once on his country's representative, and learnt from him that the First Consul's anger concerning the marriage was extreme. Nevertheless, the minister thought that he might be induced in time to relent, and meanwhile advised that Jerome should continue to reside in the United States. The exact date on which Napoleon heard of Jerome's marriage is uncertain. In January both he and Madame Letizia Bonaparte had been informed of the engagement and its breaking off, and Napoleon had immediately sent orders for his brother to return to France—orders which did not reach Jerome until May. The young man had quailed before the thought of writing to the First Consul, and he had not apparently communicated even with his mother or any others of his family when Pichon's letter of the 4th January put Napoleon in possession of the facts. This letter must have arrived in Paris, at the latest, early in March, as the news was already public when Robert Patterson reached Paris.

The Burlesque Napoleon

It had not produced on the Bonapartes generally the effect which it had on Napoleon. Joseph, according to what Livingston told Robert Patterson, was quite reconciled to the idea, and spoke about investing money in American funds to enable Jerome to go on living in the United States. Further, when Robert Patterson visited Lucien Bonaparte three days after his arrival, he was assured by him that Madame Bonaparte, he himself, and the rest of the family approved the match—all, in fact, except the First Consul, who did not for the present concur with them, his action being dictated by policy with which his family had nothing to do. He also advised that Jerome should stay in the United States, and even suggested that he should get naturalised there. In speaking as he did, Lucien, who had but recently married his second wife against Napoleon's wishes, exhibited his usual independence of character, but also his inability to estimate Napoleon's power of will. In a few weeks' time Lucien himself was in exile because of his marriage; in a few months the rest of the family was, outwardly at least, in agreement with Napoleon's policy towards Jerome.

Napoleon allowed some time to elapse before

The Bonaparte-Patterson Marriage

he took any steps. It was not until the 20th April that Decrès, Minister of Marine, wrote to Pichon to give him Napoleon's strict injunctions that no money must be advanced to Jerome; that Jerome must at once obey the orders already sent for his return on a French frigate; and that all captains of French vessels should be prohibited from receiving on board the young person with whom he had formed a connection—it being the First Consul's intention that she should not set foot in France—and, did she come thither, that she should be sent back immediately to the United States. Decrès added a kind personal letter to Jerome, urging him to obey his brother, and informing him of the fate that had just befallen Lucien. He quoted what Napoleon had said to himself: "I will receive Jerome if he leaves the young person in America and comes hither to associate himself with my fortunes. If he brings her with him she shall not set foot in the territory of France. If he comes alone I will forgive the error of a moment and the fault of youth. Faithful services and the conduct which is due to himself will regain for him all my kindness." The trial which Jerome's character was so ill fitted to resist had begun.

NAPOLEON CONQUERS

CHAPTER IV

NAPOLEON CONQUERS

AFTER their dinner with Pichon at Georgetown Jerome and Elizabeth had continued their honeymoon in the neighbourhood of Baltimore. At the beginning of February they proceeded to Washington, and took up their residence near the Capitol. If the young Bonaparte had been well received there before, he and his bride were still more warmly welcomed now. The air of romance which surrounded them was irresistible in its attraction. President Jefferson was more than benevolent to them, officials and diplomatists followed the example, and the useful Marquis d'Yrujo and Elizabeth's relatives formed almost a court around them. Pichon in a letter to Talleyrand, describing the state of affairs, says: "M. Bonaparte is constantly with Madame's friends. He seems to take and give pleasure in such society. It is vexing to see a young man of his age, in his position, and with his tastes, given up so entirely to frivolity

The Burlesque Napoleon

and idleness. Madame has anything rather than the character to lead him to serious affairs. She is proud of her position, and only thinks about enjoying all the glory which it gives her." After the slighting remark on her education, already quoted above, he adds: "At least, that is how it strikes me. It is possible, as I have seen little of Madame Jerome Bonaparte, that I am mistaken." Pichon was a harsh judge of the girl of eighteen, still practically on her honeymoon. He was, no doubt, right in considering her unfit for the task of turning Jerome towards serious things; but what woman would have been equal to that task? Pichon and Willaumez had renewed their solicitation of Jerome to embark on the *Poursuivante* as lieutenant, and return to France. The Consul could hardly have expected Elizabeth to join in persuading her husband to go to an unknown, almost certainly unpleasant, future. The Pattersons, indeed, threw their influence strongly in the other scale. They had no difficulty in inducing Jerome to stay until he heard what his brother had to say about the marriage. He told Pichon that he had given his word of honour to wait for this; and so when the *Poursuivante* sailed from Baltimore early in

Napoleon Conquers

March, Lieutenant Bonaparte was not on board.

Willaumez had left but a short time when Meyronnet returned from France with the instructions which Jerome had sent him to fetch in the previous winter. These were contained in a letter written by Decrès on the 26th January, and ordered him to embark on the *Poursuivante*, or, should she have left, by the first French frigate available, "as great events were preparing." In spite of the urgency of the command, Jerome now adhered to the view that he must stay until Napoleon had learnt of his marriage and expressed his opinion thereon. Accordingly, with the approval of his wife's family, and presumably with financial aid from them, since he had now nothing but debts left he set out on a tour through the northern and eastern states. While on this pleasure-trip he received intelligence that the French frigates *Didon* and *Cybèle* had reached New York at the end of May, coming from France by way of the Antilles. They had brought imperative orders for him to embark if he should still be in the United States; and Pichon, in forwarding the news, impressed on him that he must start at once if he wished to escape danger. The

The Burlesque Napoleon

frigates had left France before the marriage was known there; Jerome, nevertheless, hardly knew whether he could disregard the command sent to him. Torn in two directions, he compromised by delaying as much as he could, and so did not reach New York until the 12th June, when he brought Elizabeth and her father with him. The *Didon* was reputed the fastest boat in the French navy, and it was on her that the husband and wife embarked. The commander had no ground for refusing a passage to Elizabeth, the prohibition not having reached America yet, and she was accordingly installed on board. All was ready for a start when suddenly a message was brought that the English frigates *Cambrian* and *Boston*, and the sloop *Driver*, were at the mouth of the Hudson. Other vessels were suspected in the offing. It was obviously impossible to sail at once. The English warships, after protests from the United States Government, consented to move as far as to Sandy Hook, but there they remained in waiting. Jerome's delay had succeeded in preventing the escape of the French frigates, and early in July he decided to resume his tour, and visit Niagara.

In August the blow struck by Napoleon fell. His decision reached Jerome with the news of

Napoleon Conquers

the great event of the 18th May, so that the young husband knew himself simultaneously brother of an Emperor, and commanded to renounce his wife. On the 9th June Napoleon had written, through Talleyrand, to Pichon that Jerome could not have hoped to have his marriage recognised as valid, and that he, in fact, considered it null. He quoted the law of the 26 *pluviôse an XI.* (which was the law Pichon had already used, to the best of his power, to stop the wedding), and concluded with the statement that he could not permit his family to break the laws. Jerome was in despair. He sent a letter to Napoleon which is, unfortunately, lost. A covering message to Decrès, dated the 18th August 1804, betrays his wretchedness. " I beg you," he wrote, " to be so kind as to give my brother the enclosed letter. I explain to him my situation in this country, which daily becomes more cruel, and I urgently ask for orders to leave it. You have yourself been long in this part of the world, and can, best of all people, explain to him how out of place my life is here, and how burdensome a longer stay here will be to me. . . . The great events which to-day occupy the world's attention do not allow my brother, I suppose,

The Burlesque Napoleon

to send me news of himself and of my family as soon as I could wish." Two days after writing this, Jerome went to a reception on the *Didon* in New York harbour, where the ship's officers gave him the title of "Your Imperial Highness," in spite of the fact that he could have no claim to it until the Emperor so allowed. When, however, it came to a question of taking Elizabeth as passenger, the frigate's commander was afraid to disobey Napoleon's express order. Jerome thereon was deaf to the entreaties of Pichon. One attempt was made to arrange matters by sending Elizabeth from New York with General Armstrong—who was proceeding to Paris to succeed Livingston—while Jerome was to make use of the *Didon*. Jerome and Elizabeth, however, intentionally or not, reached the landing-stage after Armstrong's boat had gone. Further delay might be dangerous, and as the *Didon* could not take Elizabeth, it was decided that both should cross the Atlantic on a neutral vessel.

A brig named the *Philadelphia* was hired, and a secret start was arranged from the city of that name in October. Before he left, Jerome received an encouraging letter from his brother Joseph, which might well lead him to hope that

Napoleon Conquers

Napoleon would end by acknowledging Elizabeth. With good prospects, therefore, Jerome, his wife, and one of her aunts, Miss Spear, set sail on the 24th October down the Delaware. Still they were not to leave America yet. A storm arose on the following evening in Delaware Bay; the whole night was passed in instant fear of disaster; and on the following day the *Philadelphia* ran on to a sandbank. The task of escape was difficult. Elizabeth rose to the occasion. Though the waves were running very high she insisted that a boat must put off for the shore. "Are you in command of this ship?" asked the captain. "Yes; if necessary." "How do you propose to reach the boat?" "You must throw me in." The captain yielded; but, unfortunately, Elizabeth was thrown into the water instead of the boat, and was wet through when she was fished out. A safe landing was at last effected, a pilot's cottage was reached, and the next we hear is how Miss Spear found her niece eating roast goose and apple sauce, and called her "an irreligious little wretch" for doing so instead of being on her knees in thanksgiving. News was at once sent to Pichon, who, with what feelings one may imagine, hastened off to see what he could do.

The Burlesque Napoleon

He found Jerome and his ladies at Newcastle, Delaware, safe and sound, but penniless. He had not only nearly lost his wife, but had actually lost, according to his own account, between 2000 and 3000 dollars, in addition to over 4000 dollars of passage-money. Pichon conducted the party to Philadelphia, and on the 2nd of November they were once more in Baltimore.

Yet another attempt was now made to induce Jerome to obey the command to return on a French warship. The frigate *Président* reached Annapolis at the end of November, bringing Napoleon's ambassador to the United States, General Thurreau, who had absolute orders not to recognise Madame Jerome Bonaparte, and to avoid meeting her. Thurreau offered Jerome a passage for himself on the *Président*, which was to return to France immediately. Jerome accepted, and, arriving at Annapolis with Elizabeth, went on board. The commander received the lady politely, disregarding what instructions he may have had, and all was ready for departure when H.M. frigate *Resolution* appeared in Chesapeake Bay, and anchored alongside the *Président*. According to the French accounts, Elizabeth in her alarm persuaded Jerome to

Napoleon Conquers

disembark. The idea of leaving before the New Year was abandoned, and the Bonapartes spent the anniversary of their wedding in the States. Jerome would hear no more of returning on a warship, after the repeated fiasco, which was not so humorous for him as for spectators or the American newspapers of the day. He applied first to Thurreau, who refused, and then to his father-in-law, about hiring a vessel. Rumours had reached America of Napoleon's intention of throwing his brother into prison until he repudiated his wife, but Jerome was still confident that the sight of Elizabeth would soften the Emperor's heart. Mr Patterson furnished one of his own vessels, the *Erin*, and on the 3rd March a start was made from Baltimore unknown to all but the family. With the party went William Patterson, junior, a brother of Elizabeth; Le Camus; and Jerome's doctor, Garnier, as Elizabeth was expecting the birth of a child. This time the voyage was uneventful. The worst that Jerome had to write to his father-in-law was that Elizabeth had suffered from sea-sickness; "But you know," he wrote in English, "as well as anybody that sea-sick never has killed nobody."

The Burlesque Napoleon

Lisbon was reached on the 8th April. Napoleon had taken his measures. On the 22nd February (*3 ventose an XIII.*) a solemn protest was published, nominally by Madame Letizia Bonaparte, against the American marriage. On the 2nd March, just when Jerome was on the eve of departure from Baltimore, elated at the idea of overcoming his brother's objections, Napoleon published a decree (that of the *11 ventose*, as it was known), which, alluding to the protest of Madame Mére against "the pretended marriage of her son Jerome Bonaparte, a minor, contracted in a foreign country, without his mother's consent, and without previous publication in the place of his domicile," forbade civil officials of the Empire to receive on their registers a transcription of the certificate of celebration of the ceremony. A further decree, of the *30 ventose*, reinforced the former, and declared the marriage null, and any offspring from it illegitimate. As soon as the *Erin* reached Lisbon a French guard surrounded her, and Napoleon's Consul-General, Serrurier, came on board. Presented to Elizabeth, he inquired what he could do for "Miss Patterson." Elizabeth with spirit replied: "Tell your master that Madame Bonaparte is ambi-

Napoleon Conquers

tious, and demands her rights as a member of the Imperial family." She was thereon given to understand that on no account would she be allowed to land—Portugal, Spain, and Holland being closed to her as well as France.

For Jerome himself, his brother's orders were equally straightforward and unmistakable. Napoleon explains them himself in a letter written from the neighbourhood of Turin to Madame Mère on the 22nd April. The letter is so good an example of the vigour of the writer's style when he was resolved to be inflexible that it may be given in its entirety:

"M. Jerome Bonaparte has reached Lisbon with the woman with whom he is living. I have sent orders to this prodigal son to proceed to Milan by way of Perpignan, Toulouse, Grenoble, and Turin. I have let him know that if he diverges from this route he will be arrested. Miss Patterson, who is living with him, has taken the precaution of bringing her brother with her. I have given the order that she is to be sent back to America. If she evades the orders which I have given, and comes to Bordeaux or Paris, she will be taken back to Amsterdam, there to be put on board the first American vessel. I shall treat this

The Burlesque Napoleon

young man severely if, at the only interview which I shall grant him, he shows himself unworthy of the name which he bears, and persists in wishing to continue his intrigue. If he is not prepared to wash out the dishonour which he has brought on my name by abandoning his flag for a wretched woman, I shall give him up for ever, and perhaps make an example to teach young soldiers the sacredness of their duties, and the enormity of their crime when they desert their flag for a woman. Write to him on the supposition that he is going to Milan; tell him that I have been a father to him, that his duty towards me is sacred, and that he has no longer any salvation except in following my instructions. Speak to his sisters, that they may write to him also; for when I have pronounced his sentence I shall be inflexible, and his life will be blasted for ever."[1]

With what feelings Madame Mère received this stern, not to say brutal, letter we do not know. Her fondness for Jerome was next to that for Napoleon among her sons. Moreover, in spite of the protest just published in her name, she had consented, if only after the

[1] Lecestre, "Lettres Inédites de Napoléon," i. p. 47.

Napoleon Conquers

event, to the marriage; and legally, at the date of the affair, it was her consent, certainly not Napoleon's, the second son's, which was necessary.

Jerome lost no time in hastening to the point where he hoped to meet his brother. Bidding good-bye to Elizabeth, whom he was never to speak to again, and only once again to see, he set out through Spain, apparently in full confidence that he would bend the Imperial will, and be able to send for his beautiful wife very soon. It is fortunate for Jerome's character that we have a record throwing light on how he felt at this time, for it relieves him at least from the charge of absolute lack of heart. He had just passed Merida, in Estramadura, when he came upon Junot and his wife on their way to Lisbon, where the Marshal was about to take up the duties of ambassador. They had halted at an inn, and Madame Junot was dressing for breakfast, when the Marshal knocked at her door, and told her that a friend of her childhood had come from Baltimore, and was asking for her. She was pleased to see Jerome again. "He had always been *bon enfant*, as the world calls those who do no harm, if they do no good." Madame Permon had transmitted

The Burlesque Napoleon

to her daughter a kindly feeling for Jerome. Besides, was there not sympathy for one unhappy in love to appeal to her romantic sense? Junot, who had only seen Jerome as a child, was also glad to meet him again, and so both welcomed him to breakfast. Madame Junot was struck by the change in him; she found him sedate, almost serious, with his usually gay and mobile expression touched by a thoughtful sadness, which made him almost unrecognisable. Before he continued the journey Junot, in a fatherly manner, advised him to yield to the Emperor. Jerome answered that, since he held himself bound in honour, he did not think, having the consent of his mother and eldest brother, he had any course open to him but that which he had decided to take. His noble confidence impressed his hearers. Jerome proceeded to assert that Napoleon would listen to him. "He is kind and just. Suppose that I have committed a fault in marrying Miss Patterson without his consent, must the punishment strike now? And on whose head will it fall? On my poor, innocent wife's. No, no; my brother cannot wish to put an outrageous stigma on one of the most respectable families in the United States, and at the same time to deal a mortal blow to one as good as she is beautiful." Taking from his breast a golden medallion, he displayed a miniature of Elizabeth, who struck Madame Junot as possessed of a ravishing face, and, while resembling Pauline Bonaparte, as showing much more fire and animation. The lover besought them to judge whether he could desert such a person when united to her beauty were all the qualities which make a woman lovable. He was certain of Elizabeth's victory if the Emperor would only see her once. He alluded to Christine Boyer, *cette bonne Christine*, Lucien's first wife, who after being repulsed by Napoleon was in the end as much loved by him as his other sisters-in-law. "I am determined not to yield," he concluded. "Strong in the goodness of my cause, I will take no action of which I might afterwards repent!"

What would be more correct than Jerome's sentiments? He rode off, still in full hope of success. Madame Junot says she was agitated, nevertheless, and could not trust him to show Lucien's strength of mind. With Jerome went his friend and secretary Le Camus, who at the time impressed Madame Junot favourably, though she suspected him later of helping to persuade Jerome to abandon his wife. The

The Burlesque Napoleon

two pressed on through Spain and France into Italy. Turin was reached on the 24th April, and thence Jerome sent an appeal to his brother, who was at Alessandria. The letter does not survive; it would be an interesting document. It had no effect upon Napoleon, who absolutely refused to see Jerome until he should announce himself ready to yield to his will. Eleven days were passed by the unhappy young man with two alternatives before his eyes—either to surrender unconditionally, and be given the chance of "washing out his dishonour"; or to keep his sacred word to his wife, and undergo what disgrace Napoleon might choose to inflict on him. The Jerome of a later period might not have hesitated so long; now he was still much in love. He brought himself, however, to make the required submission—with mental reservations, as appears afterwards. He obtained permission to go to Alessandria, whence he wrote a letter, also lost, on the morning of the 6th June. Napoleon's answer, written on the same day, is in existence. "My brother," wrote the Emperor; "your letter of this morning tells me of your arrival at Alessandria. There are no faults in your conduct which a sincere repentance does not efface in my eyes. Your

Napoleon Conquers

union with Miss Patterson is null in religion as in law. Write to Miss Patterson to return to America. I will grant her a pension of 60,000 francs during her life, on condition that in no event she shall bear my name, to which she has no right, her marriage being non-existent. You yourself must make her understand that you have not been, and are not, able to change the nature of things. Your marriage being thus annulled of your own free will, I will restore to you my friendship and resume the feelings which I have had towards you since your childhood, hoping that you will show yourself worthy of them by your anxiety to earn my gratitude and to distinguish yourself in my armies."

On the same day Napoleon wrote to his sister Elisa, expressing his satisfaction with Jerome's sentiments, and stating that Le Camus was to go to "Miss Patterson" to persuade her that her marriage, null in religion and in law, must be null in her own eyes also. Twelve days later he wrote to Decrès that Jerome had acknowledged his fault, and disavowed "this person" as his wife; that Jerome had promised miracles; and that he had sent him to Genoa for a while. He had, indeed,

The Burlesque Napoleon

sent him on a special mission to Genoa after according him an interview at Alessandria. His first words to him on their meeting are reported to have been: "You, sir, are the first of the family to abandon your post shamefully. It will require many striking actions to wipe that stain off your reputation. As for your love affair with your little girl, I disregard it." The reconciliation, however, was effected, and the pardoned prodigal (who, according to the witness of Napoleon's valet Constant, left his brother's room visibly affected)[1] was despatched to forget his grief in the work of inspecting the French vessels in the harbour of Genoa. On the 18th May Napoleon appointed him to the command of the principal of these, the 44-gun frigate *Pomone*, with two brigs also under his charge. The intention was that he should devote himself entirely to the completion of his naval training, paying particular attention to gunnery. After sailing to Toulon to complete his vessels' armaments, he was to cruise in the neighbourhood of Genoa. Two more frigates were added to his squadron in the course of a few days, the Emperor writing to

[1] Martinet draws a picture of Jerome, "*l'âme déchireé, s'inclinant devant la volonté de son aîné.*"

Napoleon Conquers

his Minister of Marine that Jerome had "brains, character, decision, and enough general knowledge of his profession to be able to make use of others' talents." Napoleon can hardly have held that Jerome had deserved such a favourable report by his conduct so far in the navy. Perhaps he felt the need of justifying to Decrès, who knew so much of that conduct, the confidence which he was now showing in the young man, and therefore set himself to enlighten him as to the real worth of character which underlay his frivolous exterior. But it is at least open to suspicion that Napoleon, eager though he was to discover merit in all his family, would have hesitated to stake much on the estimate of Jerome which he gave to Decrès. Outwardly, the fact that he had entrusted him with duties proper to a rear-admiral seemed sufficiently to back his opinion.

Suffering from the wound of separation from Elizabeth, and assuredly from shame at his broken word, Jerome began to develop rapidly the extraordinary levity which marked his life. Napoleon's method of discipline was ill-chosen, indeed, for a character like his. The high functions which had been thrust on him appealed only to his hurt vanity. It was gratify-

The Burlesque Napoleon

ing to be acting virtually as a rear-admiral, and the inappropriateness of the duties to one who had reached only the rank of lieutenant could not fail to strike him. His remedy for the anomaly was to assume the honours due to a full captain. Decrès, contrasting this conduct with Napoleon's eulogium, no doubt, complained. Napoleon expressed himself in full agreement with the Minister's views, but, nevertheless, stultified himself at once by raising the offender to be *capitaine de frégate*. After his severe castigation of him at Alessandria, only on one point would he show himself relentless to Jerome. This was with regard to his wife. Jerome had made a last appeal to him at the end of May. Napoleon waited ten days, and then wrote to him from Milan, assuring him that nothing he could say would alter his determination. He held up the awful example of Lucien, bitterly censuring the "mental alienation" of one who preferred a disgraced woman to the honour of his name and his family, and whose selfishness had robbed him of a brilliant destiny. He ended a brief note with these words: "Miss Patterson has been in London, and caused great excitement among the English. This has only increased her guilt."

Napoleon Conquers

From the date, early in April, when Jerome had left her, to the end of the month, Elizabeth had remained on the *Erin* off Lisbon. The ship then sailed for Amsterdam, arriving on the 1st May. Holland, as Serrurier had threatened, proved closed to Jerome Bonaparte's wife like the rest of the Continent. Schimmelpenninck, appointed by Napoleon first Grand Pensionary of the Batavian Republic, was a good servant, and took immediate steps to prevent the *Erin* from having any communication with the shore from the moment of her arrival in the Texel. Guarded by two war-vessels, one a 64-gun ship, the *Erin* lay at anchor, virtually a prisoner, for eight days. Finally the intervention of Bourne, the United States representative at Amsterdam, procured her release, and the *Erin*, having on board Elizabeth, her brother, an American friend, Mrs Anderson, and the French doctor, made for the English coast. On the 19th May the Dover Roads were reached, and Elizabeth was beyond the power of Napoleon. No obstacle was put in the way of her landing on English soil. *The Morning Chronicle* of the 20th May had the following brief record of the event:—" It was reported yesterday

The Burlesque Napoleon

that Mrs Jerome Bonaparte had arrived in the Downs, and had applied to Lord Hawkesbury for passports to land, she having been refused leave to land in Holland. It is added that passports were immediately sent down to Deal to permit her to come ashore." From Dover she proceeded to London, avoiding publicity as much as possible, for political reasons, as well as on account of her state. In June she made a move to Camberwell, then only an outlying suburb on the Surrey side of London. Here, in a house in Park Place, on the 7th July, she gave birth to a son, to whom the name of Jerome Napoleon was given, and who became the founder of the American family of Bonapartes. The young mother proposed to stay in England during the winter, "but not in London, as my going into public or showing myself here would be highly improper."[1] She still believed in Jerome's honour, and concluded that he must be a prisoner in the power of his brother. But the news which soon arrived from the Continent changed her decision about remaining in Europe till the spring at least. When it became plain that the husband's protestations were inconsistent with his conduct,

[1] Letter to William Patterson, 14th August 1805.

Napoleon Conquers

the wife determined to accept the shelter of her former home.

In November Elizabeth returned to the United States with her child, to settle down to a position detestable above all others to her. To be merely an injured heroine of romance in Baltimore was the cruellest of fates to her who had aspired to be a princess in Europe. "Madame Bonaparte is ambitious" had been her message to Napoleon through his agent at Lisbon; and now the end of her ambitions seemed to be this, that she had become the object of wonder to her fellow-townspeople. When we consider her early pride and hopes, it is not so much curious that her disposition hardened under the treatment which she received, as that she bore her sorrow with what calm she did. Two passages in her correspondence later in life throw an interesting light on her attitude. In the first, writing to her father, she says: "I was sacrificed to political considerations, not to the gratification of bad feelings, and under the pressure of insupportable disappointment became not unjust." There is rather a suggestion of the maxim about this. In the following there is a more genuiue ring. "The Emperor," she wrote in 1849, "hurled me back on what I hated most on earth—my

The Burlesque Napoleon

Baltimore obscurity. Even that shock could not destroy the admiration I felt for his genius and glory. I have ever been an imperial Bonaparte *quand même*." Let the limitation of her desires be condemned however much, it must be admitted that the bitterness of having been so near attainment of the object was greater than that of a complete failure to attain. The self-revelation in the abundant letters of Elizabeth Patterson-Bonaparte[1] prevent her, perhaps, from being a sympathetic character. But interesting she undoubtedly was, and attractive with a certain hard brilliance. The many years which she spent on the Continent, after the downfall of Napoleon and his family, proved clearly that this pioneer of American invaders of the European marriage preserves was well adapted to shine in that society which she had proposed in her girlhood to enter. The contrast between her triumphs in Europe from 1815 to the 'thirties, and the apparently endless obscurity into which the discredited and bankrupt Jerome had sunk, must have been sufficiently piquant to her.

With the relations between Jerome and his

[1] See E. L. Didier, "The Life and Letters of Madame Bonaparte."

Napoleon Conquers

wife during the seven years following their separation at Lisbon it is convenient to deal here, leaving to their proper place the final meeting between the two and the acquaintance between King Jerome in exile and his American son. As has been stated, Napoleon made a grievance of the departure for England of the unfortunate girl whom he prevented from landing anywhere on the Continent of Europe. Jerome, too, was displeased at the step which Elizabeth took, or else, under the domination of Napoleon, he pretended to be displeased; for, so soon as he heard what she had done, he wrote a complaint to William Patterson through Le Camus. He followed this up with another letter to his father-in-law, in which he expressed the wish that Elizabeth should return to America, to wait in her former home until he should have obtained her recall from the Emperor. It is hardly possible to say that Jerome was insincere in his protestations of hope and of continued love at this period. It is true that we very soon begin to hear of a young Genoese woman, Bianca or Blanche Carrega, whom he met during his mission to her native place, and who attached herself to his fortunes in such a way as to leave no doubt of their relations. But this did not

The Burlesque Napoleon

take place at once, and we need not consider his early letters to Elizabeth as pretending to sentiments which he had ceased to feel.[1] He had nothing to gain in any material way by asserting to his "dear little wife" that all his love and his life were hers, or in beseeching her, after their son's birth, to believe he would never entertain the fatal thought of abandoning her. "I love my country, and I love glory," he declared to her,[2] "but I love them as a man accustomed to fear nothing, who will never forget that he is the father of Jerome Napoleon and the husband of Elise." Again: "Be assured, my dear wife, that I work and endure only for you and for my son. Let people say what they will. Adieu, Elisa; a thousand embraces!" And a little later still: "My first thought on waking, as my last before going to sleep, is always for you, and if I were not sure that I should have the happiness of rejoining my beloved wife I should not go on living."

Napoleon had not contented himself with

[1] Jerome's ideas of marital fidelty, moreover, were peculiar, for, as will be seen later on, he did not deem inconsistent with his undoubted attachment to Catherine, fondest of wives, a long series of scarcely at all concealed intrigues with all manner of ladies.

[2] Letter of the 4th October 1805.

separating husband and wife and declaring their marriage illegal. After a consultation with Cambacères in May he despatched Cardinal Fesch to Rome with a present of a gold diadem, decked with diamonds and rubies, for Pope Pius VII., and a letter containing a request for a bull to annul Jerome's marriage. He stated that his brother, a minor, had married "a Protestant young woman" after a month's residence only in the United States; that a Spanish priest had so far forgotten himself as to pronounce his blessing on the marriage; that he could have the union broken in Paris, but that he preferred to have it annulled in Rome, on account of the example which would be furnished. Cardinal Fesch, if we may judge by a letter which he wrote to the Emperor after an interview with Pius, expected that he would yield to Napoleon's wish. The Pope, however, did not do so, in spite of the misrepresentation of the case by his Imperial correspondent. The matter was considered very carefully, and all possible precedents examined. Finally, anxious though he might be, on general grounds, to fall in with Napoleon's wishes, the Pope was obliged to say that he found no reasons for annulling a marriage duly performed

The Burlesque Napoleon

by the Bishop of Baltimore (no misguided Spanish priest, as the Emperor had alleged); and, as for the point about the Protestant young woman, the Church, though disapproving of such marriages, acknowledged them as valid. The Vatican's answer was sent on the 26th June. Deprived of the aid of Rome, Napoleon had recourse to the Gallican Church, on which at least he could count. This involved delay; but finally, in the October of the following year, the American marriage was declared null ecclesiastically in Paris.

Jerome, though he continued to write to Elizabeth down to the year 1812, ceased, after he had been declared free of his marriage, to speak of a possibility of reunion, and interested himself in his son rather than in his wife. His communications grew scantier as well as colder. In fact, after the 17th July 1806, when he wrote very briefly to say that he was well, but full of regrets at being so far from Elizabeth, he remained silent for almost two years. In 1808 he sent from Cassel to the United States one of the Le Camus family, a brother of Alexandre, to try to bring the young Jerome Napoleon to Westphalia, with the Emperor's consent. Very naturally, Elizabeth and her

Napoleon Conquers

family entirely refused such a proposal. In November of the same year Jerome wrote to offer her the principality of Smalkalden, in Westphalia, with a pension of 200,000 francs a year. Elizabeth, though she restrained her bitter tongue as a rule from making any remarks about her deserter, could not resist the opening which this astonishing suggestion gave her. Westphalia was a large kingdom, she replied, but not large enough for two queens. Moreover, she preferred being sheltered under the wing of an eagle to hanging from the bill of a goose. The eagle, of course, was Napoleon, who kept his promise of allowing her 60,000 francs a year up to the date of his fall.[1] The rebuff kept Jerome silent for three years. Then he wrote to her for the last time as follows:—
"My dear Elisa, what a long time it is since I have received any news of you and of my son! In the whole world you could never find a better or a more tender friend than me. I have many things to write to you; but, as I

[1] Madame Patterson-Bonaparte was inconsistent in her use of the name Bonaparte, against which Napoleon had expressly stipulated. She insisted on signing her receipts in that name, and as late as 1815 used the initials "E. B." in her correspondence. After she had procured a divorce in the Maryland legislature she ceased to do so.

The Burlesque Napoleon

can but fear that this letter may be intercepted, I limit myself to giving you news of myself and asking you for news of you and my son. Be assured that all will be arranged sooner or later. The Emperor is certainly the best, as he is the greatest, of men." He signed himself "*Votre affectionné et bon ami, Jérôme-Napolèon.*" The humour of this production must have struck the recipient more than the writer. But it is worthy of note that Elizabeth, for all her silent contempt for Jerome, firmly believed in the reality of his love for her above all others. "Jerome loved me to the last," she is recorded to have asserted after his death. "He thought me the handsomest woman in the world, and the most charming. After his marriage with the Princess he gave to the Court painters several miniatures of me, from which to make a portrait, which he kept hidden from the good Catherine." She may have been right, but we do not know what evidence she possessed beyond the letters which she received from Jerome from 1805 to 1812. One is inclined to doubt whether any passion for an individual woman could maintain a long hold over Jerome. The very secret of his many years of tenderness for his second wife was that he was never "in love" with her.

THE WAY TO
A THRONE

H

CHAPTER V

THE WAY TO A THRONE

THE beginning of July 1805 found Jerome Bonaparte newly promoted to the rank of captain of frigate, commanding a light squadron of five vessels in the gulf of Genoa. On the first of the month the Emperor came to Genoa for the celebration of the union of the Ligurian Republic with France, an event which marked the end of the historic Genoese State. Genoa had fallen before Napoleon as Venice had fallen earlier, but the fall of the former took place with every outward expression of joy. For the seven days of Napoleon's visit a series of magnificent entertainments continued. Jerome naturally took his share in these, and in commemoration received the title of Commander of the Naval Forces in Genoa Harbour, as well as a special mission which promised him glory without much danger. It was on the 5th July that the order was given to him by the Emperor to prepare to sail with his squadron to Algiers,

The Burlesque Napoleon

and demand from the Dey all such Genoese, Italian, or French slaves as he might have. It was more than a month before Jerome left, for which delay he had the excuse that he had still to complete the armament of his flagship, and to make up the crews of his five vessels, for which he had to draw on the Ligurians. Unfortunately, as has already been mentioned, it is also known that he had begun to look for consolation for the loss of his American wife, and had formed an acquaintance with that Blanche Carrega who later found her reward as a baroness in Jerome's kingdom. For the present he appears to have helped her to find a husband, for she married La Flèche, a contemptible person, whom Jerome took into high favour, and afterwards carried with him to Westphalia, where he was assuredly well qualified to associate with other husbands of his kind.

The French squadron did not reach Algiers until the 18th August, having been driven into Toulon by a storm after leaving Genoa, and having stopped there three days for repairs. When he arrived at his destination, however, Jerome showed that he was at least capable of undertaking the task entrusted to him. The

The Way to a Throne

Dey was inclined to temporise, and offered to surrender thirty slaves only. Jerome sent a peremptory message that he gave him forty-eight hours before breaking off negotiations. This produced the desired effect. The Dey handed over two hundred and thirty-two slaves without further delay, and within a day and a half of the French ship's arrival the mission had been accomplished. The squadron returned to Genoa, where, after a fortnight's compulsory quarantine, the conqueror had a great reception. He was met on landing by all the military and civil officials of the place, and escorted to the Cathedral of St Lawrence to attend a solemn *Te Deum*. The rescued slaves followed him, accompanied by their families and friends, who had flocked into Genoa, and on reaching the cathedral fell down and kissed the threshold, amid the sympathetic tears of the crowd. After the service the ex-captives were entertained at a banquet on a ship in the harbour, while a dinner, illuminations, and a ball in the town awaited Jerome. A letter of congratulation came from Decrès; the Emperor expressed his satisfaction; and Jerome started for Paris in a blaze of triumph which he found very gratifying. The end for which he had sacrificed Elizabeth (though

The Burlesque Napoleon

he still professed to hope the sacrifice might only be temporary) seemed well in sight. He considered he had earned a long rest on shore, and set himself with content to run up bills in Paris.

Napoleon, however, had no intention of letting Jerome rest on such laurels as he had found waiting him at Algiers. Nor did he intend to acknowledge him as a prince of the blood yet. The reward which he offered for the expedition to Algiers was the full rank of *capitaine de vaisseau*, and this was to be exercised at once in a quarter where no little danger accompanied the chance of glory. He was himself starting on a momentous campaign in Central Europe. He had not, for all his efforts, a fleet capable of meeting the English navy; but he could harass English commerce, and this he intended to do. The man whom he chose for the work was Willaumez, whom Jerome had known, of course, in America, and who was now an admiral. The text of Napoleon's instructions to him was in the words: "Do as much damage as possible to the English." The general idea was that Willaumez should make for the Cape of Good Hope, revictual there, and after a feint in the direction of Mauritius, spend a month in commerce-raiding off Saint Helena; thence

The Way to a Throne

he was to sail to the Antilles, work what destruction he could, and return to France. He was given eight vessels, six of them of the line, and to the command of one of these six, the *Vétéran*, Jerome was appointed.

There are few more curious documents in the whole correspondence of Napoleon and his ministers than the letter of the 29th October which Decrès sent to Willaumez, containing Napoleon's desires as to the treatment of his brother. What was required in him, Willaumez was told, was "the firmness of a chief full of the sense of duty, combined with the consideration due to a personage destined to a rank which the Sovereign's will had not conferred on him yet." There must be no flattery. "The Emperor will never forgive you—weigh this expression well—for any act of adulation towards his brother." Indeed, the Emperor threatened with "humiliating remarks in the public papers" anyone adopting an adulatory tone to Jerome. A few days later Decrès himself received a letter from Napoleon to the effect that he was held personally responsible for the attitude of people towards Jerome. "He must be kept rigorously in his rank. I hope that you have written that no honour is to be paid to him

The Burlesque Napoleon

at Brest: none is due." The Admiral and the Minister of Marine had no excuse for misunderstanding Napoleon's wishes. Yet Willaumez disobeyed them almost at once. Like Ganteaume, Villaret-Joyeuse, and Villeneuve before him, he found something in Jerome which compelled a rapid advancement.

The visit to Paris had proved very expensive to Jerome, and he found it necessary to pay some of his bills before he left. Napoleon being away, he applied to Joseph, who amiably but imprudently lent him 80,000 francs. Joseph communicated what he had done to Napoleon in Austria, and asked that the money should be refunded, only to receive the reply that the Emperor intended to let Jerome be imprisoned for debt if he could not live on his allowance. "It is inconceivable," he added, "how much this young man costs me, merely to cause me vexation and to be useless to my policy." Jerome, thanks to Joseph's loan, had been able to proceed to Brest, where every honour, however uncalled for in Napoleon's opinion, was paid to him. He might not be an Imperial Prince, but he had all except the title. Willaumez hastened to disregard his very plain instructions, and announced his intention of

The Way to a Throne

making Captain Bonaparte his second-in-command. He further communicated to him the secret of the expedition, which Napoleon had charged him to reveal to none. This folly nearly caused a catastrophe. Jerome had been under the impression that the squadron was to remain in the neighbourhood of Brest. When he found that a long and arduous voyage was before him he was immensely disgusted. He showed his annoyance so strongly that Willaumez wrote to him personally on the 14th December. He addressed him in very kindly terms, but besought him not to forget that the eyes of the whole fleet were upon him, and that on his conduct might depend the success or failure of all. The sacrifice of a few months now, he urged, would be worth many years of happiness to Jerome, and would obtain for him from his august brother every satisfaction. Jerome's answer was frank and honest; it must be admitted that he usually wrote well, if with an odd familiarity to his official superiors. Nothing should turn him from his duty, he declared; all that could vex him in the Admiral's letter was that Willaumez should think him such a touchy child as to make others partakers in his disappointments.

The Burlesque Napoleon

On the 13th December the fleet left Brest. Jerome was reconciled to his fate. On the *Vétéran* he had with him Halgan and Meyronnet as officers, and the indispensable Le Camus as private secretary. Though the youngest of Willaumez's captains, and most junior in service, he was second-in-command, taking up the post officially on the 1st January 1806. To celebrate the occasion he called his crew together, and addressed them in terms which might, perhaps, have come better from a more experienced warrior. His men's ideal was to be that one day it might be said: " He was a hero, for he was on board the *Vétéran* ! " The words have the Napoleonic ring, are, in fact, modelled on what Napoleon said a month before. But Napoleon uttered his remark after Austerlitz; Jerome spoke before a naval campaign which ended in failure. Yet, on the whole, it cannot be said that Jerome made an inefficient second to his Admiral up to the point when their separation took place. Willaumez asked his advice more often than he accepted it, but his own ideas brought him to grief. What documents of the period remain among the letters of Jerome seem to show that he was at least as good a

The Way to a Throne

sailor as his chief. That he had the best-manned vessel in the fleet was less a matter of credit to him, since care was taken at the beginning that this should be so.

Willaumez found it impossible to carry out the general idea sketched for him by Napoleon. The Cape was in English hands before he could reach it, and having been allowed a certain discretion in modifying the plan of campaign, he made for San Salvador, Brazil. Leaving that port again on the 21st April, he reached Martinique at the end of June. He was now shadowed by Admiral Cochrane, with a somewhat inferior English squadron. Willaumez continued along the Antilles until, receiving reinforcements, he offered battle on the 6th July off St Thomas. Cochrane declined, the numerical odds being heavily against him—seven ships of the line against four, and, apparently, four frigates against three. He continued to watch the French with two frigates, the rest of his squadron awaiting reinforcements, which arrived in the West Indies six days later. Willaumez continued north-west without succeeding in doing more than trifling damage to shipping. On the 28th July occurred the separation of the *Vétéran*

The Burlesque Napoleon

from the rest. The circumstances are rather obscure, and Jerome's real intention is quite so. The *Vétéran* had that day captured a privateering corvette, which she was towing. This caused her to lag behind the rest of the fleet. When night fell none of the others could be seen from the *Vétéran*. She fired signals during the dark; but when day dawned all trace of Willaumez's vessels was gone. After a consultation with his officers, and after making them sign a document to show that they upheld him, Jerome opened the sealed orders which he had on board in event of such emergencies. Herein a rendezvous was appointed on the Newfoundland Great Bank. Willaumez had a few days ago given another rendezvous in the West Indies, but Jerome elected to follow the sealed orders. He was now off the Florida coast, and started north. Suddenly, and for unexplained reasons, he changed his mind, and turned southward again. He never seems to have cast his eyes towards Baltimore. On the 13th August he appeared off Porto Rico, when, hearing of an English convoy on her way from Quebec, he started in pursuit. The convoy of sixteen vessels was laden with timber, etc., and was guarded only by H.M.S.

The Way to a Throne

Champion, a frigate which was no match for the *Vétéran*. Jerome overtook the merchantmen north of the Azores, capturing and burning a number of them[1] on the 18th August. Being now nearer home than the West Indies, he abandoned all idea of rejoining Willaumez, and headed for the coast of France.

Jerome did not reach safety until after an adventure which is, perhaps, the best known of all stories connected with his name. At early morn on the 25th August the *Vétéran* sighted four English warships out of the fleet with which a blockade was being maintained from the Lizard to Finisterre. It was decided to make a run for Lorient. The pursuers gained, however, and the *Vétéran* was cut off from Lorient unless she could force her way through the enemy. She might, perhaps, have attempted this, for Jerome had no intention of going to London as a prisoner; but another way of escape offered itself. Jerome heard a Breton sailor, by name Furic, mutter to a comrade that there was a way into the bay he knew. Eagerly he questioned the man, finding that he had been a Concarneau fisherman, and was acquainted with

[1] Six, according to the contemporary English admission; eleven, according to Jerome's own report.

The Burlesque Napoleon

the channels. "Well, then, take the helm," said Jerome. Furic obeyed, and steered straight for the groups of small islands known as the Glenans, south of Concarneau; the *Vétéran* passed safely between the rocks, to the astonishment of the British, and ran into the bay of La Forêt—another example of the incredible luck of the Bonapartes, complained the English papers of the day. The *Vétéran* was taken under the guns of the French fort, and her commander set foot on shore.

As soon as he had landed, Jerome sent off to Decrès the news of his arrival at Concarneau, and on the last day of the month Meyronnet reached Paris with a report and a letter to Napoleon. The intelligence of the *Vétéran's* return was most unwelcome to Decrès, whose thoughts turned to Willaumez deprived of his best battleship. The Admiral, indeed, came entirely to grief, but hardly through Jerome's desertion of him. Usually lenient to the young man, Decrès took an unfavourable view of his conduct now. The Emperor, however, thought quite otherwise of the affair. He authorised Jerome to appear in Paris, and received him most affectionately, decorating him with his own grand cordon of the Legion of Honour,

The Way to a Throne

while Josephine fastened the cross to his breast. De Salha, a lieutenant from the *Vétéran*, whom, with Meyronnet and Le Camus, Jerome had brought with him to Paris, and whom he afterwards put over the royal pages at Cassel, describes, in a letter to Halgan, the Emperor enchanted at Jerome's return, lavishing on him every proof of tenderness, and the whole Court prostrating itself before him in a chorus of jubilation. Quite the hero of the moment, Jerome was made Rear-Admiral at once. Apartments were assigned to him at Saint-Cloud, and finally, on the 24th September, the Senate announced that he had received the rights of a Prince of France, including the reversion of the throne to him and his "rightful descendants," in default of heirs to Napoleon, Joseph, and Louis. He had wiped out at last the stain on the family honour caused by his Baltimore marriage!

Having reached the rank of Rear-Admiral before he was quite twenty-two years of age, Jerome was considered by his brother to have gained from the sea what was necessary for the training of a prince useful to his country. The Napoleonic system, however, required him to become a king outside the boundaries of France,

The Burlesque Napoleon

and to add a third to those rulers of German states secured to the Empire by the marriages of Eugene Beauharnais and his cousin Stéphanie to a Bavarian princess and to the heir of Baden's Grand Duke. Napoleon had, before Jerome's return to France, designed both a marriage and a kingdom for him, the latter depending only on his own success in the war whose outbreak was inevitable towards the end of 1806. But some military service was still necessary, in the Emperor's eyes, to fit Jerome for his position. For the dignity of his family, he must have more to offer his wife than he received from her. He must be not only a king, but a successful general too. And since Napoleon, as he told Joseph, did not believe in the proverb that to know how to command one must first know how to obey, he looked about for a post of authority to assign to the candidate for military reputation. He quitted Paris with him on the 24th September. At Wurzburg the princes of the Confederation of the Rhine waited on their master, and Jerome was introduced to his future father-in-law, Frederick II. of Würtemberg. Then, at the Bavarian town of Cronach, on the 7th October, the Emperor left his brother to await the arrival of a native

The Way to a Throne

division, which was to be put under his command. Jerome's annoyance at the idea of remaining behind in Bavaria while the Grand Army was fighting elsewhere was genuine enough. He implored Napoleon not to keep him at a distance from the field of battle, but to place him near his own person. "Sire," he wrote on the 13th October, "Your Majesty knows better than any that what I most need is to win glory. How much shall I have to lament if on my return from this campaign I can only say that I commanded Bavarians and remained at the rear!" The piteous appeal touched Napoleon, who sent permission for the Prince to leave all his Bavarians except some light cavalry, whom he was to bring with him. It was too late, however, for Jerome to see the battle of Jena, which was on the eve of commencing when he sent his appeal, and had been decided when he arrived. The only consolation which Napoleon could offer him was to take him to Berlin, where he carried out his plan of giving him the opportunity to command. Putting together two Bavarian divisions and one from Würtemberg, he gave them the name of the Army of the Allies, and set Jerome over them. A staff was formed, which included Jerome's

The Burlesque Napoleon

friends, Meyronnet and de Salha, and a Colonel Morio—who soon won his way to his chief's esteem, little to his own ultimate advantage.

The duty assigned to the Army of the Allies was to clear the Prussians out of Silesia, where they had a number of strongly-fortified places. Numerically the allied troops were sufficient for the task; but they were an ill-disciplined and unscrupulous lot, whose ideas of conduct towards the inhabitants of Silesia were most unsatisfactory to Jerome. Unfortunately Vandamme, the most able of the French generals associated with him, was an upholder of the same views about requisitions from the inhabitants as those of the Bavarians and Würtembergers. This was an immediate cause of friction between the Prince and Vandamme, placed as they were in the uncomfortable position towards each other of titular and real fighting chiefs. Jerome entered on his duties early in November with the utmost zeal to win the glory which he had said was so necessary to him. He found the siege of Glogau, a fortress on the Oder, in progress—General Lefebvre-Desnouettes, who was now on his staff, having failed to take the place by assault. Jerome was anxious to renew the assault; whereon General Deroy refused to

The Way to a Throne

guarantee the conduct of his troops, and the Prince abandoned the idea in disgust. Napoleon, though he had purposely given his brother a separate command, interfered in Silesian affairs to direct Jerome to march against Kalisch, leaving Vandamme with the Würtemberg troops only to proceed against Glogau. Vandamme profited by this to capture the fortress three days later. Further orders from Napoleon caused both Jerome and Vandamme to converge on Breslau, which he particularly wished to see in his hands at once. Although he was directing the operations here, and was in a position to check the plundering Vandamme, Jerome was very discontented at the news which reached him of an impending collision between the French and the Russians on the Vistula. He wrote to Napoleon on the 17th December, expressing the fear that he would once again lose the honour of fighting under his eyes. Napoleon, however, had that very day sent orders for Jerome to join him, leaving the siege of Breslau to Vandamme.

The Emperor explained his action in a bulletin, which stated that he had summoned Prince Jerome from Silesia in order that he should have the chance of instruction. "This Prince,"

The Burlesque Napoleon

added the bulletin, "has taken part in all the fighting in Silesia, and has often been at the outposts." A sarcastic remark by Vandamme later in the campaign would imply that Jerome did not see the outposts as often as Napoleon claimed. At the siege of Neiss, which Vandamme was conducting, Jerome, who had arrived from Breslau to hasten operations, thought fit to show himself in the trenches to encourage the troops. A shot from the town fell among the group of staff-officers, and scattered dust over Jerome. "These devils of bullets," said Vandamme, "have no respect for strangers!" Vandamme had this habit of making unanswerable remarks. When captured by the Russians in 1812, and reproached by the Tsar Alexander as a "brigand," the General replied: "I may be a brigand, but I did not kill my father." That Alexander did not find the allusion to his unexplained share in Paul's death pleasant is no matter for surprise. Apart from his quick wit, Vandamme was a courageous and ambitious young man, who undoubtedly found his association with Jerome as galling as Jerome found it himself.

It must at least be admitted to the honour of the Prince that in his despatches he gave Van-

The Way to a Throne

damme credit for his successes, though he might display ridiculous jealousy beforehand. It was so at the siege of Breslau. Jerome had joined Napoleon at Warsaw in December, but had only been with him a fortnight when he heard that Breslau was on the point of capitulation. A repetition of what occurred at Glogau was imminent. He wrote off at once to Vandamme, giving him the extraordinary command on no account to enter the place. The General was astounded, thought of throwing up his post, but obeyed to the extent of not entering the town in person. The capitulation took place on the 6th, and on the 8th the surrendered garrison defiled before Jerome, who had just arrived from Poland. The news of Breslau's fall was welcomed by Napoleon, who had looked for its military stores of all kinds and its plentiful provisions to improve the equipment of the Grand Army and to revictual the troops. As a reward he enrolled the allied troops in Silesia in the Grand Army itself, making them the 9th Corps. While the sieges of the other strongholds were to be carried on by his subordinates, Jerome himself was assigned the important, but not exciting, task of superintending the organisation of stores for the Grand Army and the

The Burlesque Napoleon

forwarding of them from Breslau. M. Martinet is lost in admiration at the energy which the Prince displayed in making Breslau supply what was required, including 100,000 pairs of shoes, in sending to Poland convoys of flour, brandy, etc., while at the same time directing the operations of three sieges, ordering attacks, modifying hospital arrangements, attending to his men's commissariat, and burning to reform abuses. It is indeed a picture of industry, but it does not seem to have much relation to fact. No doubt some useful work was done at Breslau on behalf of the Grand Army. But Jerome, after all, was only the figurehead, and had a competent staff to do the actual labour. For the rest, disappointed in his thirst for glory, of which there was little in Silesia to divide between Vandamme and himself, Jerome had a resource to fall back upon in his love of pleasure. Breslau was a sufficient Capua for the young soldier, and his interest in the remaining operations under his command was at least languid.

Napoleon himself crippled the work in progress in Silesia by taking 7000 of the best Bavarian troops to Poland. He did not, however, omit to blame Jerome for reducing the forces engaged in the sieges of Kosel and Neiss.

The Way to a Throne

Jerome, for his part, was not afraid to point out the injustice of this policy; and that Napoleon was not seriously angry appears from the fact that he advanced his brother to the rank of General of Division on the 15th March. He followed this up by a bulletin, dated the 4th April, in which he stated that "Prince Jerome, commanding the troops in Silesia, gives proof of great activity, and shows talent and prudence, usually the fruit only of long experience." Such bulletins, it will easily be understood, were for the public; and Napoleon had a strong suspicion that Jerome was not finding life too hard at Breslau. Indeed, he wrote to him, nine days after this last bulletin, mentioning that "a certain lady of Stuttgart" was complaining that Jerome was too gallant towards the ladies of Breslau. Was it true? he asked. It is not probable that the Princess Catherine had actually made any complaint, but it is more than probable that stories were current in Germany about Jerome's life at Breslau. In particular, he was known to have attached himself to an opera-singer, whom Le Camus, on his behalf, induced to come to Cassel later. Other entanglements were spoken of also. Now, though the Emperor might himself have one love affair in Poland, it was by

The Burlesque Napoleon

no means suitable that Jerome, soon to marry a princess, should have a number of affairs in Silesia. It was necessary that he should recall to him the thought of the marriage in store for him.

Jerome took the hint, and reappeared in the field. Unfortunately for him, General Lefebvre-Desnouettes won the battle of Frankenstein, against the Prussian forces attempting to relieve Schweidnitz, just before Jerome reached the front. This caused a fresh access of wrath in the Emperor. "What a lesson lost!" he wrote. "War cannot be learnt except by going under fire." The offender was already back in Breslau when he received this letter. He remained there until the 6th June, being confined to his bed by illness for two weeks. He was anxious, nevertheless, that not all the glory of the sieges should fall to subordinates, and it was thus that he brought on himself the sarcasm of Vandamme. Kosel and Neiss both fell in June, the garrison of the latter place defiling before Jerome on the 16th. Glatz soon followed. Silberberg held out longest against the French. The town was weakly held, however, and capitulated on the 3rd July, after the armistice which preceded Tilsit had been signed, but before the news reached Silesia.

The Way to a Throne

So the campaign came to a lucky conclusion. Jerome had at least done enough to parade before the world as a general as well as a rear-admiral. It was unfortunate that Vandamme and his other officers had won most of the actual glory, and also that Breslau could be said to have distracted the Commander-in-Chief from the field to more peaceful conquests. But there was a good array of bulletins to show; and with a royal title and a royal wife Jerome would make a sufficiently imposing king. Only the situation of the kingdom remained to be found. This was not difficult with Prussia so humiliated as she was now, and Alexander of Russia anxious for peace, and dazzled also by the personality of Napoleon. Already at the beginning of the previous year Napoleon had conceived the idea of new states to be formed in the vicinity of the Rhine, and had caused his Foreign Office to draw up a memorial contemplating the stripping from Prussia of her Westphalian and East Frisian provinces, and the creation of one or more new states from the spoils.[1] After he had assigned Berg and Cleves to Murat as a Grand

---

[1] *Mémoire sur les Etats à former en Westphalie et le long du Rhin.* See H. A. L. Fisher, " Studies in Napoleonic Statesmanship : Germany," p. 111.

The Burlesque Napoleon

Duchy he momentarily thought of adding Hesse-Darmstadt to that rather diminutive realm, but his schemes continued to change and develop until the idea of the Westphalian state as it was actually constituted was evolved. Thus the king and the kingdom were ready, and the rulers of Prussia and Russia were prepared to recognise both. The Tsar Alexander, it is true, seems to have tried to save Prussia's dignity by suggesting that Jerome should have the Grand Duchy of Warsaw rather than the realm of Westphalia; and there was the chance of a Saxon marriage to be considered for the Polish prince. But Napoleon preferred to adhere to his own schemes of a Westphalian state and a Würtemberg marriage. Accordingly, on the very day of the signature of the Peace of Tilsit, he was able to write to his brother, announcing to him that he had been made King of Westphalia, and bidding him prepare to come to Dresden to consult over the organisation of the new kingdom. He sent him with the letter a precise list of the territories included in his 1900 square leagues of Germany. Roughly speaking, Westphalia was made up of pieces of Prussia, Brunswick, Hesse-Cassel, Hanover, and some

The Way to a Throne

smaller items.[1] Hesse-Cassel and Prussia, in particular, Napoleon was eager to punish heavily for their treacherous conduct, as he considered it, during the late war.

There was, it may be remarked, not the slightest geographical excuse for the new kingdom, nor any approach to homogeneity among its inhabitants. Its eastern boundary was, indeed, practically formed by the Elbe and Saale, but otherwise the division of the country from its surroundings was arbitrary. Among its 2,000,000 inhabitants were the greatest diversities of character and of religious belief. Though it had five universities, those of Göttingen, Halle, Helmstadt, Marburg, and Rinteln, it had also, in the Hessian element of its population, the most ignorant of all German peoples; and in religion the divisions between the Roman Catholics, the Reformed Church, and the Lutherans were extreme. In

[1] All the territory of the Duke of Brunswick-Wolfenbuttel, who was killed at Jena, was included in the new kingdom; nearly all Hesse-Cassel; the bulk of Prussia's lost possessions on the left bank of the Elbe; Prussia's fief of Stolberg, and Hesse-Cassel's fief of Rietberg; Göttingen, Grubenhagen, and Osnabruck, belonging to George III., as Elector of Hanover; and the Abbey of Corney, belonging to the Prince of Orange ("Mémoires et correspondance du Roi Jérôme," iii. p. 40).

The Burlesque Napoleon

a way, no doubt, the lack of internal unifying influences tended towards the acquiescence of Westphalia as a whole under Jerome's rule. There was no common cause to bind his subjects together against him, and even his monstrous extravagances would not have done so had not other circumstances transformed the whole of Germany.

In accordance with his brother's command on the day of Tilsit, Jerome left Breslau, and went to Dresden. Here, on Napoleon's arrival, a preliminary discussion concerning the government of Westphalia no doubt took place. But we may suppose Jerome to have played chiefly the part of listener. The project had long been in Napoleon's mind. The two brothers made a very brief stay in Dresden, and departed for Paris on the 22nd July. When they arrived apartments were at once assigned in the Tuileries to the new monarch, and a royal household was chosen, among whom Jerome was allowed to find places for Le Camus and his friends from the *Épervier* and *Vétéran*. Nothing was left for the King-maker to do except to marry Jerome, and to send him off to reign at Cassel.

JEROME NAPOLEON
KING OF WESTPHALIA

THE MARRIAGE OF JEROME BONAPARTE.

CHAPTER VI

JEROME NAPOLEON, KING OF WESTPHALIA

SOPHIA-DOROTHEA-FREDERIKA-CATHERINE of Würtemberg, the princess chosen to be the bride of the newest king in Europe, has furnished to her contemporaries and to subsequent writers alike a puzzle for which they have found it difficult to suggest a satisfactory explanation. Merely as the faithful and loving wife of the most notorious royal rake of his day, she might be dismissed as stupid. Against such a verdict there is a powerful protest of observers during life, including not the least acute men and women of the period.[1] Napoleon himself, to the very last, had nothing but good to say of her. The tribute is well known which he paid

[1] De Norvins, perhaps, may be thought too prejudiced in her favour, since he admits that he "devoted to her an adoration which must last as long as his life." He declared her "one of the first princesses in Europe by birth, and the first beyond denial in beauty, character, wit, education, and dignity"; and thought regretfully how different history might have been had Napoleon himself married Catherine instead of Marie-Louise, and left Jerome with his American wife.

The Burlesque Napoleon

to her at Saint Helena, when he said that she had "with her own hand inscribed her name on the page of history." In her fragments of diary, and in the mass of her correspondence which has been published, we are bound to recognise Catherine's great simplicity of character; but certainly there are more evidences of amiability than of strength. Her main fault, undoubtedly, was a lack of sense of the responsibility of her position. She was pleasure-loving, too, but in no dishonourable way. How then, it has been asked, could she reconcile herself to Jerome's ideas of pleasure, the chief of which was rooted in his dishonour as a husband? Still more, how could she be satisfied with him in the midst of his Court, as she always, in the accents of sincerity, protested herself to be? If she was not stupid, she could not be blind when all around her knew so much; and if not blind, how could she find contentment with a Jerome? The secret of the latter's fascination for his "Trinette" must, apparently, remain unknown. As a rule, his power of attraction was merely superficial, or exerted itself only on worthless persons. But Catherine preferred ruin, and virtual imprisonment, with him to any easier lot without him, and declared that he made her perfectly happy.

King of Westphalia

No clue to what is perplexing in her disposition seems to exist in her ancestry. Both her parents were of uncommon character; but her mother's career was cut short by a tragedy of which Catherine was too young to appreciate the horror. Frederick of Würtemberg, whose sister Sophia, the Empress Catherine of Russia had selected as wife for her son Paul, was persuaded by his sister to come to Russia, in the hope of making his fortune in the Russian service. He had already quitted the service of Prussia, and was ready to listen to his sister's suggestions. With him he brought his wife, Augusta, who was eldest daughter of Charles Ferdinand of Brunswick by the sister of George III., and was, therefore, sister of the unhappy English Queen Caroline. The little Catherine was born on the 21st February 1788 (so that she was a year and eight months older than Jerome Bonaparte), and her early years were spent in St Petersburg. Augusta had much to complain of in the conduct of her husband, who, with or without reason, was exceedingly jealous about her. So outrageous was he at last that Augusta appealed to the Empress Catherine, who took her part. Frederick replied by confining his wife to the house;

The Burlesque Napoleon

but, as he was obliged to bring her to Court on the Empress's birthday, she seized the opportunity to throw herself at Catherine's feet, and pray for protection. The Empress received her into the palace, whereon Frederick took his children, and left Russia. In September 1788 Augusta died in childbirth, at Polangen, near Riga, being only twenty-four years of age. The circumstances were mysterious. According to some, Frederick was the instigator of the crime; but also the Russian Empress has been charged with it, a plausible reason being found that Augusta had intrigued with one of her favourites. The story is one of the many scandals of the period incapable of proof or disproof, but the deed seems altogether unlike Catherine. All that is certain is that the unfortunate woman died through want of proper assistance, and that her coffin was left unburied for twenty-eight years, her son giving it the last honours when visiting Russia in 1816. Her daughter remained ignorant of the facts of the case. She says in her diary: "I have never tried to lift the veil which to this day hides her last moments from my eyes. Whether she had faults, or whether they were the results of my father's faults, I cannot permit myself to judge.

King of Westphalia

If my unhappy mother was guilty she has long been at the feet of the Eternal One, whose infinite pity persuades me that she has found grace in His eyes, and expiated the errors which are unknown to me."

Catherine was only five years old when she was taken from her mother for ever. Frederick went first to Mayence, and then to Lausanne. He sent Catherine to the home of his father, who was younger brother of the reigning Duke of Würtemberg. With him and her grandmother, who was a charming and devoted guardian to her, she remained for nearly ten years, living at Montbéliard, Cuvier's birthplace, until the outbreak of the French Revolution alarmed the old people and drove them to the capital of the Duchy. She went with them to Stuttgart, where her grandfather succeeded his brother in 1795. To this period of ten years the child owed an excellent, if not profound, education, and the formation of a character which was very different from what might have been expected from the records of her mother and father.

At the age of fifteen Catherine was deprived of the home with her grandparents, for the Duke died in 1797, his wife following him a year later.

The Burlesque Napoleon

She came under the care of her father, now the reigning Duke, and married a second time to the Princess Royal of England. Frederick was described by Napoleon[1] as "a man of considerable talent, but unprincipled and wicked"—"a brute, though a man of talent." The rights of the case between him and his first wife, and the question of his complicity in her death being obscure, it is difficult to judge how far Frederick deserves the epithet of wicked. He was, undoubtedly, brutal to his sons, and to his daughter's husband he was very vindictive after Napoleon's fall. Towards Napoleon himself, however, before Leipzig, his conduct was an honourable exception to that of the German princes in general, for he warned the Emperor that he was obliged to follow his subjects' wishes, while he restrained the mass of the Würtemberg troops from deserting before or during the battle. Marbot, speaking of his

---

[1] In conversation at Saint Helena with O'Meara, whom he also told that the Tsar Alexander and the King of Würtemberg were the only sovereigns in Europe possessed of talent. It was certainly a tribute to Frederick's ability that Napoleon enlarged both his dignities and his territory and united him, through the daughter, with his own family. But, of course, the gain of 10,000 Würtembergers for the Grand Army was a great consideration.

King of Westphalia

behaviour in 1813, calls him "a man of violent character, but honourable." He and the Elector of Bavaria were the two new German kings whom Napoleon created at the end of 1805. De Norvins describes Frederick as taking his promotion so seriously to heart that he had royal crowns sculptured on every post in his kingdom, and a colossal gilded crown hung over his bed, which was of a size to hold the greatest sovereign in the world. He was, indeed, enormously fat—Catherine inheriting an uncomfortable stoutness from him. His Court, after he became king, was so remarkable for its magnificence that Napoleon sneered at him as "a regular Louis XIV. in miniature." But in the early days of his dukedom, Würtemberg was a most tedious place. He was not a sympathetic father, and though she was his favourite child, Catherine's feeling throughout life towards him appears to have been one of fearful respect. Her stepmother, though she impressed Napoleon favourably, did nothing to make Catherine's life less dull; in fact, Catherine found her stupid and tiresome. The idea of marriage, in itself, must have come to her as a relief in 1806, but the particular marriage which was put before her by her father alarmed her. Ger-

The Burlesque Napoleon

many was the home of strict views about misalliances, and the man proposed to her as husband had only been made prince a few months ago by his brother, himself an upstart if an Emperor. Moreover, he was of different creed. In her diary Catherine merely says that her father told her of the overtures made by France for her union with Jerome. "Not knowing him, and being occupied with other ideas, I refused. My father returned to the charge, and insisted on my consent, telling me that the happiness of all the family and the prosperity, perhaps the existence, of my country depended on it. I gave way at the end of a year, and offered myself as sacrifice to interests so dear to me. I could not then foresee that I should find therein the most pure and lasting happiness."

Whether Napoleon or Frederick first conceived the idea of the match seems doubtful. The upset of the marriage with Elizabeth Patterson showed that Napoleon had views of a politically judicious union for his younger brother, and Germany was the natural soil on which to look for princesses. When the Emperor made Frederick a king, patron and client were evidently at one. The objections, religious and

King of Westphalia

dynastic, of Frederick's wife, Catherine's stepmother, had been overcome at a personal interview with Napoleon at Ludwigsberg, where Napoleon exerted all the fascination of which he was capable, and won the English princess over to his side. She found his smile "bewitching." All that remained was to enlighten the appointed husband and wife. Jerome being away with Willaumez, his return had to be awaited; but Frederick was able to commence to persuade his daughter, with what result we have seen. As Napoleon wrote to Joseph, on the last day of 1806, asking him to find out whether "the young man" would do as he wished, it seems that he had not himself approached Jerome definitely at that date. But Jerome made no resistance. Madame Junot's premonitions had been realised. As she says, Jerome wished to taste the sweets of power like the rest of his family, and he had denied even before the cock crew.

When the European war was ended at Tilsit, therefore, all was ready, and Napoleon had only been back in Paris twelve days when he despatched Marshal Bessières and Madame de Luçay to Stuttgart with a letter to his "dear sister," assuring Catherine of his affection for

The Burlesque Napoleon

her, and his conviction that she would make his brother happy. On the 19th August he informed the Senate of the approaching union, and immediately afterwards the marriage by proxy took place at Stuttgart, Jerome being represented by Bessières. The young princess left home without delay, that the real ceremony at Paris might follow the formal pledge. Napoleon superintended all the arrangements, and according to these Catherine was not to arrive in Paris till seven on the evening of the 21st August. The early part of that day she was to spend at the chateau of Raincy, where Madame Junot was deputed to receive her, and whither a suite, chosen for her from Josephine's household, was sent to wait on her. A full record of the events of the day was preserved by Madame Junot, on whose impressions we must rely. Catherine was not altogether pleasing on first view, says this writer. She was a fine woman, however, and there was a noble pride about her head, which would have been more striking still if her neck had not been short, as was her general figure. To make the most of her inches she carried herself very upright, throwing her head back on her shoulders. She could not be called exactly pretty, though her features were all good. Her eyes looked as though they might soften; but they never did, and this gave her a very haughty if not a disagreeable expression. She seldom smiled; seriousness and calm marked her face rather than liveliness or grace. With fair hair, blue eyes, very white teeth she had a very fresh complexion, while her unfortunately inherited stoutness caused her to colour violently when agitated as she was when she reached Raincy. Her position, indeed, was a cruel one at the moment of her arrival. To satisfy the requiremeuts of etiquette, all her German attendants had left her before she approached Paris. She had not with her a single person whom she knew. Before an entirely strange household, she was condemned to wait for the arrival of one to whom she was already half married, but whom she had never seen. She played her part well. The keen eyes of Madame Junot detected no tears, but could divine from the alternations of a blush, which was almost purple, with a deathly paleness the suffering she was undergoing. She made every effort to be gracious, insisted that those in the chateau should be present at *déjeuner* with her, and accompanied Madame Junot afterwards in a carriage to a stag-hunt which had been ar-

The Burlesque Napoleon

ranged to pass the time. Jerome was not due to arrive for his bride until the evening. The remainder of the day was spent in making ready for this event.

The witness of Catherine's preparations was in despair about the effect likely to be produced upon him who had once been the husband of Elizabeth Patterson by the sight of the new wife whom his brother was giving to him. Her costume was sadly ill-chosen; indeed, it was "one for which there was no excuse in 1807, especially on a princess." To come to particulars, we learn that the dress was of white moire, the white having a bluish tinge, which was quite out of fashion. The sleeves were very tight and flat, and down the bosom of the dress was some ugly silver embroidery in a style no less than four years old. Behind was an absurd train, cut like a beaver's tail. The manner in which her hair was dressed was in keeping with her costume—that is to say, it was entirely out of keeping with her features. Two strings of pearls were around her neck, and suspended from them was Jerome's portrait, framed so heavily in diamonds that it swung about and struck her every time she moved. Thus was Jerome's young and poetical imagination to be moved; thus the image of Elizabeth on her wedding day to be effaced!

Poor Catherine, however, was, no doubt, unconscious of being badly dressed and four years behind the times. She came down with an air of as great dignity as she ever showed when the dressmakers and hairdressers of Paris had reformed her. Only at dinner did she suffer a return of her agitation. Would it not be possible, she asked, with a painful flush on her face, to be warned a few minutes in advance of the Prince's arrival? At half-past six his approach was announced. Catherine's colour became dark purple, says her cruelly observant critic, and her state was alarming. Regaining control of herself, she proceeded to the reception-room, and seated herself by the fireplace, where two chairs were set. As Jerome entered the room, ushered in by Bessières, she rose, made two steps forward, and greeted him with grace and dignity. The Prince had "the air of a man obeying orders." Madame Junot, so merciless in describing Catherine's physical defects, is certainly no more kind to Jerome at this period. The least well-looking of Napoleon's brothers, she calls him. His head was close to his shoulders—the fault of all the younger Bonapartes except

The Burlesque Napoleon

Pauline. He was pleasing neither in face nor in figure. "When I was told that in Westphalia he lived on *cœurs en brochette* I thought to myself how far the title of king goes even in love, for to act the Lovelace as he did there were needed far more arts of pleasing than one saw in him."

For the present Jerome was making no effort to please. He was merely correct. After a few words of greeting Catherine pointed to the chair beside hers. They both sat down, and a short conversation on the journey followed. Jerome then rose, saying: "My brother awaits *us*. I would not delay any longer the pleasure which he must feel in knowing the new sister whom I am giving to him." Catherine smiled, and led him to the door. When he had left her to get ready she fainted. An application of eau de Cologne revived her, and she proceeded to the second part of the ordeal at the Tuileries. The kindness of Napoleon lessened her trouble here. He came to the top of the grand staircase of the Palace to meet her; and when she tried to kneel to kiss his hand he would not allow this, but, having embraced her tenderly, led her himself to the room where Josephine, Madame Mère, the Queen of Naples, the Grand Duchess of Berg,

King of Westphalia

and the Princess Stephanie were awaiting her. To them he presented her as the new daughter and new sister. Napoleon's manner towards ladies has been much criticised, and with reason, but to his young German sister-in-law it could not have been kinder or more charming. There sprang from it a very genuine mutual esteem and affection, which endured until the Emperor's death. Catherine's merits were early recognised by the women of her new family also, and with Madame Mère she soon became the favourite among her son's wives.

The marriage-contract was signed on the night of the arrival of the bride, and the religious celebration followed on the evening of the next day. In honour of the first royal marriage of a Bonaparte nothing was left undone which could make the affair magnificent. Eye-witnesses were much impressed, it is easy to see from their accounts. The pearls, the diamonds, and other jewels worn by the ladies were astounding in number and brilliance, and the diplomatic representatives and distinguished strangers were untiring in their expressions of admiration.[1] The Gallery of Diana in the Tuileries was reserved for the ceremony. Bridegroom and bride

[1] Chancelier Pasquier, " Histoire de mon Temps."

The Burlesque Napoleon

were alike in white from head to foot, Jerome's white satin being only relieved by a profusion of gold lace. Six witnesses signed the register—Prince Borghese, the Grand Duke of Berg, and the Prince of Neufchatel, for France; and the Prince of Baden, the Prince of Nassau, and Count Wintzingerode, for Würtemberg. Truly, there was a contrast in these titles to the names of the witnesses in Baltimore on the Christmas Eve of 1803! During the marriage service a violent storm arose, which spoilt the illuminations that had been designed, and lightning struck the Tuileries. The superstitious Josephine remarked (though not in the presence of the bride) that if Catherine believed in omens she might suppose that evening presaged an unhappy fate for her. Catherine, fortunately, was of a wiser cast of mind, and, so soon as she had been put at her ease, thought more of enjoying the honours which were hers than of gathering omens from the weather.

From the date of their wedding until the following December, Jerome and Catherine remained in France, amid the luxuries of Napoleon's Court, and surrounded by a flattery agreeable enough to them both, no doubt. A series of entertainments were given in their

King of Westphalia

honour, the most striking of which was the fête at the Elysée arranged by Eugene Beauharnais on the 29th August. The feature of this was an exact representation of Catherine's favourite walk on the outskirts of Stuttgart, got up purposely to surprise her. The autumn was spent at Fontainebleau, near Napoleon himself, now in the enjoyment of a brief period of peace. As for Jerome, the cares of kingship (few cares as kingship ever had for him) might be postponed a few months. A Regency had been established at Cassel at the beginning of September, whose main duty was to collect the revenues and to pay over the money which Napoleon demanded for the upkeep of the French troops quartered in Westphalia. Four Frenchmen, Beugnot, Siméon, Jollivet, and General Lagrange, formerly head of Kléber's staff in Egypt, with a German secretary, Mossdorf — since none of the others could speak German—composed this provisional government, which remained in office until the King's arrival. Jerome further took the precaution of sending two personal representatives, one his friend Rewbell, now aide-de-camp, and the other Morio, also on his staff, to make general inquiries about the country and its

The Burlesque Napoleon

people. These two reported to him constantly, usually in the most enthusiastic terms. Morio was in particular delighted at the reception which some of the Westphalian towns insisted on according to him, in spite of his protests. Triumphal arches, a profusion of flags, carpets of flowers, and choruses of *vivats* almost overwhelmed the vicar of King Jerome. Rewbell, too, found whole provinces anxious to send deputies to Paris to lay at the King's feet the homage of a devoted people. And, in fact, a deputation did reach Paris as early as the middle of August, praying for Jerome's speedy arrival in Cassel. He might almost be excused if he thought that his subjects were consumed with anxiety to see him. But the deputation had really come to Paris, not so much to look at Jerome as to hear what Napoleon wished to say. The Emperor had summoned them to him, and he received them at the Tuileries to prepare them for the constitution which was to be their country's. They were allowed to choose a committee, before which Napoleon set his draft scheme for comment. Unfortunately, the Emperor did not find to his taste their most sensible objections to the exaction of arrears of war contribution from an impoverished land, and little heed was paid to their criticisms generally. On the 30th August they were dismissed to their homes. Jerome received them at Saint-Cloud before they left, and assured them that he was not changeable, and would leave them all that was good in the old regime. "My subjects are Westphalians, not Frenchmen," he said. "In a few years I shall speak and write German. I will appoint only natives."[1] Drawing what comfort they could from these easy promises, the delegates returned to Westphalia.

On the 15th November Napoleon delivered to Jerome the constitution now finally drawn up for his kingdom. The document is, politically, a most interesting one; a detailed examination of it, however, would be outside the scope of the present work. The general conception was truly Napoleonic. Had Jerome been a wise man, had the French Empire endured, and had sincere efforts of the Emperor to secure peace enabled him to lighten the military burdens of the vassal states, the effect of the example of Westphalia in Germany must have been immense. As it was, that example was not

[1] H. A. L. Fisher, "Studies in Napoleonic Statesmanship: Germany," chap. xi. Mr Fisher gives, from German sources, a full account of this deputation's visit to Paris.

The Burlesque Napoleon

altogether thrown away. When he founded the Grand Duchy of Berg, Napoleon had spoken of its being the *école normale* for the other members of the Rhine Confederation.[1] In the same way, or still more, a successfully administered Westphalia was calculated to be a school for all its neighbours in Germany. Here was a free and constitutional monarchy, with elective, if not popularly elected, States of the Realm and a liberal code of laws, thrust into the side of a semi-feudal country. Was it too much to expect that such a spectacle of enlightened rule would lead and transform the adjacent kingdoms, until they became an effective barrier against the old autocracies of Eastern Europe? The idea was doomed to failure, partly because the man chosen as king found in the harem and in the pomp of a court far more interest than in the affairs of his subjects; partly because the military exactions of France never allowed her dependants a fair chance of freeing themselves from debt; and, lastly, because the continuance of Westphalia's existence was bound up with that of the empire of Napoleon himself.

While handing to his brother the Westphalian

[1] Roederer, iii. p. 425.

King of Westphalia

constitution, Napoleon bade him proceed to Stuttgart to visit his father-in-law. There had been one difficulty in the way of Jerome leaving Paris, and this was that since his wedding he had spent 3,000,000 francs, which he could not pay. Early in November Napoleon authorised him to borrow 1,800,000 francs from the Sinking Fund, while instructing Gaudin, his Finance Minister, to see that the repayments were made promptly. He further permitted him to draw in advance his allowance as a Prince of France, which was to cease altogether at the end of 1807. In consideration of the advances, Jerome was to have no further debts in Paris. He should, at any rate, start his life in Westphalia solvent, Napoleon decided. The curious thing is that from this time forward, by his conduct towards Westphalia, he made it almost certain that Jerome should never again be solvent, even had he been anything else than the spendthrift and debauchee that he was. Once again there was an unfortunate contrast between admirable theory and vicious practice.

A slight indisposition of Catherine prevented an immediate start for Stuttgart; but on the 28th November Jerome and his wife reached the Court where once she had suffered so much

The Burlesque Napoleon

weariness. Now everything was as gay as the host could make it, and Jerome had little cause to suspect, from King Frederick's reception, how bitter an enemy he would find in him a few years later. After leaving Stuttgart the young sovereigns crossed the frontier of their own kingdom in the first week of December. On the 7th they reached Wilhelmshöhe, renamed Napoleonshöhe, in honour of the Emperor, by Jerome, himself but recently glorified by the addition of Napoleon's name to his own. The neighbourhood of this vast but dilapidated and poverty-stricken palace (the restoration and refurnishing of which cost its reckless new master enormous sums) was brilliantly decorated, and Jerome and Catherine drove under triumphal arches and between festooned poles and flags, amid cheering crowds of their subjects. In a carriage drawn by six white horses, preceded by scarlet-clad outriders, they led the string of coaches of their household, of whom not one lady was ill-looking, remarks de Norvins, not one gentleman could speak German. Le Camus, of course, was there, "with all his family in the baggage"; Meyronnet, de Salha, Morio, and others to whom Jerome had taken a fancy at various times; hangers-on like La Flèche, husband of

King of Westphalia

Blanche Carrega; and the ladies of Catherine's suite. The young King and Queen attracted every eye. Jerome was in a green uniform, covered with gold lace, and white knee-breeches, while a sword of gold hung at his side. Catherine was in blue taffeta, under a gold-embroidered velvet cloak; a Parisian hat covered her head, and supported the light veil which fell upon her shoulders. Her amiable expression and familiar smiles at the King were noticed by all. Jerome struck a German observer[1] as small, graceful, and spare, dark-haired and black-eyed. His cheek-bones were prominent, and slight wrinkles had already formed about his eyes, but did not disguise the pride of youth. He was fond of displaying his hands, which were small and like a woman's.

With the entry of Jerome into Napoleonshöhe the provisional government ceased. In recognition of the Regency's services the King appointed those who had formed it to the chief offices of State. To Siméon he assigned the departments of Justice and of the Interior, to Lagrange that of War, to Beugnot Finance, and to Jollivet the Treasury. He named nine Councillors of State. all Germans. Lastly, he

[1] M. von Kaisenberg, "König Jérôme Napoléon."

The Burlesque Napoleon

gave orders for all funds in the State Treasury, from the 1st December, to be held at his disposal. Then, unconscious of the coming storm, he proceeded to Cassel, on the 10th December. The capital received its King and Queen with every demonstration of joy, with salutes of honour by day and illuminations by night. Jerome hastened to put on his coronation robes, and, magnificent in velvet (but looking, it may be hoped, less ridiculous than the painter has represented him in the extant portrait of him in these robes), he received the dignitaries of his kingdom. The day passed off well, public evidences of good feeling being all that could be desired. The King issued a proclamation to his "good and faithful subjects, inhabitants of our kingdom of Westphalia," in which he pointed out to them the advantages springing from the conquests of the August Chief of his House, and promised himself to be faithful to the obligation of making his people happy. Unfortunately, though he was naturally clement and kind-hearted, the evidences of his attempts to fulfil this promise are miserably few. What he lacked, of course, was not the good will, but the exertion and self-denial required to make that good will of any effect

King of Westphalia

in relieving the distress of the Westphalian people.

The first sounds of the storm were very speedily heard. Jerome, as has been said, ordered that the funds in the State Treasury from the 1st December should be held at his disposal. As soon as news of this command reached Daru, the Intendant - General of the Grand Army at Berlin, he refused to recognise it. His duty being to look after Westphalia's contribution, among others, to the maintenance of that army, he had written to the provisional government in September, claiming payment of 35,600,000 francs, which, he said, were still owing out of the 49,000,000 due from Westphalia to France. He had secured, on account of this enormous sum, possession of all the revenues of the country during the period preceding Jerome's arrival, and had a sharp quarrel with Morio, who, on his mission from the King, had attempted to prevent the conversion to military ends of some small funds. Jerome, therefore, in December found nothing but bills in the Treasury, and on asking Daru to refund the moneys which he had exacted from the Regency during the two preceding months, met with a positive refusal. That he had a suspicion

The Burlesque Napoleon

he would find little in the chest at Cassel appears likely from the letter which he wrote to the Emperor the day after his arrival at Napoleonshöhe. "If I do not find in the Treasury on my arrival, as your Majesty assured me I should, the wherewithal to repay the 1,800,000 francs which your Majesty lent me, and to provide for the preliminary expenses of my installation, I shall be unable to meet my engagements towards the Sinking Fund, and shall myself be in the greatest embarrassment."[1]

Daru lost no time in appealing to Napoleon, who was away on a visit to Italy, and, pending the arrival of an answer, steadfastly declined to allow the King to touch the money which he demanded. Now, in the second article of the constitution of Westphalia, which Napoleon had delivered to Jerome but a month before, it had been provided that half the "allodial" domains of Westphalia should be reserved to the Emperor, to be used in rewards to the Grand Army officers for their services in the past war. The natural implication, as Jerome saw, was that

---

[1] He might have remembered that when Joachim Murat entered Düsseldorf as Grand Duke of Cleves and Berg in March 1806 he similarly hastened to the Treasury, to find it empty!

King of Westphalia

Napoleon made no claim to the remainder of Westphalia. During the provisional government, Jollivet, who thus early acted entirely in the interests of the Emperor, took care to prevent any discussion of the question of *domaines allodiaux et domaniaux*. A settlement, however, could now no longer be postponed. Jerome, faced by the refusal of Daru to give up to him what he considered his own revenues, wrote, in despair, to his brother. He represented his condition, hinted again that he might not meet his liabilities to France, and proposed, finally, to guarantee to Napoleon 1,000,000 francs a year if his own right to all property in the country, allodial or other, were recognised. The answer of the Emperor was entirely favourable to Daru. He wrote to Jerome from Milan on the 17th December, reserving to himself half of the entire lands of Westphalia.[1] He would not object to the money which Jerome claimed for the months

---

[1] In a subsequent letter (to Jerome, 4th January 1808) he showed a most improper disrespect for the legal terms *allodial* and *domanial*. He was much worried, he wrote, about these ridiculous distinctions between allodial and non - allodial estates. His intention was to reserve to himself the clear half of the estates in Westphalia; apart from which Jerome would be giving him nothing, and the Grand Army would be without recompense.

The Burlesque Napoleon

of October and November being paid over to him *as soon as his Ministers had settled accounts with Daru.* As for the suggestion that the debt to the Sinking Fund might not be met, Napoleon refused to credit this. "It would be a bad beginning for your reign," he added, "and would suit your credit ill if you started off by not paying your debts."

Jerome could not extract any comfort from this letter. He wrote to explain that he could not impose any fresh taxes without rendering himself unpopular in Westphalia. Two days later, on the 25th, he wrote again, saying that on his arrival he had found all payments ten months in arrears, and all funds closed against him. He was obliged, nevertheless, to spend money. He had counted on the October and November revenues, and he once more asked the Emperor for these. "Your Majesty knows that on my departure I was without money, and that I left in the assurance of finding resources here to repay your Majesty the sum advanced, and to provide for my government here." Jerome supported his case by procuring a report on the financial state of Westphalia from Siméon, Beugnot, and Jollivet—all three appointed originally by Napoleon, it must be

King of Westphalia

remembered. These ministers declared that there was a deficit of 6,000,000 francs, to which there was further to be added another 3,000,000 for the excess of actual over estimated expenditure on the upkeep of the troops of the Grand Army in Westphalia. They could only advise that a loan should be raised to pay off this debt of 9,000,000 francs.

THE ART OF
BANKRUPTCY

CHAPTER VII

THE ART OF BANKRUPTCY

AT the end of 1807 Jerome was still awaiting the decision of the Emperor about Westphalia's debt. But this dispute over his country's finances and the enormous claims of the Grand Army was not the only cause of trouble with Napoleon in the first month of Jerome's reign. One of the most prominent traits in his character was his passion for liberality to those whom he made his friends. Among all his circle there was no one whose services he esteemed more highly than Alexandre Le Camus. From the early days of the San Domingo expedition the young Creole had never left him. Jerome could do nothing without him—not even go to sleep, one of Napoleon's agents at Cassel wrote scornfully to his master. Since his patron had become a prince it was the general opinion that Le Camus added to his other duties the rather less than respectable task of assisting him in his

The Burlesque Napoleon

love affairs. One supposed instance has been mentioned already; his talent in this line was to have more scope later. Yet the man was one who created an excellent impression at first sight. Possessed of good manners, calm, very correct in his language, yet affable, he conveyed an idea of distinction with which his mental and moral attributes accorded ill. His address, however, made the fortune of his family, who all followed him to Cassel. One of the King's first acts was to bestow on him a token of esteem in the form of the title of Count of Fürstenstein, with the property of the old family of that name, and an income of 40,000 francs a year. Napoleon's annoyance when he heard of this was extreme, as was natural, seeing that Jerome, almost in the same breath, announced this creation and his own desperate financial condition. He had never heard of so mad a proceeding, he said, fatal to the State, and, above all, fatal to Jerome. "What has the Sieur Le Camus done?" he asked. "He has not performed a single service for the country—only for you personally. Is this a reward proportionate to the services which he has performed for you? Since I began to reign I have never dreamt of so arbitrary an

The Art of Bankruptcy

act. I have more than ten men who have saved my life, to whom I pay no more pension than 600 francs. I have marshals who have won ten battles, who are covered with scars, and who have no such reward as you are giving to the Sieur Le Camus." Either Jerome must recall his gift or Le Camus must renounce French citizenship; for if Le Camus had 40,000 francs a year, what should Berthier, Lannes, Bernadotte, and others have? Jerome chose the latter of the two alternatives offered to him, and Le Camus kept his title and pension. The new Count adopted the arms of the old Fürstensteins and their liveries. Unhappily, he could not adopt their pronunciation of the name, so that the favourite amusement of the Court for a time was to ask him who he was, whereon he invariably replied: "The Count of Furchetintin."[1] He was always the first to laugh over his own blunder, however—and he could afford to laugh. Jerome did not cease to advance him, in spite of what Napoleon had said. He made him Minister of Foreign Affairs —such affairs were indeed foreign to him, de Norvins remarks—and in 1809 found a wife for

[1] With the French nasal sounds, that is to say. De Norvins gives this story.

The Burlesque Napoleon

him in the Countess of Hardenberg, daughter of the Grand Huntsman of Westphalia. The German nobility was horrified, for the Hardenbergs were very blue of blood; but the Count of Fürstenstein could put up with their horror. It is to be noticed that he was commendably careful of his wife's reputation. He knew the Westphalian Court; above all, his illustrious benefactor. He succeeded in obtaining excellent marriages for two of his three sisters, who were all possessed of good looks; and a brother was employed also at Cassel, and sent later to America on a mission to Jerome's first wife.

Apart from his friction with the Emperor, Jerome very early began to experience other difficulties. He had written on the 23rd December that it would be unwise to make him unpopular by the imposition of fresh taxes in Westphalia. He had, however, been less careful in other respects about his reputation; and in Cassel at least his early popularity was distinctly on the wane, if we are to believe Jollivet. The latter, though still acting as a Minister of Jerome to the end of 1807, also filled the post of spy on Napoleon's behalf. He commenced that very entertaining series of bulletins, afterwards continued by Reinhard, which kept

The Art of Bankruptcy

the Emperor informed about Court life at Cassel, and which are our chief authority about that life. So now, near the end of the first month of Jerome's reign in Westphalia, we find Jollivet writing:

"The people of Cassel have grown singularly cold since the King's arrival. Distress and complaints are general. Things are not going as they promised. The French who came to Westphalia are leaving in crowds, utterly discontented. They are wearied in the town, bored at the Court, where neither money nor pleasure is to be found, people say. Everyone is gloomy. The King meets with few signs of respect. He is rarely saluted in the streets, where he often rides. He has sunk in public esteem. Certain gallant adventures have already done him harm. It is publicly known that one of the Queen's ladies has been dismissed because of him. The Chief Chamberlain (M. Le Camus), nevertheless, discovered a way of keeping this woman in Cassel on behalf of his master. The Queen insisted that she should leave. At length the police got rid of the woman for her. M. Le Camus is reputed to be an obliging servant of his master. A Breslau actress, whose acquaintance the King

The Burlesque Napoleon

made on his Silesian campaign, must have been attracted to Cassel by the efforts of M. Le Camus, and at his master's orders. Other stories of the same kind are being told. The mothers of Cassel with pretty daughters are afraid to let them go to the Court balls and festivals. The Queen is beloved, and many fears are expressed for her domestic happiness."

"All goes very badly," concluded Jollivet; and it does not appear that he was exaggerating the gloominess of the picture he drew. With regard to the dreariness of the Court at the beginning of Jerome's reign, we have similar evidence from a very different source—one certainly not hostile to the King. De Salha, formerly of the *Vétéran*, and now aide-de-camp to Jerome, writing in the middle of January, tells Halgan (whom Napoleon had not allowed to accept Jerome's invitation to Westphalia) that "our Civil List of 5,000,000 is very scanty for two young sovereigns equally magnificent in their tastes." Salha went on: "We ought to have elbow-room here, instead of which we are thwarted by the desires of the King of Kings, who maintains a special superintendence over this new kingdom. We are only half reigning in a home where it is very

The Art of Bankruptcy

hard to banish dulness." This was in spite of the fact that "the King often gives balls and sledge parties; and we have also a Comédie Française under the direction of Le Camus."

Without wasting sympathy over Jerome's inability to find sufficient amusements to banish dulness from the Court of Cassel, we must still recognise that Napoleon displayed injustice, if not actual bad faith, in putting out of his brother's reach all the ready money in the kingdom. Leaving aside the question of his claim, on behalf of the Grand Army, to half the entire dominions of Westphalia, we can but suppose that he intended Jerome to keep up some state at his capital. Yet, knowing that he left Paris without any balance to his credit after paying his debts, but, on the contrary, with a loan to repay, and having evidently allowed Jerome to think that there would be some ready money at least in the Treasury when he reached Cassel, Napoleon unhesitatingly supported Daru's uttermost claims to the only available cash in the kingdom. Having plenty of spies in the country, he knew well enough that it was nearly reduced to bankruptcy already, and could not stand further taxation. How did he expect Jerome to pay his way at the begin-

The Burlesque Napoleon

ning? He recommended to him the strictest economy—and this was the right policy to pursue. But even the narrowest parsimony would not provide the money required at the commencement of the new reign. Moreover, Napoleon was acquainted with Jerome's character. Could he hope for economy from him? Or did he think that Westphalia would produce so great a change in him? It is difficult, indeed, to judge what he expected. Jerome, at any rate, made no attempt to solve the problem which Napoleon set him. Having no money, he proceeded, almost immediately, to the greatest lengths of extravagance. Holding, apparently, that the Emperor must some day relent and give him financial assistance, he lived on that hope for years, and at no time did he abate at all his ideas of the style necessary for a king. Napoleon was adamant; but so was Jerome. The one continued to exact the money which the other was so anxious to keep; but the other spent its equivalent none the less. The sufferer was the unfortunate country over which one governed and the other nominally ruled.

Had he been quite other than what he was, Jerome might have set his kingdom's finances straight in time. His biographer, du Casse, sees

The Art of Bankruptcy

no reason why a Civil List of 5,000,000 francs a year should not have sufficed not only to keep a Court going in a small German state, amid a people of simple ideas, but also to provide money to pay off other debts. Jerome's predecessor at Cassel had, indeed, lived on so mean a scale as to be a laughing-stock among his neighbours. All the royal buildings were falling to ruin, and so much had all luxuries been discouraged by the Elector that Catherine complained that she could not find a piece of ribbon for sale in Cassel when she first arrived. Acting as the Elector had acted, Jerome might, no doubt, ultimately have had a reasonable balance-sheet. But between King Jerome and the Elector of Hesse-Cassel there was not the slightest resemblance, and no one knew this better than Napoleon. Nor did Jerome lose any opportunity of emphasising the difference.

The first act of 1808 was, indeed, a striking example of the change which had come over the land. On New Year's Day it was arranged that the ceremony of the swearing-in of the Westphalian deputies should take place. The *Moniteur Westphalien* gives a long account of the affair, which, to its courtly official eyes, seemed full of charm and brilliance. All was

The Burlesque Napoleon

ready in the assembly-room by eleven o'clock in the morning. The decorations were elegant, we are told. At the end of the room was a canopy of white satin with a golden fringe, surmounted by the royal escutcheon. Under this was the King's throne, adorned with the Westphalian colours of white and blue. Behind the throne was a laurel-wreathed bust of Napoleon, who thus seemed to associate himself with his brother on the solemn occasion. The Queen's seat faced the throne.[1] At 11.30 salvoes of artillery announced the arrival of Catherine, "the beloved of two kingdoms." She was introduced by her Grand Mistress and the ladies and officials of her household. A quarter of an hour later came Jerome himself, heralded by a salute of twenty-one guns. His carriage drew up before a loyal deputation of his subjects, who escorted him to the steps of the throne. The Minister of Justice and the Interior addressed to him the speech of welcome; the deputies then in turn took the oath of allegiance; and finally Jerome delivered a speech concerning the great task which he was undertaking, and the mutual duties of

[1] Catherine wished to sit beside Jerome, but his royal dignity would not allow this.

The Art of Bankruptcy

sovereign and subjects. Great applause followed; and the King took his departure in the same manner as he had arrived, preceded by his household, and followed by the Ministers and deputies. The Queen left shortly after the King, impressing all by her graciousness. The *Moniteur* sees ample grounds for satisfaction over the ceremony; and, no doubt, the day seemed to the good people of Cassel a revelation after the parsimonious times of their old Elector.

With the advent of the new year Jerome was pleasantly surprised by receiving from Napoleon the Order of the Iron Crown. In writing to express his gratitude he spoke of the certain proof which the gift furnished him of the Emperor's continued kindness. Unfortunately, there were more proofs forthcoming of the very strict watch which Napoleon was determined to keep over the kingdom. He commenced by appointing Jollivet his commissioner to arrange the division of the Westphalian revenues, thus removing him from the Westphalian service. On the 4th January he sent Jerome no less than five letters, of which that has already been quoted which refers to the excessive honours conferred on Le Camus. Three of the other

The Burlesque Napoleon

four are equally severe in their comments on the King's public acts. Jerome was assured in one that he had no jurisdiction whatever over Frenchmen sent to him by Napoleon, and, if this did not suit him, he was to send them back to France, and to govern with Germans. In another he was informed that, in paying his Ministers as he did, he was "putting his country upon a footing which would bring it to ruin." There was, indeed, justice in this complaint, as all his principal Ministers had 60,000 francs a year assigned to them—a figure ten times as much as Murat was allowed to pay his Ministers in Berg, and one which Westphalia could not possibly afford. All that Jerome could plead in response was a misunderstanding of the Emperor's wishes on the subject; he could not now reduce the salaries.

In comparison with the value of the abilities of the majority of them, the Ministers of Jerome were certainly overpaid. Of the former members of the Regency, among whom Jerome temporarily divided the chief offices of State when he assumed the royal power, Jollivet dropped out at the beginning of 1808, when Napoleon appointed him to the commissionership. General Lagrange followed a few days later, leaving suddenly

The Art of Bankruptcy

without warning, after a disagreement with the King. Napoleon handled Jerome severely for his treatment of Lagrange; but that officer, though an excellent soldier in most respects, was one of the brigand type, like Vandamme, whose distastefulness to Jerome is not a matter for blame. This left of his first advisers only Beugnot and Siméon, Ministers of Finance and Justice; for Siméon maintained the Ministry of Justice, while resigning that of the Interior. These two men, both of whom had been proscribed during the Terror, but had risen rapidly afterwards, worked in harmony up to the time of Beugnot's departure from Westphalia, and may be held responsible for the best work in the early organisation of the kingdom. Siméon, from all accounts, appears an admirable old man, only lacking in the force of will necessary to cope with his giddy but obstinate King. A clever lawyer, upright in character and of gentle manners, he was a rare example in the Court of Cassel. Beugnot was also an able man, but more of a theorist than a sound politician—vain, oratorical, and not distinguished for tact. De Norvins, who (for his sins, as he afterwards considered) allowed himself to be persuaded by Siméon to enter the Westphalian service, and was soon after, through his influence, made editor of the official *Moniteur*, says in his "Souvenirs" that the two Ministers and himself came to form a *petit conseil privé*, a sort of inner Cabinet to advise the King—Siméon and Beugnot both having considerable influence over him. De Norvins seems to have acted as a general secretary to them. For a few weeks Johann von Müller, the Swiss historian, was also in this Cabinet; but he found the post of Secretary of State little to his taste, and at his own request he was made Councillor of State and Director-General of Education, resigning the more arduous office. This man has been gravely attacked on moral grounds by scandalmongers; but the picture which de Norvins draws of him is charming and sympathetic, and such is the general reputation of "the German Tacitus." He was a member of the deputation which went to Paris before Jerome's arrival in Cassel, and even before that he had attracted Napoleon's favourable attention in Berlin in 1806. When he gave up the Secretaryship of State, Fürstenstein was appointed in his place, joining to it the Ministry of Foreign Affairs—a rather unnecessary post in Westphalia. Another personal friend of the King succeeded Lagrange at the

The Art of Bankruptcy

War Office, in the person of Morio, just made a General. Claims of friendship had already been recognised, in the appointment to intimate offices at Court of Meyronnet, now Count Wellingerode, Grand Marshal of the Palace; de Salha, head of the College of Pages; Rewbell, aide-de-camp; La Flèche, Master of Ceremonies, etc. Further, the unfortunate Pichon, who had suffered so much on account of Jerome in America, appeared in Westphalia, and was appointed to superintend the public treasury. On his return to France he had been accused by Napoleon of embezzlement of 3000 francs, which he claimed to have used on behalf of French refugees in America, and was compelled to pay part of that sum. Jerome, who had spent some at least of the money in question, endeavoured to make up to Pichon now for part of his sufferings, and readily forgot their differences. But Pichon did not remain to the end at Cassel, being disgusted, it was said, at not being made Finance Minister.

In keeping, no doubt, with the well-salaried Ministers, but little in harmony with the condition of Westphalia, the whole Court of Cassel was on an elaborate scale. Du Casse goes into the question minutely, and shows that the King's household consisted of some sixty, and the

The Burlesque Napoleon

Queen's of nearly twenty, persons, apart, of course, from servants. Some light on the ways and the duties of the household is thrown by the memoirs of de Norvins; but the remarks may be reserved to their proper place, for it was not until September 1809 that he became attached to Catherine personally, and the ceremony of the Court had been considerably developed then. From the very beginning, however, the scale on which Jerome planned his surroundings was singularly inappropriate in a country placed as Westphalia was financially. The standard to which everything was referred was the King's sense of dignity, not the resources of the kingdom; and Jerome took his royal dignity very seriously in outward matters.

It was not without considerable difficulty that an arrangement was at last came to about the Westphalian contribution to France. Jollivet, released from his ambiguous position under Jerome, proved himself almost as hard to deal with as Daru. Finally, he and the King's representative, Malchus, succeeded in fixing the annual sum to be paid to Napoleon at 7,000,000 francs, and Jerome gave his assent to this on the 23rd February. The

The Art of Bankruptcy

report, which Jollivet, in conjunction with Beugnot and Siméon, had made in December on Westphalian finances, was rejected by Napoleon, who produced on the other side a memorial by his own Finance Minister. The latter stated that the Westphalian Ministers had under-estimated the country's revenues by 4,000,000; but he allowed that Westphalia could not provide the war contributions immediately, and so he too advised a loan. This, indeed, was compulsory at once. Apart from the demands of France under the arrangement of Jollivet and Malchus, Jerome had to meet the clamorous requests of his officials for their arrears of salary, and to pay for the current expenses of his kingdom and Court. In March the Caisse d'Amortissement of Paris came down on him for repayment of the 1,800,000 which he had borrowed in the previous November, the request being supported by a note in Napoleon's own writing. Jerome, by dint of paying interest of seven to eight per cent., succeeded in borrowing 2,000,000 from a Jewish banker named Israel Jacobson, an excellent man apparently, who secured the removal of all his co - religionists' disabilities in Westphalia in partial return for his assistance to the King.

The Burlesque Napoleon

But of this money Jerome could find none to give to the Sinking Fund, devoting all to his other expenses. Napoleon's anger must be braved; Jerome sent merely a request for extension of time with regard to the 1,800,000 francs. In the meanwhile he had gained a respite, and had some funds with which to carry on his government and his amusements.

He was by no means unaware that his brother was kept informed as to the nature of these amusements, as well as of his manner of government. He knew, moreover, who was the principal source of information. At the beginning of the year he had asked Napoleon to recall Jollivet, for whom he had no longer a post, he said. He would have liked in his place at the Treasury to put a man called Hainguerlot, but Napoleon denounced him as a forger and the perpetrator of criminal acts which had made him the horror of France.[1]

---

[1] So strong was Napoleon's prejudice against the man that, in a letter to Champagny from Schönbrunn on the 8th October 1809, he wrote: "Inform Reinhard that, if the King employs H——, he is to ask for his passports, and to let it be known that he has orders to declare positively that I will not allow such a blackguard to remain near the King." The reason of Jerome's persistent regard for Hainguerlot is unknown.

The Art of Bankruptcy

Jerome was obliged to do without Hainguerlot, and to put up with the continued residence at Cassel of Jollivet, whose appointment as Napoleon's commissioner promised him a long career in Westphalia. All that he could do was to treat the obnoxious ex-Minister with coldness. On the birthday of the Queen there was no invitation for him or his wife. Anticipating Jollivet's complaint, Jerome wrote to Napoleon explaining that the fête in honour of the day had been quite a private affair, held only in a country house, and that, while two French Councillors of State (Siméon and Beugnot) had been invited, the Westphalian War Minister had not been asked. Moreover, he complained of Jollivet and his wife refusing former invitations to Court, or, when they accepted, being so rude as to leave early, before himself and the Queen. He could not, of course, mention the chief cause of his objection to Jollivet, which was natural, if not creditable to either. A king could not be expected to be amiable to a spy on the royal gallantries. Jerome summed up the matter concisely, from his point of view, when he said later: "*A quoi bon écrire à Paris que j'ai donné un diamant, que j'ai couché avec une belle ? Un Ministre ne*

The Burlesque Napoleon

doit pas s'occuper de ces bagatelles ; il doit mander que le Roi se porte bien, que la Westphalie marche dans la système de la France, et voilà tout!" But Jollivet's instructions from Napoleon, of course, expressly prevented him from ignoring the *bagatelles*. Personally, he does not seem to have been the most agreeable of men as a spy, though reputed exceedingly able in finance. He had started as a land surveyor in Poitou, and according to his former colleague, Beugnot, had worked his way like a mole. De Norvins describes him as a type of the most vulgar *bourgeoisie*, and his wife as resembling *une vieille loueuse de chaises*. Napoleon, however, esteemed him highly, and, from the *18 brumaire* onward, had constantly made use of his talents. In the proceedings against Lucien Bonaparte he had been serviceable, which was another reason for the dislike felt by Jerome, whose affection for Lucien was unaltered by the latter's disgrace.

The stream of reprimands, just and unjust, from the Emperor, flowed on unceasingly. Jerome had asked Siméon and Beugnot to take an oath of allegiance to him. Napoleon wrote to him on the 6th March that the idea was ridiculous, and added: "I have met few

The Art of Bankruptcy

men with so little sense of proportion as you. You are ignorant of everything, and you follow merely your own fancy. Reason decides nothing with you, impetuosity and passion everything." In the postcript, in his own writing, he added the consoling phrase: "*Mon ami, je vous aime, mais vous êtes furieusement jeune.*" Indeed, there can be no doubt of Napoleon's affection at this period; but its expression was limited, while the attitude of the master towards his pupil was painfully evident to the pupil. Early in June, just after Jerome had returned from a short tour in the Magdeburg district, he received a letter from Berthier, complaining on behalf of the Emperor that the French troops in Westphalia had been ill-treated and refused admission to the hospitals, and threatening to send 15,000 men into the kingdom. Jerome replied, with some spirit, that he had directed his War Minister to answer the false calumnies in circulation, and that as for the 15,000 men, the Emperor might send them. In spite of his subjects' poverty he would readily share with the soldiers all that was left. His own dearest title was that of a French Prince. "Can the Emperor believe," he asked, "that I forget for a moment that my first country is France, and

The Burlesque Napoleon

that my greatest glory is the fact that I quitted her only to serve her as an outpost?"

Undoubtedly Jerome had the gift of stating his case well. But the case was a bad one. Now worse trouble was in store for him. The debt to the Paris Caisse d'Amortissement, of course, still remained unpaid, and it was not to be hoped that either Béranger, the Director, or Napoleon would forget it. Some steps must be taken. On the 2nd July Jerome convoked the Estates of the Realm. He determined to take the opportunity to lay before them a proposal for a loan. The spectacle of this first free Parliament in Germany was a curious one. The deputies met in the Orangery in the Park of Cassel. Jerome drove to the place of assembly, clad in his favourite white satin, covered with a purple cloak, his head adorned with a plumed and diamond-decked toque. The brilliant costumes of the royal household lent splendour to the scene; already the Court of Cassel was winning for itself a reputation for pre-eminence in dress, masculine as much as feminine. Jerome was most gracious, most paternal. The deputies did not fail to be impressed, if, perhaps, they were covertly amused

The Art of Bankruptcy

at the youthful father of his people.[1] The proposal for a loan met with approval. It was agreed that an attempt should be made to raise 20,000,000 francs in Holland. Unfortunately, when negotiations opened it was found that France was just floating a loan there, and the Westphalian attempt failed completely. Then suddenly arrived three letters from Napoleon, all written on the same day, the 16th July, at Bayonne. The first must be quoted in full. "You owe 2,000,000 to the Sinking Fund," wrote the Emperor. "You have allowed your bills to be dishonoured. That is not the act of a man of honour. I never allow anyone to fail me. Sell your plate and diamonds. Cease indulging in the foolish extravagances which make you the laughing-stock of Europe, and will end by rousing the indignation of your subjects. Sell your furniture, your horses, and your jewels, and pay your debts. Honour comes first of all. It ill becomes you not to pay your debts, when people see the presents which you give, and the unexampled luxury you live in, so

---

[1] "A light ironical smile" is mentioned by an eye-witness quoted by Mr Fisher ("Studies in Napoleonic Statesmanship: Germany," p. 242).

The Burlesque Napoleon

disgusting to your subjects. You are young and inconsiderate, and you never pay any attention to money matters, above all at a time when your subjects are suffering from the effects of a war."

In the second letter Napoleon impressed on Jerome the necessity of respect, gratitude, and attachment to himself in the first place, and to France in the second; and finally, "the severest economy, to avoid the contrast between the burdens weighing upon your people and an unbridled luxury and extravagance; an economy necessary for all sovereigns, especially for the king of a simple people; an economy necessary at all times, especially at the beginning of a reign, when public opinion is taking shape; an economy so great that not only will you have no debts, but further, on your Civil List of 6,000,000 francs you will spend 3,000,000 francs on your household, and will keep 1,500,000 francs for unforeseen expenses—such as marriages, festivities, and the construction of palaces—and 1,500,000 francs to form in ten years a reserve fund of 15,000,000 francs, which you will meanwhile lend to hasten the formation of your army." The third letter referred again to the prohibition to have any dealings with Hainguerlot.

The Art of Bankruptcy

The reproaches of his brother, however merited, did not discover to Jerome any way of meeting the claim for 1,800,000 francs immediately. He saw, therefore, no other resource than to write in the hope of touching the heart of Napoleon. "What can I reply, Sire," he asked on the 28th July, "when your Majesty tells me that I do not act like a man of honour? Beyond a doubt, I am truly unhappy in that I cannot die after reading the words. If I have not paid the 1,800,000 francs which I owe to the Sinking Fund, it is because I have not the money and did not think that your Majesty's intention was that I should pay ruinous interest to get rid of my debts to you. But, Sire, I have just ordered an immediate loan to meet this call, whatever the interest required, and before three months have passed my bills shall be withdrawn. Sire, I am of your blood, and never have I quitted the path of honour which your Majesty has marked out for me!"

The immediate loan which Jerome alluded to was one obtained for him from some local Jewish bankers by von Bülow, his new Finance Minister. Beugnot had left Westphalia for France at the end of May, for family reasons, as he alleged, and, deaf to Jerome's entreaties to continue in

The Burlesque Napoleon

his service, would not come back. Napoleon had given him permission, as he had to Siméon, to remain with Jerome or to return to work in France. But whereas Siméon preferred the Westphalian service, Beugnot, in spite of Jerome's esteem for him, was tired of Cassel, and was glad to accept an appointment to administer the Grand Duchy of Berg. Von Bülow showed some talent in the raising of money, but the small sum which he managed to obtain now would not cover the debt to France and current expenses. Jerome did not hesitate: the Sinking Fund must again wait.

Early in September Napoleon wrote to inform his brother that he was going to meet the Tsar Alexander at Erfurt at the end of the month. On the 3rd October Jerome left Cassel with his wife, being called to make one of the brilliant "parterre of kings" which there gratified the sight of Napoleon, while he and Alexander discussed the affairs of Europe and the developments since Tilsit. The King of Westphalia was, of course, but an insignificant factor in Europe, and of his part in the proceedings no record remains beyond some scandalous, and probably not at all trustworthy, tales of his revels with the Grand Duke Constantine, the

The Art of Bankruptcy

Tsar's brother. Jerome was only away from Cassel eight days altogether. Another story seems authentic, since it is told by de Norvins, of Napoleon's question to Jollivet, who accompanied Jerome to Erfurt—scarcely, it may be imagined, by the King's desire. "Well, M. Jollivet," asked the Emperor, "how does my brother Jerome get on?" "Sire," answered Jollivet, "the young prince does not yet appear to me ripe for kingship." Possibly it was this remark of Jollivet which decided Napoleon to send a special representative to Cassel to watch affairs. He certainly seems to have conceived the idea when he was at Erfurt. Hitherto France had no representative at the Westphalian Court except Jollivet, who was not an ambassador. Now such an official was appointed; and Napoleon's choice fell upon Reinhard, a Würtemburger by birth, who had settled in France at the age of sixteen, and had embraced a political and diplomatic career. He met with success, and in the closing days of the Directory had risen to be Minister for Foreign Affairs. His progress continued under Napoleon, who appointed him his representative at Hamburg, to watch over the so-called neutrality of the Hanseatic towns; at Jassy; and finally, in 1808, at Cassel.

The Burlesque Napoleon

Reinhard, after being notified of his appointment, was sent to Paris to receive instructions as to his duties from the Minister for Foreign Affairs, Champagny. It was impressed upon him that his work was of a special nature. "His Majesty the Emperor and King," the written instructions stated, "having very much at heart the personal welfare of his august brother and the prosperity of his people, desires to be informed of all circumstances which might affect one or the other." Again: "His Majesty charges me to tell you that your despatches will not be seen, and that the source of the information given by you will be forgotten." To his despatches he was commanded to append unsigned "bulletins," containing society news, common talk, and the anecdotes, true or false, in general circulation.

Fortified by his instructions, Reinhard arrived at Cassel at the beginning of December. His reception was favourable, and most satisfactory to himself, and his early impressions were astonishingly advantageous to the King's character and the government of his realm. His first important despatch was written after he had been at Cassel six weeks.[1] It is very long, and

[1] "Memoires et Correspondance du Roi Jérôme," iii. pp. 198-214.

The Art of Bankruptcy

gives a general sketch of the state of affairs in Westphalia. The most interesting and most personal passages are those which follow:—

"The Court is young and brilliant. The evenings are divided between play and conversation. Sometimes there is chess; sometimes games of chance, the royal munificence providing the expenses, to the extent of a moderate sum decided on beforehand. The King delights in giving presents, such as shawls, watches, and jewels; the Queen has abundance of dresses to distribute, since she is constantly renewing her wardrobe. The hour of bed, except when there is a ball, is nine o'clock. The Queen's affections are constant; only one or two ladies have gained her confidence. The King's affections vary more, but they always return. In the society which throngs about their Majesties may be seen abundance of estimable as well as amiable characters. The King's noble mind has allowed him to make no mistakes in his choice, and all that one could wish is that he had given a greater share to age and experience. . . . I need name but one person, whether on account of the influence which she is supposed to have over their Majesties or on

The Burlesque Napoleon

account of the opinions held about her. That person is Madame la Comtesse de Truchsess. I have always found her amiable, clever, and thoughtful; she seems to have few friends, or rather I know of none, and, new-comer as I still am, I find in this a further reason for suspending my judgment.

"The ease and dignity with which the King sustains his part are unequalled. There is no learning nor study. The crown does not weigh heavy upon him, one can see, because he feels himself worthy of wearing it. The Queen, whose charms of soul and mind seem to unfold more graciously in intimate society, rather tolerates the pomp of large assemblies than takes pleasure in it. The attitude of the King and Queen towards each other in public leads one to think that in private too they are in harmony. . . .

"All those who work with His Majesty are full of admiration for his insight and perspicacity, and his talent for summing up a case is unique. It is plain that work holds the King's attention and interests him. His decisions are the result of that quick conviction which flashes forth instantaneously. . . . Perhaps, if trammelled by preliminary study,

The Art of Bankruptcy

his insight would be less correct and less decisive."

Reinhard obviously forced the note of admiration, but in praising the King's rapidity of judgment he mentioned the one quality admirable in a public man which Jerome's critics are disposed to allow him. Concerning other virtues of which he speaks in this preliminary sketch of Jerome and his kingdom, Reinhard saw reason to modify his views later. Of the enigmatic Madame de Truchsess he soon had occasion to write again, as we shall see a few pages further on. He concluded the report with a description of the condition in which he found Westphalia, particularly with reference to finance. He admitted that his sketch was a rapid one, and only provisional. But it is curious that he took a rather optimistic view. He pointed out that all European countries except France were suffering at this time from a common malady, and he thought Westphalia's state less grave than that of most.

The long report sent by the Ambassador met with Napoleon's approval, for in the postscript to a letter to Champagny on the 25th January he writes: " I have read M. Reinhard's report

The Burlesque Napoleon

of the 15th January with pleasure.... I keep an Ambassador at Cassel in order to know what happens in Westphalia." In the body of the same letter he directs Champagny to impress on Reinhard that he must write in detail, and to assure him that his letters will be kept secret, and that the Westphalian Government will not know the source of the Emperor's information. As a matter of fact, this was more than Napoleon could guarantee. Jerome knew that he had now two spies on his conduct, and, moreover, he let them know that he knew. He took a very early opportunity of enlightening Reinhard on the matter. The interview (which is described fully by Reinhard in his letter of the 28th February to Champagny) was a remarkable one. The French representative had asked for an audience in order to communicate to the King some views of Napoleon concerning the Westphalian military contingent. Fürstenstein, introducing him into Jerome's presence, told him that the King had been sleeping badly. "He has been up late," suggested Reinhard, thinking of the two balls on successive nights in honour of the Queen's birthday. "Yes," replied Fürstenstein; "the King often works very late into the night." When the Count

The Art of Bankruptcy

had withdrawn, Jerome, after a few minutes' conversation, suddenly began speaking about Jollivet and his minute exactions in the division of the Westphalian domains. Jerome's irritation seemed natural to Reinhard; but he then proceeded to talk about the watch kept over his actions. "What was the result of this espionage? A moment of anger! But two brothers might quarrel and be reconciled, and after an explanation the blame would fall finally on the cause of the misunderstanding." Reinhard found Jerome's tone changing to apostrophe, addressed, he assumed, to the absent Jollivet, but also uncomfortably capable of including himself. "If *you* give information as to what goes on in my kitchen even, I shall treat *you* like the Ministers for Bavaria or Würtemberg, not as the Minister for the Family. I shall only admit *you* on occasions of State." While Reinhard was wondering whether the King had read his last despatch to France, Jerome went on: "Besides, M. Jollivet has never been accredited to me. I might regard him as a stranger, and even, if he meddles, might ask him to leave. He is an honourable man, an excellent man, but he loses himself in details. If *you*" (again you!) "were at the Bavarian or Würtemberg

The Burlesque Napoleon

Court—well, then, it would be right to watch and write about everything that happens. But all that my brother wishes to know I will write myself; and to stand well with the Emperor a man must stand well with me." At last Reinhard found an opening. "Your Majesty has taught me a lesson. You are preaching to a convert, and I beg you to be convinced that my ardent desire is to win and deserve your confidence."

The audience was over, and Reinhard was glad to escape after a trying half-hour. In spite of Jerome's manner of life, the reader of Reinhard's bulletins cannot help sympathising with the King in this interview. But neither Reinhard nor Jollivet seems to have felt any degradation in the work of investigating "what went on in the kitchen." Jollivet, almost at this very time, was sending to Champagny a strong denunciation of Jerome and his government. "I have lost hope," he wrote, "that His Majesty the King of Westphalia, in spite of his excellent qualities and his extreme sagacity (the attribute of his family), can extricate himself from the embarrassing position into which he has been brought by evil counsels, inexperience of ruling, over-ardent passions, and his irresistible tendency towards prodigality."

The Art of Bankruptcy

Unfortunately for Jerome, there was no overstatement in these words of the more hostile of his two spies. The few hundred thousands which von Bülow had obtained from the Jews for the King's Civil List had satisfied only for a short time even the household expenses. Von Bülow, being Minister of Finance, had to justify his position; as the aid of Holland was cut off he could only suggest the desperate expedient of a forced loan. This was adopted, and on the 19th October 1808 the loan had been offered to the people of Westphalia. Every inhabitant possessing over 5000 francs was called upon to subscribe, according to his income. 100,000 200-franc bonds were issued, bearing interest of six, five, and four per cent., according to date of issue. The unhappy Westphalians, however, already so severely bled by France's exactions, showed little anxiety to take up the bonds, and at the time when Jollivet was writing his letter quoted above, only some 6,000,000 or 7,000,000 francs had been secured. The King's Government prolonged the facilities for subscription to the 1st March, and held out threats of strong action in the event of the money not coming in; but the whole was never secured. In the meantime

The Burlesque Napoleon

Jerome saw a chance for economy in closing some of the universities in his kingdom, which he proceeded to do, in spite of the vigorous protests of Johann von Müller. The resourceful von Bülow, not content with the forced loan, set himself to work again in Holland, and in April 1809 succeeded in getting about 6,000,000 francs for the Westphalian Treasury from Dutch bankers, the security being the products of the salt-pits and the Harz mines.

Thus, though the year 1809 had opened with the blackest of prospects, there was at least some money available in the spring. It did not, however, appear possible to Jerome yet to pay the debt to the Sinking Fund. Napoleon might write to him, as he repeatedly did, to point out that he was expecting the money; but the money remained in Westphalia. "Keep your engagements to me," said the Emperor, "and remember that no man ever made such engagements without fulfilling them." Again: "You must be scrupulously exact, and you would do better to keep your engagements than to make presents."[1] Jerome was hardened

---

[1] Letters to Jerome of the 11th February and 15th March. In the former Napoleon says: "I have nothing

The Art of Bankruptcy

against such appeals. He would neither retrench his personal and Court expenses nor pay his debt to the Caisse. On his return to Cassel from Erfurt he appeared quite another man. So at least his Grand Equerry d'Albignac told Reinhard. His talks with the Emperor had changed him; but in eight days (added d'Albignac), the women, the Queen, the intriguers had got round him again. It is curious to see Catherine here included among the bad influences. There is little justification for the reproach, except in her excessive amiability. But d'Albignac was right in his estimate of the brief duration of Jerome's reform. His extravagances and follies increased instead of diminishing; and as we now have Reinhard's regular bulletins to supplement the ordinary sources of information, the picture becomes almost overcrowded with detail. Hitherto

---

to do with the condition of your Treasury and your administration. I am aware that both are in a very bad way. This is a consequence of the measures you have taken and the luxury in which you live. All your acts have the stamp of folly. Why should you confer baronies on men who have done nothing? Why display a luxury so out of harmony with the country, and a calamity to Westphalia, if only for the discredit it casts upon your administration?"

The Burlesque Napoleon

Jerome's debts rather than his intrigues occupied the attention of those deputed to watch the King; but from this time the latter occupy an even larger place than the former in the accounts of his conduct.

THE KING IN COURT AND CAMP

CHAPTER VIII

THE KING IN COURT AND CAMP

IT will have been gathered that the domestic life of Jerome Bonaparte, from the time when he married the Princess Catherine, had been far from blameless. Even in the honeymoon period, at Fontainebleau, he was alleged to have shown very marked attention to the Grand Duchess of Baden. But as Stephanie Beauharnais and he had been friends in childhood, the malicious comments were quite possibly unfair. In the first month of his reign at Cassel, however, we have seen Jollivet writing of " certain gallant adventures " which had damaged the King in public esteem, of a Court dame on whose dismissal the Queen had insisted, and of the Breslau actress whom Le Camus had brought to Cassel at his master's desire. The latter lady, it appears, had been considered by Jerome a suitable wife for his head valet Albertoni; but the ingenious plan had not been very successful, for Albertoni,

The Burlesque Napoleon

though he received a dowry with his bride, found her too good-looking for life in Cassel, retired from the King's service, and took her to Paris. Other actresses were connected by Court scandal with the King, and the lesser stars of the dramatic profession certainly seemed to have a strong attraction for him. One, it was said, was secretly deported from Westphalia in a closed carriage, by no less orders than Napoleon's, much to Jerome's disgust. Usually, with the aid of obliging courtiers, he found little difficulty in lodging a temporary favourite discreetly in his capital; often, indeed, at his Court; for Catherine was marvellously unsuspicious about the appointment of her maids-of-honour. Jerome suffered little interference in his faithless career.

None of these early affairs of the King had much influence on events in Westphalia beyond the fact that they required money, which could only be provided by the neglect of other claims. Another intrigue in which he engaged had further consequences. A remark has already been quoted from the long report of Reinhard in January 1809 concerning a Madame de Truchsess, on whom Napoleon's envoy decided to reserve his judgment. She was not, indeed, of a character which it was easy to read hastily.

The King in Court and Camp

The Countess of Truchsess-Waldburg was the first Grand Mistress of Catherine's household. She was a Hohenzollern by birth, and her husband, who succeeded Le Camus as Grand Chamberlain in Westphalia, had formerly been Würtemberg's Minister in Paris. She was a woman of striking appearance. Reinhard goes so far as to describe her as "the ornament of a Court not lacking in beauties," and speaks of the grace and seductiveness which supplemented her looks. In the Palace she was naturally more popular with men than with women. But she was very reserved towards all except the sovereigns themselves, and paid the penalty for this in being an object of suspicion. The manner in which she appealed to Jerome it is unnecessary to specify. Over the Queen she had a strong influence, which Catherine appeared to tolerate easily, but also rejoiced to shake off ultimately. The Countess dominated her by a combination of charm and of imperiousness. So far was she able to carry this domination that the Queen came to pass nearly all her days *tête-à-tête* with the Grand Mistress, and was thus cut off from other influences. The Court in revenge called her Catherine's *gouvernante*, and accused her of plying the Queen

The Burlesque Napoleon

during the hours they spent together with scandal concerning itself. In particular, the French section of the Court alleged that the Countess poisoned Catherine's mind against the French at Cassel. It does not seem that this was true. Madame de Truchsess was a German, like her Queen, and there was a distinct division between the French and German members of the Court. But Catherine neither now nor afterwards showed any lack of loyalty to the nation into which marriage had brought her. All that could be said against her at this period was that she allowed her Grand Mistress to isolate her to a great extent from all the ladies of her Court.

The resentment of the French party, nevertheless, was directed against the supposed underminer of their characters (very poor characters, it must be confessed), and circumstances combined with the disposition of Madame de Truchsess to put her downfall within their power. Le Camus, though now a Fürstenstein and a Westphalian, not a French, subject, was a leader of the French party. He retained his influence over the King undiminished, and his thorough acquaintance with Jerome's nature gave him great advantages in the attack against

The King in Court and Camp

the Countess. He was credited with an elaborate plot by which to rouse suspicions as to her faithfulness to her royal lover, getting some accommodating friends to compromise her. Jerome, moreover, was very easily distracted in new directions, and seldom found one affair sufficiently engrossing to exclude others. He soon showed that he was tiring of the Countess. She did not intend to let him go without a fight. Holding now only the Queen for certain, and with all the Court unsympathetic, part of it actively hostile, she was in a desperate position, where a mistake would be fatal. She made the mistake, and her defeat was final. The defects of her own character brought about her ruin. She had a quickness of wit which, in addition to her ambition and reserve, caused her to be regarded with a respect that was almost fear. Had she been able to control her tongue she might have continued to hold her place. Here she failed; and the story of her failure, very impartially told by Reinhard for Napoleon's edification, is a curious one.

It was at the end of January that Count Wellingerode, Grand Marshal of the Palace, *alias* Meyronnet, leaving for a holiday at

The Burlesque Napoleon

Marseilles, addressed himself to Madame de Truchsess, and jestingly observed: "Well, Grand Mistress, I am off. Try to turn the time to profit. I shall be away a month, and if you don't prevent it I shall come back." "A month, Grand Marshal? That's very short; but we shall see!" What Meyronnet knew cannot be said, but it looks as if there were some ulterior meaning in his words. A few days later a Court ball was given, at which the guests were all to appear masked. Among those present was Madame de Launay, daughter of the respectable Siméon. Jerome had already shown favour to this young lady, which may account for the attack made upon her. At the ball she exchanged some jests with Pappenheim, one of the Masters of the Ceremonies. Her words were overheard by Madame de Truchsess, who did not fail to recognise Madame de Launay, and proceeded to spread her version of what had been said among the dancers. On the next day the remarks were repeated to the Queen, "with the comments suggested by the charity of the Court," says Reinhard. Catherine manifested annoyance, and the news reached the ears of Siméon. The old Minister was as distressed as his daughter, and went off at

The King in Court and Camp

once to the King to complain. Jerome, now completely cured of his love for the Countess, angrily denounced her as an inventor of tales, and said, impolitely, that she was a liar, her father was a liar, and so was her brother, the husband being the only one in the family worth anything. Herein his verdict coincided with that of the French party at Court, except, perhaps, as regards the husband. When Madame de Truchsess appeared in the evening of the same day she was received by Jerome with coldness so marked that she wept, shrieked, and fainted. The game appeared lost; but she decided to try a last card. Going home, she wrote at once to offer her resignation. The King read the offer with pleasure, but Catherine, we are told, with regret at the loss of one who had so much influence over her. The Countess had not imagined that she would be allowed to execute her threat, and was aghast at the acceptance which awaited her when she awoke in the morning. She was not yet deserted by her courage, nor altogether by hope. On the following day there was another Court ball, to which she received an invitation. She asked to be allowed to be received still as Grand Mistress, but was plainly told that henceforth

The Burlesque Napoleon

she could only be regarded as wife of the Count of Truchsess-Waldburg. She went, nevertheless, to the Palace. She approached the reception-room slowly, her face betraying great agitation. Addressing a few of the ladies she saw, she was reassured by the fact that her greetings were returned (her enemies still feared her enough to dissemble their exultation), and went bravely through the humiliation of entering after all the dames of the household. For the rest of the evening, Reinhard says, she played her part admirably, Two days after she and her husband gave a party to celebrate the opening of their new house, from which, but a little before, the unresisting Finance Minister had been turned out at forty-eight hours' notice, to oblige Madame de Truchsess. Here she put an excellent face on the affair, and talked of her forthcoming visits to her parents in Italy, and to Paris. The guests, however, were somewhat embarrassed, and devoted themselves assiduously to supper. The disgraced favourite even talked about her dread that her holiday might be spoilt by pressing invitations to return. But for the present, as Reinhard says, she was being pressed to go. Further, her husband had to go too, resigning his post of Grand Chamber-

The King in Court and Camp

lain, which now fell to de Salha. On the day they left the King and Queen honoured with their presence a select masked ball at Siméon's house, where the royal kindnesses shown to Madame de Launay were noticed by all. Jerome had sent her some shawls and a magnificent dress, and Catherine was most gracious. Her vindication was complete, and the Truchsess-Waldburgs were seen no more in Westphalia. Thus ended Jerome's only experiment in favouritism on the lines of Louis XIV. and XV.; for though other Court ladies subsequently occupied the position of Madame de Truchsess, none of them wielded any political power.[1]

Such an affair could not be allowed to disturb the amusements of the Court, any more than the general distress of the country restrained its expenses. In fact, the round of pleasures seemed to go more merrily, since the Queen, usually rather reserved in large gatherings, at this period began to exhibit a charming gaiety, which people attributed to relief at the departure of her *gouvernante*. In consequence,

---

[1] The Countess is said to have procured his place as Finance Minister for von Bülow, who was accused by the French party of being their enemy. Certainly von Bülow was on the worst of terms with Bercagny.

The Burlesque Napoleon

the Carnival season of 1809 saw the Court of Cassel at its lightest. Reinhard's bulletin gives an amusing description of a masked ball which wound up the season. As a reward to the townspeople of Munden, who had by their prompt help extinguished a fire in a neighbouring village, Jerome had sent tickets to all their notables, who appeared to the number of seventy-five, in a string of ten carriages. One worthy was in despair, for he had lost his ticket, and was afraid that the King would notice his absence, and put it down to want of manners. The ball was a fine sight for the rustics. Nine hundred guests were present, and the King and Queen were received by garlanded shepherds and shepherdesses, who formed with their crooks an arch for the sovereigns to pass under. The ball opened with a Spanish quadrille, and continued until five in the morning. Even Reinhard himself unbent so far as to head a masquerade in the guise of an Egyptian Bey, who, accompanied by his harem, passed in procession before the enthusiastic King. All round the dancers a fancy fair was in progress, arranged by the Queen, and among the side-shows was a puppet-theatre, managed with unique talent by General du Coudras. The General was aide-de-camp to

The King in Court and Camp

Jerome, and had just been created by him Count Bernterode—rather on account of his wife than through any merits of his own. He was one of the ignoble crowd of complaisant husbands in which the Court of Cassel abounded. The Countess, a woman of a very different stamp from Madame de Truchsess-Waldburg, had stepped into a share of the vacant place in Jerome's heart after the latter's fall. She did not keep it long.

One of the bulletins tells of a ball given by Bernterode at which the King and Queen were present, and at which there was a display of fireworks in the courtyard to entertain the royal guests. Now, fireworks were forbidden by the municipal regulations, and next morning Jerome sternly imposed fines alike on Bernterode and on Bercagny, the head of the police, who had been present, and had taken no steps. Catherine consoled the Countess with a present of an amethyst and pearl necklace. There was no consolation awaiting Bercagny, a man who can only have been appointed to his post on the principle of setting a thief to catch a thief; for this ex-priest and jack-of-all-trades was of execrable character, and lived mainly by blackmail. Bercagny before long found an oppor-

The Burlesque Napoleon

tunity, in the course of his professional duties, of avenging himself for the monetary loss which he had suffered. He was in the habit of making a daily report to the King on the affairs of the town. He, no doubt, could always make these reports interesting, for his great notion of police work was an elaborate system of espionage. He now had great pleasure in announcing to his Sovereign that the Countess of Bernterode was carrying on an intrigue with a Government underling. This insult to the royal dignity was intolerable. Bercagny was ordered to seize the lovers at one of their meetings, put them into a closed carriage, and drive them over the frontier. The command was faithfully obeyed, and the career of the lady in Westphalia closed. Her husband remained behind, lamenting his misfortune, but retaining his post.

Reinhard's painstaking bulletins about this time contain the names of various persons whom something more than suspicion connected with the King. Sometimes he is discreetly reticent as to their names, as when (in the bulletin of the 17th March 1809) he informs Napoleon of one "Madame de X——," who is said to be enjoying the King's confidence at the moment. "It is asserted," repeats the ambassadorial

The King in Court and Camp

scandalmonger, "that she has not yielded yet. If she can keep herself a desirable object for long, and the King's passion is strong enough to prevent him seeking distractions elsewhere, she will have deserved well of the young prince." Reinhard, apparently, did not recognise that it was beyond the power even of an unyielding Madame de X—— to keep the young prince from "seeking distractions."

But for a time distractions of a very different kind from those alluded to by Reinhard threatened to occupy the King. Already, in March 1809, Central Germany was full of rumours and plots. War with Austria was daily expected—Jerome had been ordered by Napoleon to hold himself in readiness to lead an army corps — and a rising in the German States under French rule was considered likely. Prussia was the headquarters of the conspiracy, but a network of secret societies spread over Westphalia. Feelings had altered since first Jerome came to Cassel in 1807. In the beginning the liberality of the constitution compared with the old German systems, the enlightened finance, the large proportion of Germans employed throughout the Government departments, and, no doubt, also the superficial qualities of

The Burlesque Napoleon

the King, had inspired his subjects with something approaching to enthusiasm.[1] But the military exactions, the forced loan, the extravagance and corruption of the Court in the midst of distress of the rest of the country, soon produced great changes of sentiment. The *Tugendbund* found ready adherents in Westphalia. The dangers of the situation forced themselves on the view of the rulers. Towards the middle of April Jerome and Catherine left Cassel on a short tour to Brunswick and Magdeburg. Their reception by the people seemed favourable; but on their return Bercagny warned the King about the alarming fermentation going on. Already, before the tour, an unsuccessful attempt to provoke a rising and seize Magdeburg had been made by a Prussian officer, Lieutenant von Katte. It had failed completely; but the Westphalian Intelligence Department knew that there was worse to come. The King decided to send Catherine on a visit to Josephine in France, while he prepared to assume command of the 10th Army Corps. The Queen left Cassel with great reluctance. Writing to the Emperor, she said that she was making "a sacrifice necessary

[1] H. A. L. Fisher, "Studies in Napoleonic Statesmanship: Germany." See especially pp. 245 *ff.*

The King in Court and Camp

for the safety and tranquillity of the King"—his anxiety for her disturbing his peace of mind. Strange though it may appear, this was true. His constant infidelities left his regard for his wife unimpaired.

The expectation of immediate trouble in Westphalia was not falsified. Catherine had hardly left when a conspiracy was discovered in which a colonel in Jerome's own Guard was implicated. A Baron von Dörnberg, a Hessian, who had served in the Prussian army as late as the campaign of Jena, had since settled down in Westphalia, in apparent acquiescence in Jerome's rule, and had accepted a commission in his forces. All the time, however, he was a member of a secret society, and he was now designing to break into the Palace of Cassel by night, make the King a prisoner, carry him off to the coast, and hand him over to the English. On the 22nd April the plot exploded prematurely. All was discovered; and Dörnberg, flying from Cassel, appeared at Napoleonshöhe, put himself at the head of a number of deserters from the army and some thousands of peasants, and marched on Cassel, where, being well prepared, General Eblé, far the ablest of Jerome's various War Ministers, met them with a heavy

The Burlesque Napoleon

fire, killing or capturing many, and dispersing the rest. Cassel itself had remained quiet and apathetic, the army stood firm, but, as Jerome wrote to Catherine, he discovered traitors about him every day, and could trust few but the French in his kingdom. An unconscious answer to this complaint reached him from Napoleon two days later. Addressing him from the Bavarian frontier on the 29th April, the Emperor said:

"Your kingdom is without police, finances, or organisation. It is not by inordinate display that the foundations of monarchies are laid. What is happening you now I have been expecting. I hope it will teach you a lesson. Take on yourself manners and habits to match those of the country which you govern. In that way you will win over the inhabitants through esteem. . . . Still, I feel that this is not the time to preach to you. Make severe examples!"[1]

Even while Napoleon wrote this letter, further events occurred in Westphalia, giving Jerome the chance of making the severe examples which the Emperor commanded. Prussia, for all her nominal neutrality in the Franco-

[1] Napoleon to Jerome, Burghausen, 29th April 1809.

The King in Court and Camp

Austrian struggle, left no room for doubt as to her sympathies, and exercised little restraint over individuals who desired to manifest their sentiments more openly. On the 28th of the month a major in the Prussian army, Schill by name, left Berlin for the Westphalian frontier with a band of followers, and, announcing everywhere that he led but the vanguard of the Prussian liberators, made a desperate attempt to seize Magdeburg, the loss of which had been the great humiliation of Tilsit to his country. The plan failed; the Westphalian troops hastened to attack the raiders, who, making for the coast, were overtaken at Stralsund, Pomerania, and destroyed. The Prussian Government entirely disowned Schill, and proclaimed him a traitor; but the situation remained threatening. Jerome endeavoured to meet the difficulties of his position, while awaiting Napoleon's order to begin active service, by plentiful reviews of his troops. Thus he hoped to produce also a good effect on the country people, whom he was unwilling to treat with severity, in spite of their doubtful loyalty. He deluded himself to the very end of his reign with the idea of his personal popularity among the Westphalians. Nevertheless, it must be

The Burlesque Napoleon

accounted to him for merit, that he was reluctant to take the stern advice of his brother, and "make examples" among his subjects.

Although the Queen was away, and the King might be supposed to have plenty to occupy his mind, the anxieties of politics were not allowed entirely to banish gaiety from the Westphalian Court. The marriage of Count Fürstenstein with the daughter of Count Hardenberg was duly celebrated on the 3rd May, in spite of war and threats of revolt, and furnished Reinhard with a new scandal to insert in his bulletins. Fürstenstein before his marriage had a *liaison* with a lady whose name appears simply as "Madame de P." Always respectable, the Count broke his intrigue off now that he was to be united with the blue blood of Germany. In doing so he spoke very eloquently to the King of the virtue and character of Madame de P., and Jerome was at once inspired with an admiration for her whom his favourite so extolled. "From this time," wrote Reinhard, "all the honours were for her." Vexatious affairs summoned the King to Saxony, and he was obliged to postpone his suit. On his return the Court talked of an agreement being signed, the terms being very high. The lady's husband,

The King in Court and Camp

Chamberlain at Court, went away on a special mission (similar to, but not so dangerous as, the mission of Bathsheba's husband), but suddenly returned. "We may still believe in the virtue of Madame de P.," delicately writes Reinhard. And so, amid all the grave perils surrounding them, Jerome continued to carry on his intrigues, and his guardian, "the Family Ambassador," to describe them for the leisure reading of the man who was convulsing Europe.

What called Jerome away from his siege of virtuous Madame de P. was the command of his brother to take the field with the 10th Corps, and to cover from Austrian attacks his own kingdom, Saxony, and Southern Germany. Saxony in particular was menaced by two legions, collected by the dispossessed Dukes of Brunswick and Hesse, who were on the Bohemian frontier at the end of May, only awaiting Austrian help to march on Dresden. They actually crossed into Saxony with 10,000 men on the 10th June, and entered the capital next day. Jerome, on his side, was slow in his preparations, and Napoleon threatened, in a letter to his Chief of the Staff, to remove the King, and nominate another commander for the 10th Corps. Jerome accordingly put him-

The Burlesque Napoleon

self at the head of his 12,000 men—Westphalians, Saxons, and Dutch—and made ready to enter Saxony. The motley character of his forces, among whom, as among their generals, jealousy was rife, no doubt contributed to the tardiness of the army's movements; but Jerome further hampered himself by taking with him all the diplomatists accredited to his Court, and a large part of that Court itself, including Fürstenstein and other professedly non-military persons, with a whole train of pages and servants. Thus unconsciously laying up for himself a violent rebuke from the Emperor, he crossed the River Saale on the 24th June, driving the enemy's outposts before him. Leipzig was entered two days later, the Austrians and their allies making no resistance until Waldheim, where d'Albignac defeated them. This success of his General enabled the King to occupy Dresden. It was, apparently, Napoleon's design that the 10th Corps should continue to hold the town in force; but after a stay of three days, during which he attended a *Te Deum* service at the cathedral and a performance of the opera, Jerome evacuated Dresden, and retired gradually on Weimar. Reports had reached him that the English fleet was menacing Holland,

The King in Court and Camp

and the Duke of Brunswick preparing to enter Westphalia. He contemplated therefore, on his own responsibility, a return to Westphalia and a march to the coast. Napoleon, however, at the end of June had despatched the Duke of Abrantès to take command of the "Reserve of the Army of Germany," with which Jerome was instructed to co-operate. Like all operations involving joint action with other commanders during Jerome's military career, the scheme was a complete failure. To crush the Austrian General Kienmayer in Bavaria it was arranged that Junot should drive him from the south, Jerome from the north. In place of this, first Junot and then Jerome saw their forces confronted by the whole Austrian army, and, so far from catching Kienmayer between two fires, were compelled to retreat. Jerome retired hastily on Leipzig, only saved from disaster by the just-concluded armistice of Znaim, according to Napoleon. The Emperor wrote a furious letter to the blunderer from Vienna on the 17th July. Ridiculing an order of the day issued by Jerome, Napoleon told him that it was necessary to be "a soldier in the first place, a soldier in the second, a soldier in the third."

" You should have no Ministers, no Diplomatic

The Burlesque Napoleon

Body, no display; bivouac with your advance-guard; be in the saddle night and day; march with the advance-guard to secure information—or else stop at home in your seraglio. You make war like a satrap. Is it from me that you learnt that? Good God! I, with an army of 200,000, lead my own skirmishers, and do not allow even Champagny to follow me, but leave him at Munich or Vienna. . . . Stop making yourself ridiculous; send the Diplomatic Body back to Cassel. Go without baggage or suite. Have no table but your own. Make war like a young soldier in need of glory and reputation. Try to deserve the rank you have attained to, and the esteem of France and of Europe, whose eyes are on you; and, in God's name, learn sense enough to write and talk as you should!"

The *bon Dieus* and *pardieus* were a sufficient sign of Napoleon's fiery indignation. But Jerome had already not merely sent the diplomatists to Cassel, but started thither also himself. On the day after his arrival, the 20th July, he wrote to Napoleon that, after hearing of his great victories, and of an English landing in the north, he had decided to march on the Baltic. Though he had learnt, on the 18th, that there was an armistice, he still thought it better to

The King in Court and Camp

continue in the direction of Hanover, whither he meant to go as soon as he knew definitely that the English had disembarked in force. This, however, he now considered an unlikely event. It may easily be imagined that this communication did not soothe Napoleon's feelings or make him more favourably inclined towards this very independent General, who on the top of his failure to co-operate with Junot had drawn up a new plan of action for his own corps. Accordingly, he now wrote off the longest and most severe of all his letters to Jerome.[1]

" I have your letter of the 20th [said Napoleon]. The letter you have received from me since that of the 14th will have informed you of my position and intentions. I consider that you have thoroughly misconducted yourself during this campaign. It was no thanks to you that Junot was not well thrashed, and that Kienmayer did not advance against me with his 25,000 men; seeing that, except for the armistice of Znaim, I should have pursued Prince

[1] Napoleon to Jerome, Schönbrunn, 25th July 1809 (Lecestre, i. pp. 330-333). The version of this letter above is taken, with a few slight alterations, from Lady Mary Lloyd's translation of Lecestre.

The Burlesque Napoleon

Charles to Prague. You have commanded a warship; you have abandoned the sea, and left your Admiral without orders. You have put forward all sorts of suppositions, which have not taken in either myself, or my Minister; but one ship is a small matter, and I was too willing to overlook that incident. I see you continue to carry on the same system; you think other people are deceived, but you take in nobody. During the whole of this campaign you have constantly been just where the enemy was not. You say the Duke of Abrantès' retreat on the Danube forced you to take up a position at Schleitz, and to cease acting on the offensive. The Duke of Abrantès' retreat was brought about by your absurd manœuvres. If you had moved to your right, as I ordered you, to join the Duke of Abrantès—if, after having driven the enemy out of Bayreuth, you had marched on Dresden—this would not have happened. If, instead of remaining three or four days in the same place, instead of being slower and more irresolute than the Austrians themselves, you had marched with the alertness and eagerness befitting your age, the enemy would not have masked his movements, and concealed them from you. . . . Finally, you run away in

The King in Court and Camp

shameful fashion, and bring disgrace on my arms, and on your young reputation.

"As for the English, your cunning march on the Baltic cannot take in anyone but fools. You knew very well that the English had not landed, and if they really had disembarked, what else ought you to have done, except join the Duke of Abrantès and the Saxons, and not break up your own corps? 3000 Saxons, 10,000 men of your own, and 7000 or 8000 belonging to the Duke of Abrantès, would have put you in a position to drive back the English; you could not do anything alone; a single victory does not decide a war. According to my calculation, I should have found you at Dresden, and following the enemy into Bohemia. Your march on the Baltic was intended to conceal your return to Cassel, and your shameful desertion of Saxony. . . .

"I am sorry, for your sake, that you give so little proof of talent, or even of good sense, in military matters. It is a far cry from the profession of a soldier to that of a courtier. I was hardly as old as you when I had conquered all Italy, and beaten Austrian armies three times as numerous as mine. But I had no flatterers, and no Diplomatic Body in my

The Burlesque Napoleon

train! I made war like a soldier, and there is no other way of making it. I did not set myself up as the Emperor's brother, nor as a king. I did everything that needed doing to beat the enemy. . . .

"As regards the future, I do not desire to disgrace you by relieving you of your command; but, nevertheless, I do not intend to risk the glory of my arms for the sake of any foolish family considerations. One warship more or less was a trifling matter, but 20,000 men more or less, well handled, may change the fate of Europe. If, therefore, you intend to continue as you have begun, surrounded by men who have never made war, such as d'Albignac, Rewbell, and Fürstenstein, without a single good adviser, following your fancy and not carrying out my orders, you may stop in your seraglio. Be assured that, as a soldier, I have no brother, and that you cannot hide the real motives of your conduct from me under frivolous and absurd pretexts. I should be glad, so as to save you from the danger of such results, to see you make over the command of your troops to the Duke of Abrantès. You are a spoilt young fellow, although you are full of fine natural qualities. I very much

The King in Court and Camp

fear it is hopeless to expect anything of you.

"If you continue in command of your troops, you are to proceed at once to Dresden. I will send you a Chief of the Staff possessed of common-sense. . . . Do away with your Court and your retinue, and make war as befits a man of my name, who thirsts for glory more than for any other thing. If hostilities are reopened, Bohemia will be the seat of war, and you will have to play an active part. . . ."

There was some mitigation of the severity of language in the latter part of this letter[1]; and in his instructions to Reinhard through Champagny Napoleon let it be seen that he did not blame Jerome alone. Though he was "distressed" at the result of the 10th Corps' expedition, which

[1] With regard to the truculent tone of Napoleon's letters to his youngest brother, it must be remembered that Jerome was not alone in the family in receiving such harsh reprimands. Instances to the contrary are abundant. To Louis in 1809 the Emperor wrote requesting him to mention him no more in his speeches. "It is mere hypocrisy," he said, "when you know very well that everything you do is opposed to my opinion." "You have only used the palladium of my name to serve my enemies." In May 1810 he desired Louis to "send him no more of his twaddle," and told him that he (Napoleon) would never write to him again —though he did, of course. Towards Lucien and his

The Burlesque Napoleon

had not, as he had hoped, increased his brother's military reputation, still he thought it "less the fault of his Westphalian Majesty, whose youth would not lead one to expect great experience, than of those in whom he places his confidence." The Ambassador was, therefore, told to obtain interviews with Fürstenstein, Rewbell, and d'Albignac, and to warn them seriously about the use which they made of their influence with the King. Rewbell was away from Cassel on a military expedition, of which we shall hear later, but Reinhard was able to fulfil his instructions with regard to the other two. He went to d'Albignac first. The General, reputed an open and honest man, was taken entirely by surprise. He protested vehemently that he was only a soldier and could but obey orders. The King

"shameful passion" (for Madame Jouberthon, who became his second wife) it is unnecessary to quote Napoleon's many bitter remarks. Nor did his elder, Joseph, escape. In Napoleon's letters to his Ministers may be read wholesale condemnation of the man to whom he ascribed the blame for everything that happened in Spain for five years, and whom he accused of "the greatest of all immoralities, to engage in a profession of which one knows nothing"— in Joseph's case the military profession. His sisters, too, had to listen to some very plain speaking; and Eliza at least was warned that she was in danger of imprisonment in 1809. If Napoleon suffered for the weaknesses of his family, he made them feel it.

The King in Court and Camp

would take advice from no one—was, indeed, the most absolute man he had ever met. "I am in despair," said d'Albignac; "but I have no influence—*and none of us have.*"

Count Fürstenstein did not allow himself to be caught unawares like the General. He barely waited for Reinhard to open the attack when he broke in with the words: "This does not concern me. I am altogether unacquainted with military affairs. Besides," he added, "the King does not permit advice to be offered to him. . . . I am attached to him, and try to serve him faithfully, but I have no influence over him." Reinhard produced Champagny's letter to himself, and showed it to Fürstenstein, who promptly offered his resignation. No, said Reinhard; his help was wanted to save the King from sorrow. Why should not Siméon and Eblé, who were Napoleon's subjects as well as Jerome's Ministers, be consulted? Fürstenstein did not welcome the idea, and then, changing the topic of conversation, began to complain of the false reports about the King. The interview lasted an hour, Fürstenstein neither explaining nor justifying anything, but cleverly carrying the war into the enemy's country. Reinhard could only console himself by writing a character

The Burlesque Napoleon

sketch of the baffling Minister for Napoleon's perusal.[1] He sought out Siméon and Eblé also; but they could merely confirm to him what d'Albignac and Fürstenstein had said, that no one had any influence over the King. Jerome, indeed, was convinced of the truth of a remark which he was fond of repeating: "The Emperor likes one to have character"; and how could one have character if one sought other people's advice?

As the result of his conversations with the Westphalian Ministers, Reinhard was convinced that the necessity existed for assistance to the King in his proceedings, and that no one in the country was equal to the task. The suggestion, of course, was that the Emperor himself should furnish someone who would be able to guide Jerome aright. But all that Napoleon did now with reference to his brother was to put the Saxon troops hitherto under his command under the Duke of Abrantès. Jerome could

[1] While paying a tribute to his natural intelligence and agreeable manners, Reinhard complained that he never had filled, and never would fill up the gaps in his education. "M. de Fürstenstein," he concluded, "is guilty of hardly any evil except that he does hardly any good. He is an excellent favourite, but a bad Minister" (Reinhard to Champagny, 8th August 1809).

The King in Court and Camp

not well complain, since he had practically accepted the less glorious of the alternatives offered to him by Napoleon, and, not having proceeded to Dresden in accordance with the instructions given on the 25th July, had himself given up the leadership of the 10th Corps. Nevertheless, he was hurt at the idea of being commander of 6000 Westphalian recruits only. "There will only be left to me the sorrow of being unable to take part in the war, if it takes place," he wrote, when it was still doubtful whether the struggle would not break out afresh after Wagram. But Napoleon had no intention of giving him further responsibilities yet; and so Jerome had to content himself with "stopping in his seraglio"—unhappily, the course which best suited his disposition.

PALACE LIFE
AT CASSEL

CHAPTER IX

PALACE LIFE AT CASSEL

JEROME had reached his capital to find affairs going anything but well. This did not surprise him; indeed, it would have surprised him to find them otherwise. He had said to Reinhard once, during the Saxon campaign: "As soon as I leave Cassel everything goes wrong. The head is lacking!" He firmly believed this to be the case. Now, though he was back in Cassel, he had still to suffer from the blunders of his subordinates in other parts of his kingdom. Only ten days after his return, Count Wellingerode, conducting a Westphalian regiment in the direction of Hamburg, allowed himself to be caught off his guard, with all his men, at Halberstadt, by the Duke of Brunswick. This fervent enemy of Westphalia, the country which had swallowed up his inheritance, was deserted by the Austrians after the armistice of Znaim, and left to his fate. With his " Legion of Vengeance " alone, about 2000

The Burlesque Napoleon

men in all, he decided on a desperate course. He would either rouse his father's old subjects against their foreign ruler, or failing that, would cut his way from the edge of Bohemia to the Baltic coast. He found, to his disappointment, that the people of Brunswick would not risk a rising; but in the alternative part of his scheme he succeeded so well that, after capturing Wellingerode and his regiment, and entering the town of Brunswick itself, he administered a check to Rewbell, who was charged with the duty of cutting him off; then, eluding his pursuit, he reached the mouth of the Weser, and on 7th August embarked at Elsfleth, whence he proceeded to England by way of Heligoland.

Rewbell's inability to catch the Duke of Brunswick was annoying enough to the King, but when he wrote asking that his men might be indemnified for the spoils of the town of Brunswick, which he had promised them, he committed a mistake far more fatal to himself. Rewbell should have known his patron well enough to be aware of his aversion to the bandit-soldier. When his infamous request reached Cassel, Jerome at once issued a decree depriving him of his command, and declaring

Palace Life at Cassel

him for ever incapable of serving him. He wished, however, to soften the blow to Rewbell's wife, associated as she was with his own early romance in Baltimore. Unfortunately, his scheme for breaking the news gently was extremely clumsy. "Betty, I have something to tell you," he said to her suddenly. She turned to him with a smile, to hear him add: "I have deprived your husband of his command. All that I can say in consolation," he continued, "is that it would have been better for you and for him that he were dead." This odd consolation was unavailing. Rewbell did not die, but left with his wife for her native town in America. Jerome and his kingdom saw them no more. Rewbell was no real loss to his master, for he was fully as incompetent as most of those with whom Jerome surrounded himself, and the King's anger against him was fully justified; but the cruel speech to the wife is curiously at variance with Jerome's general manner.

If military matters were progressing ingloriously for Westphalia, financial affairs were still worse. Von Bülow, it was true, kept up his character for optimism, and continued to insist that the resources of the country were sufficient

The Burlesque Napoleon

by themselves to meet a regulated expenditure. Perhaps he was right, even in spite of the accumulation of debts since the beginning of the reign; but Jerome had no idea of regulating his expenditure in the way which von Bülow meant. His one notion of finance lay in the raising of loans. Accordingly, when the banker Jordis proposed to borrow from Hamburg, though von Bülow disapproved, Jerome gladly consented. Jordis was one of the Westphalians whom he had admitted to his friendship, to no small profit of the banker. Having lunched one day at his subject's country house, half way between Cassel and Napoleonshöhe, the King as he left said to the gardener: "This house belongs to me." He paid Jordis 30,000 thalers, though Jordis had only given 7000 and had spent another 5000 thalers on improvements. As may be imagined, this story was duly told to Napoleon. What was more serious, however, was the report which he heard that Jerome was endeavouring to get his personal expenses included in the Westphalian budget. This was not to be tolerated. The Emperor wrote to Reinhard, through the usual medium of Champagny, that if the King's Civil List were increased in contravention of the Constitutional Oath, the

Palace Life at Cassel

Ministers of Finance and of the Public Treasury would be held responsible. Von Bülow had thus more than ever reason for keeping a tight hand on the King, and it is easy to understand that the Minister's position became constantly more precarious.

Napoleon, no doubt, acted rightly in preventing Jerome from inserting his private debts in the general accounts of his country. But the Emperor himself was making far more grievous inroads upon the revenues of Westphalia. The "Continental System" was being enforced with great severity, and, in spite of the protests of Jerome, a ring of custom-houses now encircled his kingdom. The King did not confine himself to mere verbal objections; he at least connived at clear infractions of the Imperial regulations. A report even reached Napoleon that during the 9th-13th September more than 300 carts full of English goods were brought across the Westphalian frontier, under escort of armed gendarmes and crowds of peasants. He indignantly expressed his astonishment that, of all countries, Westphalia should occasion him the most difficulty in his war against England. It is true that he addressed the same complaint to Hol-

The Burlesque Napoleon

land, but that did not lessen its impressiveness at the time of writing. The Westphalian King, however, was growing desperate, and on the 20th September wrote personally to his brother that distress had reached such a pitch throughout his realms that, if assistance were not forthcoming from the Emperor, things could not go on for another two months. "In spite of all the attention which I pay to my administration," he said, "I believe that it is impossible to keep it going any longer, and I beg your Majesty to allow me to return to France. There, as everywhere else, I shall strive to prove that there is no one more devoted to you than I. All such measures as your Majesty may see fit to take to assure the future of my realms shall be approved and seconded by me to the utmost of my power."

It would be difficult indeed to withhold sympathy from the King had he only supplemented the alleged "attention to his administration," by a further attention to the regulation of Palace life in a bankrupt State. On the manners of the Court of Cassel at this period we have the independent testimony of de Norvins to corroborate that of Reinhard. De Norvins in the autumn of 1808 had been appointed secretary

Palace Life at Cassel

to General Eblé, the new Minister of War, then commencing his task of cleansing the Augean stables (as he expressed it himself) of the Westphalian army. After six months' very hard work with Eblé he was given the post of Westphalian *chargé d' affaires* at the Court of Baden. Returning to Cassel in the September of 1809, he was appointed Chamberlain to Queen Catherine and official introducer of ambassadors. He was at once struck by the changes which had taken place since he left. The richness of the costumes at Court, he writes, was "appalling." Extravagance of dress and of entertainments was at its height. Jollivet alone was not in debt. There was, indeed, a special reason for Jollivet standing so well financially, for, as we shall see, Jerome had by no means received him into favour again, and he was not called upon to vie with the rest of the Court in spending his income. The others, willing or unwilling, followed the lead of the Sovereign, and kept their place as best they could in the round of gaieties which Jerome, after his wont, hesitated not to lead at the very time that he was writing of the impossibility of keeping things going for another two months.

The loan planned by Jordis was carried through

The Burlesque Napoleon

by the assistance of Bourrienne, then representing Napoleon at Hamburg, but it only amounted to 300,000 francs. Nevertheless, the grateful King sent to Bourrienne his portrait framed in diamonds, which the Emperor promptly made him return. Von Bülow gradually failed to fulfil his early promise of resourcefulness, and the opposition to him grew stronger as the King grew more discontented. The French party had always hated him, and now their most vigorous member, Bercagny, made an attempt to secure his immediate downfall. The head of the police, true to his methods, wished to search von Bülow's papers, hoping to find something compromising among them, and bribed one of the Finance Minister's servants to help in the job. The man, however, told Madame von Bülow, who instructed him to say nothing to anyone else, but to get from the police a written promise of reward. On the night of the 3rd October von Bülow was out at dinner, when he received an urgent message from his wife. Hurrying home, he learnt that she had entered his private room to find a police agent hunting among the papers in his desk. The scandal was great. Von Bülow's complaint to the King could not be neglected, and Bercagny and his chief subor-

Palace Life at Cassel

dinate were necessarily removed from their posts. Bercagny, his disgrace modified by his appointment as Commissary-General at Magdeburg, remarked: "Had I succeeded I should have gained the Grand Cordon. I failed. Can the head of the High Police afford to fail so?" He was at least a philosopher.

Jerome's complicity in the plot is not established, though he aroused suspicion by showing disapproval of Madame von Bülow's conduct in laying the counter-trap. For the present the Finance Minister was stronger than ever, and Fürstenstein and de Salha, now leading the French party, lacked the vigour of the scoundrelly Bercagny. Perhaps it was due to von Bülow's triumph that Jerome now consented to some "*reformes de valets*" in the Palace. But as Reinhard, while announcing these, remarked,[1] "partial reductions of expense do not form a complete system of economy"; and the Ministers' united efforts were busily employed in resisting the King's tendency towards expenditure totally disproportionate to his resources. Jerome knew that his advisers had the hearty support of Napoleon, and that all his own attempts to combat them were noted by the keen eyes of

[1] To Champagny, 18th October 1809.

The Burlesque Napoleon

Reinhard and Jollivet, and reported to the Emperor. With Jollivet at last he reached the limit of his patience. How this happened is explained in the following letter, which he sent to Napoleon on the 20th October:—

"Sire, in spite of the complete oblivion in which your Majesty seems determined to leave me—for I receive no answers to my letters—I cannot refrain from informing you of the scandalous conduct of one of your agents. . . . This scandal has reached such a pitch that the dignity of your brother can suffer it no longer. I have myself surprised one of my servants searching my papers in my private desk, and when I called on him to tell me what made him commit so criminal an act, he threw himself at my feet, and declared that for a year past he had been in the pay of Count Jollivet, who had told him that it was by the Emperor's orders! Your Majesty's name was employed to procure such conduct! . . . Sire, it is to your Majesty that I appeal for the recall of M. Jollivet. It is impossible that you desire to dishonour me so. I should be unworthy to be related to you if I tolerated near me, and appeared to have a regard for, so contemptible a man."

Palace Life at Cassel

Ten days later, receiving no answer, Jerome wrote again, not mentioning Jollivet's name this time, but asking to be relieved of the government of Westphalia if he could not act as King. His present position was entirely false, he said; he loved neither German nor Germany, and was altogether French. "I did desire, no doubt, to have a people to rule over. I should now prefer, I confess to your Majesty, to live as a private individual in your empire rather than be as I am, a sovereign without a nation."

The Emperor tacitly admitted that there was some justice in his brother's complaints by summoning him to Paris. Jerome left Cassel at the beginning of December, and spent a month in France, to the apparent advantage of himself and his kingdom. This was the period when the arrangements for the divorce of Josephine were carried out; but Napoleon found time to discuss Westphalian affairs with Jerome. He promised him the cession of a large portion of Hanover, entrusting the negotiations to Champagny and to Fürstenstein, now granted the Legion of Honour. He further added to this generosity by assenting to one of the darling wishes of the King, who had been writing to him about it since July. This was the foundation of an

The Burlesque Napoleon

Order for Westphalia on the lines of the Order of the Iron Crown. Jerome had secured the necessary money from the revenues of the Abbey of Quedlimberg, about 300,000 francs a year (which he did feel it incumbent on him to devote to the relief of his bankrupt kingdom), and he was certain it would please the Germans.[1] He had himself designed the badge, which introduced a number of animals, including the Napoleonic eagle, and the ribbon of royal blue. Napoleon is reported to have remarked sneeringly, with reference to the design: "*Il y a bien des bêtes dans cet ordre-là.*" But he wore the Order, nevertheless, with Jerome and Berthier, on New Year's Eve 1809. On the following day Jerome left with Catherine, who had joined him in Paris, and returned to his kingdom, well pleased with his seeming success. Reinhard remarked in him new kindliness and contentment. "His time is divided, as before, between work and pleasure," he wrote.[2] "Spectacles, excursions to Napoleonshöhe and to Schönfeld, the little country house bought some time ago from the banker Jordis; and balls, especially in masquerade, which give equal pleasure to

[1] Jerome to Napoleon, 11th July 1809.
[2] To Champagny, 2nd February 1810.

Palace Life at Cassel

King and Queen, occupy the evenings of their Majesties."

This winter, indeed, after the return of the sovereigns from Paris, was the gayest of the many gay seasons of the Court of Cassel. De Norvins and Reinhard have both left descriptions of its leading features. The excursions alluded to by the latter are more fully detailed by de Norvins. On such occasions the King insisted on full dress, and it was expected that all the Court should be present, Ministers as well as the rest. Even on the sledge-rides in the depth of the Westphalian winter, for instance, old Siméon had to make one of the merry party, thrusting his plumed hat over his powdered wig to keep out the cold, and afterwards plunged in doubt how to carry the whitened hat under his arm without soiling his uniform. The gentlemen of the enormous royal household, in scarlet coats embroidered with gold lace, clung to the sledges, exposed to the freezing winds. At last de Norvins boldly brought with him a vast blue cloak, in which he wrapped his scarlet bravery. Royalty looked disapprovingly on him; but the fashion soon became general. This cloak was the only institution due to himself in

The Burlesque Napoleon

Westphalia, says the writer, except the official Gazette.

The glory of the sledge-excursions paled entirely before that of the Court balls. Jerome and Catherine had the precedent of Napoleon himself for their devotion to the *bal masqué*. But, whereas the great man was wont to wear a simple black domino, and to preserve his incognito strictly, his young relatives dressed with extravagance, and did not trouble to keep the secret of their disguises. Though Jerome might change "like a very chameleon" in the course of the evening, his courtiers failed not to recognise him in every dress, and to observe his movements. On one of these occasions Reinhard describes how the King left at midnight and went to spend the night at Shönfeld. It was not noticed, he adds, that one of the Court ladies left also. It may be suspected that there was little that went on which the Court did not know as well as Reinhard. The Queen, it is true, was apparently ignorant. Her ladies professed the utmost zeal in shielding their mistress. It was better for their own reputations with her that she should not know too much. De Norvins speaks of the amusement caused in him and his bachelor fellow-chamber-

Palace Life at Cassel

lains by the affectation of prudishness on the part of these "startled doves" of the Court. One cannot help wondering that he did not himself feel tempted to undeceive the poor Queen, seeing how evidently genuine were his love and respect for her. He appears rather to exaggerate the picture of Catherine dying of ennui but for the distraction of the library in the Palace, for there is no evidence that her pleasure in the constant masquerades and balls was entirely assumed. We may regret that she did not divine how great was the harm that these extravagant entertainments were causing to her husband's kingdom; but an examination of the daily journal which she began to keep a year later forbids us to think that she realised such a thing.

That the masquerades cost enormous sums can easily be understood from the mere descriptions of them. At one, characterised by Reinhard as especially brilliant, in the Carnival season of 1810, three elaborate changes of dress were made by the maskers in the course of the evening. First a Piquet pack came on; then the cards were metamorphosed into the towns and rivers of Westphalia; and finally the King took part in a quadrille where all the Court ladies were

The Burlesque Napoleon

in Egyptian costume. Still more ruinously expensive, according to the chroniclers, was the ballet of "Figaro's Wedding," towards the end of February, produced under the direction of Taglioni, father of the dancer; while Blangini, whom Jerome had during his visit to Paris engaged as *maître de chapelle*, at a salary of 12,000 francs a year, conducted the music which he had composed for the occasion. The King, as Figaro himself, danced to the sound of castanets with Madame de Boucheporn, and distributed flowers all round. After supper "Figaro" gave place to the "Cairo Caravan." At another wedding ballet, the "Noces de Gamache," Reinhard was particularly struck by the Queen's skill in showing herself in turn as an old Jewess, an American squaw, and a Black Forest peasant. The ladies all on this occasion had the pleasing task of disguising themselves as old hags! On Mardi Gras the royal buffets were "simply devastated," and the tradespeople of Cassel for the moment rejoiced. But Napoleon's envoy found it necessary to groan in sympathy with those who, looking at the Carnival bills, perceived the cost. The courtiers groaned, too, when orders for some particularly elegant travesty went round. Once de Norvins describes

Palace Life at Cassel

the household as about to give notice in a body. Jerome and Catherine, "sitting in choregraphic council," had decided that nothing but velvet and satin should be worn at the next dance. Happily, a message arrived from the King that he would pay for all the wardrobes, male and female, and the news was followed by the Court tailor waiting to take the measurements. Jerome was not ignorant of the extent to which his ideas of kingly state emptied the purses of his intimate circle; and to him royalty chiefly meant the pleasure of giving—as he told his councillors on one occasion. Very probably, too, he considered that the recent addition to his realms justified a little extra display—even though he might be about 10,000,000 francs in debt, according to rough computations.

There was never a greater mistake, really, than to imagine that Napoleon's gift of December 1809, had benefited Westphalia. Jerome's Ministers recognised this before their King.[1]

---

[1] Even Reinhard took a very pessimistic view of the advantages accruing to Westphalia from the new territory. The Westphalian public debt, he wrote, was already 93,000,000 francs; with the addition of Hanover's liabilities it would reach 180,000,000. The joint revenues, on the other hand, would never exceed 40,000,000 francs (Reinhard to Champagny, 25th May 1810).

The Burlesque Napoleon

Nominally, 300,000 new inhabitants and a large territory, with a strip of coast between the mouths of the Elbe and Weser, were incorporated in Westaphalia. But the debt of Hanover had to be taken over; the Emperor reserved to himself more than 4,500,000 francs from the revenues for a period of ten years; and the obligation of maintaining another 6000 French troops fell to Westphalia. It was soon reckoned that what the new territory involved to Westphalia was a further deficit of 10,000,000 francs a year. Yet for the present Jerome was disinclined to look the gift-horse in the mouth. He preferred to rejoice in his apparent good fortune, and to make displays of that kindliness and contentment which Reinhard noticed in him at the beginning of the year. His thoughts even turned again to his son in America. He sent a brother of Le Camus in February on a mission to Baltimore, to try to obtain Elizabeth's consent to part with the young Jerome Napoleon. He assured the mother that time had not effaced her from his memory, and that he had still the tenderest feeling for her. Elizabeth refused to give up her child, and Jerome had to wait another sixteen years before he saw his firstborn.

Palace Life at Cassel

On the whole, in spite of debt, affairs seemed to be going very well for Jerome. His increased dignity as lord of Hanover was grateful to him; and the winter season at Cassel had been splendid. In March he learnt that the hated Jollivet, whom he had kept away from his Court as much as possible, was leaving Westphalia; and he received for himself, Catherine, and their suites the command to attend the wedding of the Emperor with the Archduchess Marie-Louise at Compiègne. Here was a chance for the Court of Cassel to shine before the world—and it was not thrown away. Amid all the brilliance of dress at the Tuileries there was nothing which could match that of the Westphalians. The chamberlains, with their scarlet velvet mantles, collars of cloth of gold, white satin sashes with golden tassels and bows, lace scarves, and plumed toques, eclipsed all save, perhaps, their King, in his gold-embroidered white satin suit, and his black velvet toque with diamond clasp and white ostrich feathers. It has not been thought worth while to record the ladies' costumes. At the Court of Westphalia the male bird had the finer plumage. Napoleon hardly showed himself grateful for the way in which his brother honoured the occasion. The

The Burlesque Napoleon

Westphalian courtiers on their return to Cassel did not appear much pleased with their journey to Paris, according to Reinhard. Some remarks of the Emperor were quoted by them concerning the luxurious dress of the Westphalian Court and the rapid promotions witnessed there; and these remarks gained currency at Cassel. Towards one of his brother's suite Napoleon was more than severe. His eyes falling on Morio at a State reception at Compiègne, he took the opportunity of publicly insulting him twice during the evening, calling him a coward, and telling him to take off the uniform of a general. The violence of his dislike for Morio is inexplicable. It never affected, however, the regard for the man which his Sovereign had.

Jerome had brought practically the whole of his household to France with him—at what cost to his Civil List may easily be imagined. After the wedding ceremonies were over the bulk of them returned to Cassel. One lady he had already found it necessary to send back. Madame de Keudelstein, whose career in Westphalia had been infamously conspicuous, even amid its surroundings there, and who had narrowly escaped banishment a few months before, so misbehaved herself in France that the

Palace Life at Cassel

King ordered her home at once. Jerome and Catherine themselves were invited to accompany the Emperor and Empress on a tour through Northern France, including the present Belgium. Catherine has left a diary of the journey in the form of letters to her aunt Emmy, wife of Prince Louis of Würtemberg, the best loved of her family; but there is not much of general interest in this simple record of visits to Antwerp, Brussels, Ghent, and the French coast towns. A month was spent in this way, a few more weeks in France followed, and it was not until the end of June that the Westphalian Sovereigns returned to their kingdom, whose history during their absence had been for the most part uneventful. One affair, however, had succeeded in enlivening society there, even though the King was away. It was connected with the scandalous story of the lady mentioned above, Madame de Keudelstein, the outlines of which may be briefly given here.

As has been stated already, Jerome made the acquaintance of Blanche Carrega when he was at Genoa, mourning for the loss of his first wife. He had assisted her to marry a Frenchman named La Flèche, whom he took very much into his favour as the reward of a base com-

The Burlesque Napoleon

placency. On his elevation to kingship he appointed La Flèche Master of the Ceremonies to himself, and Blanche maid-of-honour to the Queen.[1] After this charming arrangement he proceeded to create La Flèche Baron Keudelstein, and shortly afterwards Councillor of State and Superintendent of the Civil List—a post which gave him plentiful opportunities of increasing his own income. As an example of the rapid promotion of Westphalian dignitaries, the case of La Flèche might well have excited Napoleon's wrath. But the Baroness was singularly deficient in gratitude for her husband's advance and the affection shown to herself. True to her original character in Genoa, she did not remain faithful even to the King. In the course of her straying, she formed an acquaintance with an officer in the Westphalian Light Cavalry, the Marquis Armand Guerri de Maubreuil, certainly the greatest ruffian in the country, though so far his public career had been honourable. Maubreuil was twenty-seven

---

[1] "The functions and duties of the maids-of-honour," gravely stated the book on "The Etiquette of the Royal Court of Westphalia," "are determined by inside regulations"—so much inside, comments de Norvins, that during his period of office as Chamberlain to Queen Catherine they escaped him as completely as they did the maids themselves.

Palace Life at Cassel

years old when he entered Jerome's service. He had done well in the recent war, and the King made him one of his equerries, and put him in his cavalry. His relations with the intriguing Baroness abruptly ended his first term at Cassel. Learning that she was favouring the suit of a young Frenchman engaged at the War Office, he proceeded with a horsewhip to verify the report. According to Reinhard, he was reputed to be "a terrible lover," whose custom was to present himself, sword in hand, before anyone who dared address a word to a lady on whom he considered that he had a claim himself. In the present case, however, he substituted the whip for the sword, and finding the two offenders together, he administered a severe thrashing to both. The King was duly informed of the affair, which caused him no little annoyance. Maubreuil was sent off to Spain to join the Westphalian contingent, the other rival of his master was banished from Westphalia, but the real cause of all was suffered to remain. In spite of the insult to his dignity, which was of a kind peculiarly bitter to him, Jerome could not force himself to part with her.

Late in 1809 Maubreuil reappeared in Cassel,

The Burlesque Napoleon

having been severely wounded in Spain, where he had won his captaincy and the Legion of Honour—with which he gracefully decorated his horse's tail in 1814 to show himself a Bourbonist. He might have posed as a hero in Westphalia; but his manners had not mended since he left. Not content with his affair with the royal favourite, he paid addresses also to her sister-in-law, Jenny La Flèche, whose character was similar to hers. This lady too refused to limit her attention to the Marquis, who thereupon had a public scene at one of the Court balls with the man whom he suspected. A duel was to have followed; but Jerome's patience was now exhausted. Maubreuil was put under arrest, and was given indefinite leave—in other words, his dismissal from the Westphalian service. Madame de Keudelstein was but remotely connected in this new scandal, and was allowed to accompany Catherine's suite to the Imperial wedding at Compiègne. Even Jerome, however, could not overlook her behaviour in France. On her return to Cassel in disgrace, the noble Baron, her husband, was very indignant—at the injury done to the King, says Reinhard's bulletin—and thought of packing her off to Genoa. But she determined to

Palace Life at Cassel

try to live the scandal down, giving out that she was remaining at home for the next two months. After all, Cassel was a good place in which to conceal a bad reputation. Unfortunately, the vindictive Maubreuil was still to be reckoned with, for he seems the most probable author of the next blow to the injured lady's character. While Jerome and Catherine were still on their tour with Napoleon and Marie-Louise, sixteen copies of a scurrilous lampoon in verse, entitled "An Epistle to Blanche," were distributed by the post at Cassel, the recipients including the Head of the Police, the Countess of Fürstenstein, Blanche herself, some of her friends, and her husband; but the Baron was away at the time. "It is useless to characterise this production," writes Reinhard, as he sends a copy for the Emperor's perusal; "on any supposition it is a calumny, and it can only inspire indignation." He suspects Maubreuil of being the author, in spite of the fact that some said that he could not write verse. Probably no great poetic talent was displayed.[1] But the libel

[1] De Norvins was accused by some of being the author, as he was known to write verse. But de Norvins was a gentleman. He had just decided at this period to quit the Westphalian service and re-enter Napoleon's.

The Burlesque Napoleon

succeeded in doing what it was intended to—that is, in further covering with contumely the wretched Blanche. The lash of the verse was worse than that of the whip.

It required the character of a Blanche Carrega to survive the combination of disasters which had befallen her. She survived it more than two years. Her retirement from the world was very brief, and her conduct was no better after than before. Her next exploit was to fascinate her Queen's brother, the Prince Royal of Würtemberg, who, after a visit to Catherine, began to show great family affection, necessitating frequent journeys to the Westphalian Court. The too amiable Catherine was touched by this display, as entries show in the diary she was now beginning to keep. The Prince was at Cassel for the whole of January 1811, and only left when imperatively commanded by his father to do so. Perhaps King Frederick knew something of what was going on. Catherine did not, and was hurt at the conduct of her father. Four months later the Prince visited her again, when she was taking the waters at Ems, accompanied, of course, by her suite of ladies, and was kind enough to remain a few weeks with her. But

Palace Life at Cassel

now the reason began to be only too plain; the intrigue was a matter of gossip, and Jerome, on his arrival from Paris, had an angry interview with the ever faithless Blanche. Still he did not remove her from Court nor from the company of his wife, although Catherine herself was forced at last to see how mistaken she had been. Her brother's visit to Ems was shown to her in its true light. In consequence, when the Prince Royal (who had, by the way, a wife of his own, with whom he refused to live), wrote proposing a short stay at Cassel, he was grieved to find that no convenient date could be arranged; and the outbreak of the Russian War prevented him from applying again. Catherine remarks in her journal that she knew now that the real attraction at Cassel was "the pretty Madame ———"; and she naively adds that neither she nor Jerome approved of the intrigue! How she amid all her Court could be ignorant of the King's own relations with the Baroness is beyond comprehension. Certainly "the startled doves" of whom de Norvins wrote must still have played their part admirably in keeping the Queen from contact with realities.

The career of the adventuress rapidly drew to an end now. She departed with her sister-in-law to Genoa, intending to return shortly. Meanwhile Jerome, through the industry of his head of police, Bongars, who succeeded Bercagny, was put in possession of the whole correspondence which his brother-in-law maintained with Madame de Keudelstein, and discovering that Baron Otterstadt, his Inspector-General of Forests, was the medium through whom the Prince conveyed his letters to their destination, banished him from Court. Otterstadt's wife was a maid-of-honour to the Queen, having been her intimate friend at Stuttgart in childhood. She attempted to put pressure on the King to obtain her husband's recall, and offered her own resignation when he refused. Jerome accepted the offer at once, in spite of the Queen's unwillingness to lose her friend. Reinhard records the departure of the Otterstadts, which made a great stir at Court, at the end of August 1812. Blanche herself, still at Genoa with Jenny La Flèche, at the same time received an intimation that neither of them was any longer desired at Cassel. This time her disgrace was final. The King had just taken Madame de Löwenstein into high favour; and besides, he had already departed far from his usual unforgiving attitude towards acts of un-

Palace Life at Cassel

faithfulness to himself. Madame de Keudelstein saw that there were no further prospects in Westphalia, and took refuge in a villa on the shores of Lake Constance, bought for her by the Prince Royal of Würtemberg. As for La Flèche, his peculations in connection with the Civil List had already been discovered, and he had been removed from office for that office's good.

So ends the story of Blanche Carrega, Baroness Keudelstein. It can, perhaps, hardly be called typical of Westphalian Court life, since the heroine was so much the most outrageous of the ladies who figured at that Court that she stands on an eminence of notoriety by herself. The various episodes, however, are fairly illustrative of the general moral degradation reached at Cassel, and to give a picture of that in a brief space the outlines of this story serve well. No features are lacking. The wanton wife, not even faithful as a mistress; the complacent salaried and titled husband; the astonishingly trusting Queen; the corrupt and venal satellites of the Palace; and the King himself in the midst, bent on the pursuit of pleasure in its crudest form—all of them are here. To throw them still further into relief,

The Burlesque Napoleon

there is the background of ruined Westphalia, with its people sunk in hopeless poverty, according to their ruler's own testimony, only wondering how much longer they can manage to endure before the end comes which they see to be inevitable. It is difficult, often, to resist the impression that the majority of the scenes which have come down to us of life at Cassel are grossly over-coloured, but after all the bare framework of facts, when we can get at it, is sufficiently startling.

THE VOLCANO'S EDGE

CHAPTER X

THE VOLCANO'S EDGE

It is necessary now to return to the period succeeding the King's tour with the Emperor in Northern France. After a brief visit to Hanover in company with the Queen, when the reception accorded to the Sovereigns appeared very satisfactory, Jerome prepared to settle down to the ordinary routine of life at Cassel. Madame Mère was expected at the end of August, and when she arrived consented to spend a month with her son and her daughter-in-law. But the clouds were gathering again thickly in Westphalia. At the beginning of 1810 General Eblé had quitted Jerome's service in disgust at the lack of necessary funds and the interference of Count Bernterode in War Office affairs. D'Albignac, who succeeded him, quickly fell into disgrace with the King, being a man of violent character. De Salha was appointed to the post in September, and created Count Höne. He found his

The Burlesque Napoleon

Department in the state of bankruptcy universal in the country. 1,000,000 francs were owing for the upkeep of the French troops, and France was pressing for the payment. Jerome, nevertheless, was bent on establishing a fortified camp outside Cassel, and had already commenced to have the scheme carried out, taking the opportunity of entertaining his Court with appropriate spectacles. Napoleon no sooner heard of this than he ordered all such preparations to be stopped at once. At the same time he furiously denounced the treatment of his troops in Westphalia. "Good God!" he exclaimed,[1] "will you put an end to this?"

Without waiting for an answer, he made the backwardness of the Westphalian payments an excuse for an extreme step, on which he had already decided. Westphalia, he said, had broken her engagements with France; consequently he took from her Northern Hanover and the department of the Weser, part of Jerome's original realm. The outraged King sent a very reasonable letter of protest. He pointed out the peculiar injustice of depriving him of the revenues of Hanover, while still leaving on him the burden of its administra-

[1] To Jerome, Fontainebleau, 4th October 1810.

The Volcano's Edge

tion (as, indeed, Napoleon at first proposed to do) and the upkeep of the extra 6000 French troops. The Emperor made no answer to this letter, and the Senate on the 13th December passed a decree uniting the territories in question, together with Holland, to the French Empire. Louis, "the incorrigible," had already fled from his kingdom rather than endure any further the mockery of his kingship. His younger brother could not bring himself to follow his example. Royalty was still too amusing to him. However hardly the Continental System ground down his country[1] he still fought for the shadow of power. In the endeavour to retain Hanover he sent von Bülow on a special mission to make terms. The mission failed. On the 22nd January

---

[1] Dr J. H. Rose in his "Napoleonic Studies" quotes a Cassel letter in the *Allgemeine Zeitung*, 28th August 1810, which says: "In consequence of the royal decree whereby the new duties on colonial products are arranged according to the example of France and the other states of the Confederation of the Rhine, all colonial wares are so increased in price that everywhere in Westphalia men are thinking either of weaning themselves from them entirely or of finding substitutes for them." The royal decree mentioned here was the sequel of the Trianon decrees of Napoleon, which imposed duties of 50 per cent. *ad valorem* on colonial products.

The Burlesque Napoleon

Napoleon decreed the immediate incorporation of the territories with France, promising some insignificant compensation to Westphalia; and in May he persuaded von Bülow to sign a treaty recognising what had happened, while doing nothing more for Westphalia than relieving her of the extra 6000 Frenchmen and annexing to her that part of Hanover which had already been under her King's rule a year.

By his signature of this treaty von Bülow gave away, on behalf of his master, some 23,000 subjects and, nominally, between 5,000,000 and 6,000,000 francs of revenue. From Napoleon he received the Legion of Honour; from Jerome his dismissal. The King denounced the signature as dishonourable, the terms of the agreement having merely been dictated by France. Still, he could do nothing but yield. He had, indeed, already addressed a wonderful proclamation to the Hanoverians whom he was losing, bidding them show to the Emperor the same love, devotion, and fidelity of which they had so often given himself proofs—in the course of a bare year! With regard to the dismissal of von Bülow, he had long been anxious to get rid of him, but the astute Minister had given him no opportunity. Now Jerome professed to have

The Volcano's Edge

received from his police a secret correspondence in which von Bülow betrayed all his doings to Prussia. He accused him, moreover, perhaps justly, of not doing his best at Paris. The grant of the Legion of Honour involved fatal suspicions.

The arduous post of Finance Minister was now conferred on Karl August Malchus, whom Jerome had first employed in the negotiations with Jollivet over the Westphalian contribution to France. Malchus was suspected by von Bülow of having plotted his fall, though he swore that this was not so. But Malchus was of a character to arouse distrust. First heard of as a family tutor at Hildesheim at the end of the eighteenth century, he had risen to positions in the official world by twice betraying the hiding-place of buried treasure—first to Prussia after the treaty of Ratisbon, and then to the French after the foundation of Westphalia. In his new country Reinhard declares that he was neither esteemed by the King nor liked by the people, and his own verdict on him was that he was "*sans conceptions et sans entrailles.*" Hard-working he was admitted to be, but his ambition was feared and his arrogance condemned. He was, how-

The Burlesque Napoleon

ever, more conciliatory to the French party than von Bülow had been. He commenced his term as Finance Minister by reaping the advantages of his predecessor's labours, for the forced loan, as far as its collection had been possible, still secured at least six months' comparative freedom from embarrassment. Needless to say, the money was being devoted to current expenses rather than to the extinction of past debts. No abatement of the royal splendour was permitted, and the New Year season of 1811 was spent in true Westphalian fashion.

Suddenly, on the unhappy country there descended another requisition from Napoleon, and, worst of all for the King, the man to whom was entrusted the task of enforcing it was Marshal Davoust, Prince of Eckmühl. Very early in his career Jerome had come into collision with one member of this family; but the little, bald-headed martinet was far more terrible to deal with in 1811 than his young brother had been in 1800. In May the Marshal claimed from Westphalia the repair of the fortress of Magdeburg and its complete provisioning. The cost was estimated at 3,000,000 francs, and was to be covered by duties imposed

The Volcano's Edge

on such colonial commodities as continued to come into Westphalia. Davoust further established an agent in Cassel who, Jerome complained, actually threatened to seize Magdeburg unless work commenced at once on the fortifications. Fürstenstein had an interview with Reinhard, and declared to him that this requisition was simply the last straw. On the Budget of 1811 there was a deficit of 14,000,000 or even, according to Pichon, who was still at the Treasury, 18,000,000; while the 1812 deficit could not be calculated, so great was it. The King's Civil List was 600,000 francs in debt to the Sinking Fund. Pichon also told Reinhard that Jerome insisted on maintaining the Civil List at 6,000,000 francs a year instead of the original 5,000,000, although he had urged that this was impossible. Pichon was contemplating a retirement to Paris, whence he could refuse to serve Jerome any longer, except on his own terms—which would, no doubt, include the Ministry of Finance in the place of Malchus. Reinhard could see that he already looked on himself as the coming Minister. Pichon failed, nevertheless, to make his terms. He left for Paris next year, and did not return.

In his first indignation at the Magdeburg

The Burlesque Napoleon

requisition and the brusque disregard of his feelings by Davoust, Jerome refused to entertain at all the idea of doing as he was ordered. When, however, an invitation came to be present at the baptism of the little King of Rome, he went, and before the influence of the Emperor his determination fell. The new burden was accepted, only to be followed at once by others, and he watched his kingdom growing weaker and weaker, its debts larger day by day. The number of French troops in the country increased steadily until it was more than doubled. French soldiers garrisoned all the principal towns, and the householders sacrificed their homes at any price rather than stay to be fleeced. "Nobles, bourgeois, and peasants," wrote Jerome in the course of a long letter to his relentless oppressor, "overwhelmed with debts and want, seem to expect no other aid than vengeance, for which they pray with all their force, and to which they direct all their thoughts. This picture is true in every part. Not one of the thousand reports which reach me daily contradict it. I repeat to your Majesty, I ardently hope that you will open your eyes to the state of affairs here, and that you will bring all your high talents to bear

The Volcano's Edge

on it, to take the steps and precautions which may seem to you fitting."

Napoleon returned a most unsympathetic answer to this dismal but not overdrawn description of Westphalian affairs. "I have constantly recommended you, on principle, to keep down the enemies of France, not to repose excessive trust in them, and by according greater trust to the generals commanding at Madgeburg, to insure the safety of that important fortress; lastly, to put order and economy into the finances of Westphalia, which is the worst-governed state in the Confederation. . . . When you have *facts* to tell me I will listen to them with pleasure. When, on the contrary, you desire to send me pictures, I beg you will spare me. In teaching me that your administration is bad you teach me nothing new."[1]

Brutally though he appeared to reject Jerome's *tableau*, Napoleon, nevertheless, considered it so much worthy of attention that he instructed Reinhard to confer with the Westphalian Ministers, and, if he found that the facts were as the King represented them, to consult them concerning remedial measures. This softening of the blow was withheld from Jerome at first,

[1] Napoleon to Jerome, Paris, 10th December 1811.

The Burlesque Napoleon

and he seems to have plunged with the energy of despair into the whirl of winter frivolities. It might have been thought that, apart from the threats of coming European war and the miseries already entailed on his kingdom by the preparations, there was enough to damp his ardour in other misfortunes which befell him. Half the royal palace at Cassel was burnt down on the night of the 24th November, and Jerome himself narrowly escaped suffocation in his sleep. Then, a month later, his friend Morio was murdered by a French shoeing-smith. Morio had survived his disgrace as War Minister and the savage attack on him by the Emperor at Compiègne, and was still holding the post of Grand Equerry when he met his death—an act of vengeance for his policy of employing Germans as well as Frenchmen in the royal stables. Jerome appeared much distressed at the tragedy, but in spite of this the Carnival of 1812 suffered little or nothing by comparison with its predecessors. Reinhard writes of eight masked and three full-dress balls given at the Court by the Sovereigns or by high officials. The Cassel public declared that money was being thrown out of the windows of the Palace simply because the King knew that Cassel would not be his

The Volcano's Edge

home much longer. The townspeople, at least, got some of the money thus prodigally scattered. In the country the wretched people suffered far worse. Even Reinhard is touched at their sufferings under the burden of taxation imposed upon them. "Hesse and Paderborn are not at all rich districts," he writes; "they have no resources—nothing but tears." Could he have put the position better? And in the same month he had written of the lavish way in which the King had been scattering pensions on his intimates and on the husbands of his various feminine favourites.

Jerome had at this time, as Reinhard carefully pointed out in a letter[1] to the Duke of Bassano (the recipient of his letters and bulletins after the retirement of Champagny), a magnificent opportunity of displaying self-sacrifice. "The whole of the State funds," he might have said, "are not sufficient to meet the current expenses. But time is pressing. Here are 6,000,000 on my Civil List. I devote 1,000,000 to the upkeep of my brother's troops. No more masked balls, no more presents for costumes, until I have provided what is necessary. The funds which the Emperor has granted me shall be

[1] Reinhard to Bassano, 30th January 1812.

The Burlesque Napoleon

used for the army." But no one could imagine Jerome speaking in this strain. 240,000 francs between them to Prince Hesse - Philippsthal, Royal Chamberlain, and his bride; 200,000 to Fürstenstein as a present on the Queen's birthday; another 200,000 as a dowry to the daughter of Counsellor Coninx; innumerable smaller gifts all round the Court—these the King delighted to pour out. But a contribution to military expenses forced upon his kingdom he, no doubt, rejected on principle. It might be wondered how he managed to find the sums necessary for his displays of liberality. It seems that Jordis, the banker, induced some Frankfort financiers to advance 3,000,000 francs to the Westphalian Government. For Jerome the partition between his Government's funds and his own was small. Perhaps the worst of his financial acts at this time was when he induced the people of Cassel to make a present of 400,000 to the Queen as a birthday present. Unhappily, Catherine was too simple and too lacking in the sense of royal responsibility to decline such a gift. Truly, his subjects might suspect that Jerome was anticipating a speedy and eternal farewell to them.[1]

[1] Others than his subjects suspected it too. The Prussian

The Volcano's Edge

The events which were ultimately to bring this about were fast approaching. The war with Russia was on the very eve of breaking out. In March Jerome went to Paris secretly, by order of Napoleon, and returned with the commission to command the right centre of the Grand Army. His chief ambition in military matters seemed to be fulfilled—the ambition which had persuaded him to fall in with Napoleon's desire of increasing the Westphalian army, in spite of the financial and personal distress entailed on his people and the drain on the ready money so useful for his own pleasures.[1] At last he was to see under his orders 60,000 men, no less than three army corps, and to make war on the grand scale. Early in April he started for Kalisch, where his headquarters were temporarily fixed. Ar- representative at Cassel declared at the end of 1811 that Jerome had three horses saddled and bridled every night, and six horses ready for Catherine's carriage, in case a hasty flight should be necessary.

[1] By the terms of the constitution Westphalia was to furnish 25,000 men, half of them being French troops paid for by the country occupied. In an army bulletin of 1809 Napoleon speaks of 15,000 Westphalians. 16,000 went with the Grand Army in 1812, and in all, by the end of Jerome's six years at Cassel, conscription took, out of a population of 2,000,000, 600,000 men, of whom 38,000 fell in war (*Vide* Fisher, "Studies," p. 305).

rangements for the government of Westphalia in his absence were made by Napoleon when he arrived at Dresden, on his way to the front. He summoned Catherine to meet him there, had several interviews with her, and sent her back to administer the kingdom with the aid of the Ministers—a high proof of the confidence which he had in her. Jerome himself, freed from the responsibility of civil government, was on his way, as he hoped, to set the crown upon his military reputation. This he did, but in quite a different way from what he expected. At the very beginning he could not restrain himself from displaying his desperate and incurable levity. He had recently been captivated by the charms of a young girl, whose parents had shown a perfect willingness to sacrifice her in return for an official post for the father. In order to keep her near the Court, the king had found her a husband, in pursuance of his usual method, and rewarded this miserable creature also with a post. When he left Cassel on his way to Kalisch, though he continued to write to the Queen daily, the Court and townspeople did not fail to notice that Madame Escalonne—such was the new favourite's name—had also left; and the next heard of her was that she

The Volcano's Edge

was at Kalisch. Yet the profligate commander was not only trusting to win himself immortal fame as a general, but also entertained expectations of being made King of Poland.

This is not the place to discuss Napoleon's general designs concerning Poland, but the point when they touched the history of Jerome is of some interest. In 1806-7 the youngest Bonaparte was at least a possible candidate for the throne of a re-established Polish kingdom. Murat, however, was then considered a more likely king. He certainly thought himself to have a good chance, and gave himself airs in accordance with his hopes. But the Emperor was most discreet and vague towards Polish expectations. "Let the Poles show a firm resolve to be independent," was all that he would commit himself to. "Let them pledge themselves to support the King who shall be given to them, and then I will see what is to be done."[1] He was not going to draw on himself new foes for one province, as he said. The only result of Tilsit for Poland was the establishment of the petty Grand Duchy of Warsaw, which as early as 1808 Davoust called "a languishing and almost agonising body," and

[1] J. H. Rose, "Life of Napoleon," II. chap. xxvi.

The Burlesque Napoleon

which suffered perhaps, even worse than Westphalia, from the military tyranny of its French protectors. Yet in 1812 there was at least the appearance of enthusiasm in the reception given by the Poles to the French army. This strikes Lejeune more than it does Marbot, who says that there was no display of national spirit outside the Grand Duchy. A good number, however, of the Poles evidently still cherished great expectations of what Napoleon would do for them. As a matter of fact, he was even more reluctant to gratify them in 1812 than in 1807. In his own phrase, he was far from wishing to be the Don Quixote of Poland. He had now both Prussia and Austria to consider, either of whom would be entirely alienated by the re-creation of the Polish kingdom, which they had assisted Russia to dismember. He would do little more, therefore, than encourage the Poles to think about the idea. Their commander's insincerity of attitude did not, of course, prevent the French officers in general from talking about the coming kingdom. According to Lejeune, the two favourite candidates were Davoust, Prince of Eckmühl, and Joseph Poniatowsky, the Polish prince unhappily drowned in the retreat from Leipzig. Jerome

The Volcano's Edge

must, however, have had some reasons for hope, for it was common talk at Cassel in June that a certain lady of the Court had received a promise that she should follow the King if he were transferred to Poland; and in August Jerome himself wrote to Catherine that he "believed that the Emperor had at first wished to give him the Polish throne" but had changed his mind.

Jerome arrived in Warsaw early in June, after the bulk of the Grand Army had passed through. Had he been able to make his troops move as quickly as his Court, it was said, he would not have been in the rear. He was not sorry, however, to have an opportunity of breaking his march at Warsaw. An account of his visit there is to be found in the memoirs of the clever but malicious Countess Potocka.[1] This Polish lady had seen Jerome at Warsaw in 1806, when she was inspired to remark how petty and absurd all the princes of Napoleon's family seemed to

---

[1] Her malice was, naturally, directed most against her own sex, as against the "wooden face" and "large, pale blue porcelain eyes, staring and fixed," of Marie-Louise. She speaks enthusiastically of Pauline Borghese's classical beauty—the type to be found in Greek statues—and her delicate and regular features, "to which she added an admirable figure, too often admired."

The Burlesque Napoleon

the Poles beside the Colossus who overshadowed them. In 1812 she draws a just enough picture of the young man. On his arrival, she says, he at least played the King. He immediately announced an entertainment, stating that he would be pleased to receive the ladies desirous of being presented to him. The Polish women, noted for their beauty, were divided in sentiment. Many thought that Jerome was making too much of his kingship, and, in spite of the French Ambassador's representations that Napoleon's brother should not be refused, the attendance at the reception was not large. Jerome, somewhat offended at this, nevertheless endeavoured to organise a ball, but, all the young men being away with the army, he was obliged to abandon the idea. A few tedious dinners were all that could be arranged, and Jerome found that such Polish gentlemen as did remain in Warsaw brooked ill the etiquette which commanded them to stand in his presence. The situation was relieved when, probably through Napoleon's orders, conveyed through de Pradt, the French Ambassador, the Westphalian Sovereign departed for Russia.

The Countess's personal sketch of Jerome at this period is not without interest. He was

The Volcano's Edge

wrongly accused, she writes, of being destitute of advantages. "He had a quick and apt mind. With a touch more of the legitimate sovereign and a touch less of puerile vanity he might have passed for a distinguished prince; but, being a spoilt child of Fortune, he used and abused her bounty. . . . It was stated that every morning he took a bath of rum, and every evening a bath of milk. His servants, they said, put up the liquor in bottles, and sold it at a rebate. He pushed elegance so far that he never wore certain of his clothes twice; so much so that a Parisian hatter, to whom he owed a considerable sum, brought a most unpleasant action against him. The Emperor would never hear of his brother's debts — and a little King of Westphalia was hardly free to do things so grandly without making trouble for his Budget." The baths of rum and of milk may, perhaps, be called fancy touches in this picture. Jerome, indeed, was accused in Westphalia of having invented a bath of Bordeaux wine, but it is not stated that he took one habitually. The practice of bathing in milk was attributed to his sister Pauline. The idea of a rum bath is too grotesque to be taken seriously.

Jerome had already dismissed to her home in

The Burlesque Napoleon

Cassel Madame Escalonne, with whom travelled her devoted mother, and when he left Warsaw prepared himself for the sterner side of military campaigns. His 60,000 men, though they were late in arriving at Warsaw, were declared by Lejeune, who examined them on behalf of the Emperor, to be well armed and well equipped. They were not the least formidable section of the Grand Army. Nor, indeed, was their service in the fatal year of 1812 discreditable to them. For their commander, however, Fate was not slow to reveal what it had in store. The opening features of the campaign which culminated at Moscow are well known. The Russians allowed their forces to be cut in two, and widely separated. While Barclay de Tolly was retiring on the Dwina before Napoleon's main army, Bagration, with 40,000 to 60,000 men, was still on the Upper Niemen, in the rear of the French. Jerome's troops were among those entrusted with the duty of covering the main army, as well as Warsaw, from Bagration's attacks. The smaller Russian force was in great peril of capture if Napoleon's scheme should prove practicable. To cut the enemy off from escape eastward by Minsk, and so ultimately to the Dwina, Davoust was directed to start from

The Volcano's Edge

Wilna, and strike at him from the north, driving him on Jerome. The latter would check him on the south, and so, caught between the two columns, Bagration would be forced to surrender. Jerome had, as a matter of fact, reached Grodno on the 30th June, the day on which Davoust left Wilna; but having arrived there he rested until the 4th July, whereby he was too late to catch Bagration. Bad weather and the exhaustion of the soldiers by heavy marching are pleaded as an excuse by du Casse[1]; but Jerome himself, not making much of this point, seems to admit that he was remiss. The Emperor, at any rate, was violently enraged at the miscarriage of his plans. As early as the 4th July he wrote to his brother bitter complaints both about his delay and about his neglect to send intelligence to headquarters. "It is impossible to make war in this way. You only busy yourself about, you

---

[1] "Mémoires et Correspondance," vol. v. Du Casse declares that Jerome, with his numbers reduced by sickness to 45,000, could not in any case have carried out the scheme. In the "Souvenirs d'un Aide-de-Camp du Roi Jérôme" he maintains that Napoleon, being obliged to give up the idea of a Polish kingdom, which he had at first cherished, was not sorry to have an excuse to deprive Jerome of a command which was beyond his ability, when there was no longer need for him to be paraded before the Poles. The censures on Jerome's tactics du Casse considers unjustified.

The Burlesque Napoleon

only talk about trifles, and I grieve to see how petty everything is in you. . . . You are compromising the whole success of the campaign of the right wing. It is impossible to make war in this way," he repeated. Two days after he wrote to Davoust that, in the event of a junction with Jerome's forces, he was to assume command of the whole right wing; he was, however, to keep this order secret, and only reveal it when the junction occurred.

Bagration, having avoided the net which Napoleon endeavoured to throw round him kept retiring farther east, while Davoust and Jerome pursued him on lines roughly parallel to each other. On the 14th July Jerome sent from Neswij an aide-de-camp to Davoust at Minsk, proposing to concert movements. The Marshal sent a curt reply, announcing that he alone was in command of the right wing, and enclosing a copy of the Emperor's secret order of the 6th. Jerome, who had been kept in entire ignorance of such an idea, in spite of several communications from the Emperor since his letter of the 4th, sat down the same night and wrote to Napoleon that he had resolved to serve under no other orders than his; that, though he cherished no resentment against Davoust after

The Volcano's Edge

their former altercation, yet that was publicly known in Westphalia, and so this subordination would be a humiliation; and that he, therefore, asked to be allowed to retire. He told Napoleon that he would await his decision at Neswij; but he also wrote at once to Davoust, telling him what he had done, while he ordered his generals to consider themselves under the Marshal's command.

Had he done as he said he would, and waited at Neswij for an answer from the Emperor, it is quite possible that Jerome might have been reinstated. But only two days later he withdrew with his bodyguard from the town, and retired to Grodno, whence he wrote again, complaining of the way in which he had been subordinated to Davoust without any warning, of the Marshal's constant hostility to him, of his own unfortunate inability to please Napoleon. "It rests with your Majesty to ruin or to save me," he concluded, "for I resigned the command three days ago; and, having retreated with my Guards and announced that your Majesty has summoned me to another point, I cannot return." He asked for a coast command, to guard against the event of an English descent on Hanover.

What Napoleon might have done had not

the decision been taken out of his hands can only be guessed. He reprimanded Davoust for exceeding his orders in not waiting for a junction to be effected before assuming command over Jerome; and his despatches of the 20th July seem to imply an expectation that Jerome would return. But the King had continued his retreat on Warsaw, full of bitterness and injured pride. "I cannot do otherwise than return, to save dishonour," he wrote to Catherine. "What! Am I, the commander of the Right Wing, composed of four army corps, to be under the orders of a mere Marshal who commands but a single corps? ... It is desired that I shall serve—I, the commander of the Right—under the orders of a Marshal. I do not desire this, and I cannot, that is all. I resign. It is quite simple." To add to his rage, he knew that a version of the affair had reached Cassel. At Warsaw he received a letter from Catherine, who was extremely upset over the story, and could ill conceal her pain. His answer deserves quotation for its delightful tone of superiority. "I have received your long letter of advice," he wrote. "I thank you for your good intentions; but I never thought I had left room for doubt

The Volcano's Edge

that I am not one of those who suffer dishonour, and I do only what I ought to do. I find it also rather rash of you, my dear, to speak at such length on a question about which you know nothing, and I have the right to suppose I have inspired in you sufficient confidence to reassure you entirely as to my conduct, which is never guided either by temper or by mere caprice. The Emperor never deprived me of the command of my troops, either Saxons or others. So you see that what you say to me in your letter of the 23rd is one of the innumerable ridiculous fables circulated in Cassel. . . . You must simply say that I have demanded leave to return home, being unable to stand the changes of climate, and that the Emperor has granted my request." In a postscript he added that he had that moment received a very satisfactory despatch from the Emperor, who seemed convinced that he could not have acted otherwise than he had done, and enjoined on him to return to Westphalia, but only on condition that the matter was kept secret, and that the state of his health should be alleged as his reason for home-coming. This letter from Napoleon, it should be mentioned, has been lost; and some have even doubted

The Burlesque Napoleon

whether it was ever written. Certainly the Emperor took long to forget the affair, almost entirely ceased to write to his brother, and refused him a command in the summer of 1813 except on humiliating conditions.[1] It was not until shortly before Waterloo that he really forgave him.

This episode in Jerome's career has been dwelt on at what may be considered disproportionate length. It seems, however, of considerable importance in forming an estimate of the man, while the facts have been very frequently distorted. Among his contemporary critics Marbot makes the best attempt to be fair to the King. "The rigorous and necessary step of dismissing Jerome from the army" (as he assumes Napoleon to have done) "produced in that army an impression very unfavourable to him," he says. "But was he to blame? His first error had been to think that his dignity as Sovereign prevented him from re-

[1] " He shall never have any command in the French army, unless (1) he makes it known that he condemns his conduct last year in quitting the army without my permission, and that he is sorry for it; and (2) in taking service in my army he submits to the authority of all Marshals in command of army corps whom I have not specially put under his orders" (Napoleon to Berthier, 31st July 1813).

The Volcano's Edge

ceiving the commands of a mere Marshal. But had not the Emperor, who knew very well that this young prince had never in his life directed a single battalion, nor been present at the smallest fight, to reproach himself for giving him his debut an army of 60,000 men, and that in such grave circumstances?" Marbot is inaccurate, of course, when he says that Jerome had never directed a battalion nor been present at the smallest fight; but he is right in blaming Napoleon for assigning to Jerome a task beyond his capacities. This defence, it will be seen, is damning to Jerome's military reputation. But that is past saving, even if we admit him to have been unduly censured over the escape of Bagration in 1812.

THE END OF
WESTPHALIA

CHAPTER XI

THE END OF WESTPHALIA

It was on the night of the 9th August that Jerome reached Napoleonshöhe from Warsaw. Next morning a salute of guns announced to the people of Cassel their King's return, and the town was loyally illuminated in the evening. In spite of the complete dashing of the hopes with which he had started from his capital four months before, to outward appearance all was well with Jerome. Reinhard declared him in good health—which went badly with his excuse to the public for his return from Russia—affable, and gay. Pichon, it is true, who was now finally making up his mind to quit Cassel, detected in the King bitterness and chagrin, and hinted to Reinhard that it needed a tempering of the Emperor's just severity with generosity and kindness to cure his brother. But Jerome, chagrined or not, threw himself eagerly into new schemes for spending money on the palaces of his kingdom—and, needless

The Burlesque Napoleon

to say, into new and old amours. The industrious Reinhard was soon writing how Madame de Löwenstein had enjoyed the King's favour since his return. Löwenstein, the husband, was one of those charming chamberlains of the Cassel Court whose advancement was due to no aptitude of their own; the Countess was able and corrupt. She had attracted Jerome before his infatuation with Madame Escalonne, and patiently waited for him to get over that. "The King returned to her," says Napoleon's agent. Had he not indeed written long before, in his first report on Westphalia, that the King's affections were in the habit of returning? The favourite signalised her triumph over her rivals (including the Baroness Keudelstein, now at last banished for ever) by appearing at Court in a new dress, so elegant as to cause despair in the breasts of the Palace ladies. Yet she did not reign alone if the rumours were as true as Reinhard believed them to be. A Polish lady made her appearance in Cassel soon after the King's return, and everyone assumed that there was a connection between the two events. This was not necessarily the fact, of course—as, indeed, may be said of many of his alleged intrigues

The End of Westphalia

—but Jerome's character was such that the presumption was always against him.

Whether he was now unfaithful to his Queen with one or more favourites, the King was undoubtedly unfaithful to his country in many more ways than one. His senseless extravagances were in no degree restrained by any consideration of the affairs of either Westphalia or the French Empire. Earlier in this year Reinhard could only reckon the Westphalian balance-sheet thus: Expenses, 60,000,000 francs; receipts, 40,000,000; deficit 20,000,000.[1] Matters had not improved even by the four months' absence of the most expensive item of the State and the temporary administration of Ministers anxious to check the approach of ruin. The outlay from August to the end of the year soon compensated for the saving between April and August. The solaces necessary for a wounded pride involved a heavy expenditure on excursions banquets, concerts, etc. More than ever before was spent on the Cassel Opera House. To procure the funds to provide Blangini with the means of engaging artists, the army treasury was turned to account, the bulk of the forces being away on service, while the remainder's pay

[1] To Bassano, 19th May 1812.

was allowed to get far in arrears. This was about the period of Borodino and Moscow, when the Westphalian contingent in Russia was pouring out its blood in the great advance into the heart of Russia. In November we hear, through Reinhard, of the magnificence of the Opera performances at Cassel, which fully rivalled those at Paris. This was the time when the Grand Army was falling back in the awful retreat to the Niemen. Could any contrast be more grim?

Of all the periods in Jerome Bonaparte's long life of frivolity these months of August to December 1812 are those for which it is least possible to find any excuse. Although he may be entitled to sympathy for the usage he underwent at the hands of Napoleon and Davoust in July, there can be found nothing to palliate the manner in which he spent the time when the Grand Army, with 20,000 of his subjects in its ranks, was fighting, suffering, and finally being almost annihilated, in Russia. Accordingly it is not surprising to find that, in the writings of his eulogists, this part of King Jerome's life is hurriedly passed over. There is nothing to be said in defence.

As soon as he heard of the approach of

The End of Westphalia

Napoleon on his lightning journey from Smorgoni, the gay monarch showed at least sufficient seriousness to endeavour to obtain an interview with him. On the 16th, and again on the 18th, December he sent messages to his brother asking to be allowed to see him as he sped through Germany. But Napoleon had no time to stop, even if it were to consult about the security of Westphalia in the coming storm. He considered his presence necessary in Paris at once, and passed on without granting an interview. It was not that he had no thought of Westphalia, however, for at the end of this very month we find him obtaining from Reinhard character sketches of all the King's Ministers and principal men. Moreover, he sent a brief reply to a further request that he should at least receive the King at Paris. "I think your presence will be more useful in your kingdom at this moment than in Paris," he wrote. "There is nothing left of the Westphalian army with the Grand Army, and all seems to point to a crisis next spring. Let me know what you have sent to fill up your contingent again, what you can do to complete your artillery and cavalry, and finally what you are in a position to do about provisioning and thoroughly protect-

The Burlesque Napoleon

ing Magdeburg against any event. A perusal of the reports and your news direct from the Grand Army may have told you that it has been obliged to take up winter quarters on the Vistula after undergoing considerable losses."[1] There seems a note of sarcasm in the last sentence. Though he might not be fully aware of the way in which his brother had celebrated his removal from the Grand Army, Napoleon may have seen some of Reinhard's recent reports.

The New Year season of 1813, the last year of the kingdom, was far the quietest in the history of Westphalia. Reinhard records less extravagance in entertainment, and in the whole manner of expenditure more order and wisdom, which he attributes to the departure of La Flèche. It is probable that Jerome himself was really sobered by the details reaching him of the retreat from Moscow and by the gravity of the military preparations he was called upon to make. His gallantries had not, of course, entirely ceased. It was common report that he had had some trouble with Catherine, and even with his father-in-law, about a lady whom he had appointed reader to the Queen. Catherine, as

[1] Napoleon to Jerome, Paris, 23rd December 1812.

The End of Westphalia

ever, had ended by being convinced by his protestations. This drove Reinhard to remark that "her eternal apathy, real or apparent, was injurious and discomforting," and that about the best one could now say of her was she never did harm—a remark, it will be remembered, very like that which he made about the totally dissimilar Le Camus. It is not likely that Catherine had complained to her father, but very possibly Frederick may have heard of his son-in-law's conduct through other sources. A year ago he had declared that Jerome took pleasure in annoying him ("How wrongly my father judges my husband!" exclaims Catherine in her journal), and the episode of the Prince Royal of Würtemberg and Madame de Keudelstein had made him furious. Jerome was certainly not to blame for the robbery of his own mistress, but he had to suffer, nevertheless. Frederick had not very long to wait for his revenge.

Signs of the coming end of Westphalia were fast accumulating now. To Napoleon's demand for the strengthening of Magdeburg his brother returned the query whence he was to get the money. Reinhard's reports about the lessened expenditure at Cassel had apparently had an

The Burlesque Napoleon

effect, for the Emperor promised to grant 500,000 francs. He subsequently cut this down to 250,000, and then sent the money too late to enable the place to be adequately protected. Jerome was beginning to feel so nervous about the state of the country that he desired Catherine to go to France. Napoleon wrote that she was to do so as soon as the Russian forces entered either Dresden or Berlin. She was most loth to go. The Russian entry into Berlin took place on the 4th March, but she did not leave Cassel until the 10th. Then she only did so because, as she wrote to Napoleon, "I thought it my duty to sacrifice my wish to live and die at the King's side to the requirements of his peace of mind and to your Majesty's views." Jerome escorted her to Wabern, and then rode back to Cassel.

The Russians were in Berlin, and Prussia was on the point of throwing off the mask; but as yet Westphalia and the neighbouring Rhine States were not menaced with instant invasion. Nor was there any attempt at a general rising, although Jerome might talk to his brother's Ambassador about the certainty that the Westphalians would prefer to die under fire rather than by sheer hunger. The

The End of Westphalia

exhaustion of the country by conscription, no doubt, had much to do with its passivity. Moreover, Napoleon's tremendous efforts, since his return to Paris, had been duly noted. Only four months after that return he had 200,000 men ready to march into Germany. In the middle of April he was at Mayence, himself preparing to meet the Russo-Prussian coalition. It was from this place that he wrote attempting to spur Jerome on to the necessary exertions on his part. "Make the King understand," he told Reinhard, "the insanity of his present position." He had failed to take the advice to get together a trustworthy bodyguard. Even now it was, perhaps, not too late. Had he taken the advice six years ago he would have had a magnificent body of Westphalian Guards; now they would only be conscripts. The King's great fault (he continued) was ignorance of history and of political principles. Here was the result — that though his army was between 15,000 and 20,000 men he was on the brink of being driven from his capital by two or three squadrons of possibly inferior troops![1] Jerome acted upon these admonitions in a way scarcely contemplated by the Emperor. Marbot

[1] To Reinhard, Mayence, 20th April 1813.

The Burlesque Napoleon

had been sent back to France to organise new cavalry forces for the French, very weak in that arm since the retreat from Moscow. A body of 150 mounted men, one of four "superb" squadrons raised by Marbot, was passing through Cassel, some time in July or August, when they caught the King's eye. He immediately stopped them, and incorporated them in his own Guard, and to Napoleon's orders to give them up represented how untrustworthy were his Germans, and how expensive the uniforms which he had purchased for these involuntary recruits. To Marbot's disgust the Emperor yielded. In a similar way Jerome was allowed to annex a body of dragoons passing through his kingdom on their way to the front. But his petition to be assigned a command was rejected sternly, with the before-mentioned allusions to 1812.

The general result of Napoleon's attempt to awaken Jerome to a sense of his "insane position" were small. He had but little diminished the scale of living at the Court. He took up his quarters at Napoleonshöhe, it is true, the Cassel Palace being under repair, and paid occasional visits to Schönfeld. He also breakfasted and dined for the most part alone, according to Reinhard, who spent a week at

The End of Westphalia

Napoleonshöhe in May. But concerts, comedies, and whist-parties occupied his evenings, and numerous guests were entertained. A special costume was invented for this country life, consisting of a blue uniform with silver lace, and finished off with riding-boots. Jerome was described now as "always amiable," but apparently more grave than before, while "order and decorum ruled everywhere." Less than two weeks later, unfortunately, the Ambassador finds occasion to speak of the King "giving way to apathy, seeking distraction in pleasures whose secret is so badly kept that the effect on the public is annoying." It was but another chapter of the old story. While there still remained a shadow of his kingly power, and while his position furnished him with access to the money which his liberality demanded, there was bound to be at the Westphalian Court enough of the society which he preferred about him.

While the King was engaged on drinking the very dregs of his royal draught in Westphalia, the fate of the country was being decided outside. The armistice signed at Pleisnitz ended on the 10th August. Austria was now in the Coalition. The defeats of the other

The Burlesque Napoleon

French generals rapidly destroyed the effects of Napoleon's victory at Dresden. Two allied armies crossed the Elbe; Bavaria deserted the French; and the day of Leipzig was approaching. On the 27th September news arrived in Cassel that Tchernichef and his Cossacks were at hand, and at daybreak the next day firing was actually heard at the Leipzig gate of the town. Owing to a fog, the 5000 Russians had managed to get through the Westphalian troops and gendarmery, and, had they passed on, might have taken the King in his bed. They stopped, however, to fire at the gate, so giving the alarm. No thought was entertained of making a determined stand. Desertions had been numerous in the Westphalian army during the summer—those going over to the enemy including Hammerstein, in whom Jerome had put much confidence. When the fusillade was heard, all was confusion. The King hastily dressed, and mounted his horse. General Allix rallied all the troops in the town, which he defended while King and Court fled to Marburg, and from there to Coblentz, where Jerome gathered some more troops. Allix, after holding Cassel until the fugitives were in safety, surrendered it to Tchernichef, on con-

The End of Westphalia

dition that he was allowed to march out with arms and baggage. The Cossacks entered on the last day of the month, and were joyfully welcomed by the townspeople, among whom the worst element attacked and plundered the few remaining French civilians. The Westphalian General retired slowly to Marburg and Coblentz, but on the appearance of 5000 to 6000 troops from France, marched on Cassel again, and re-occupied it—Tchernichef having left, taking the mayor and other officials as hostages. The local Garde Nationale had restored order before the royal troops' re-entry, and Allix issued a proclamation in the King's name praising the general conduct of the town, and stating that only a few *misérables* had joined the Cossacks, a remark which must have been very gratifying to the Cassel people.

Jerome followed Allix after a few days, and on the 13th October re-entered his capital for the last time. His advisers were anxious for him to make examples, Bongars being particularly fierce. Large numbers of suspects were thrown into prison, but Jerome was unwilling to proceed to extremities. In gratitude to Allix, he created him Count Freudenthal, with a visionary pension of 6000 francs a year. He

The Burlesque Napoleon

also filled up the vacant posts in the Government, and nominated a number of people to the Crown of Westphalia. The little pretence at royalty, however, was speedily over. On the 25th intelligence reached the King of the disaster of Leipzig. This news was not common property yet, and very early next morning Jerome left Cassel quietly, with a specially selected bodyguard, mainly French, and started for the Rhine. Allix and the bulk of the French troops remained at Cassel to cover the second retreat of the Court, which was conducted without precipitation. Numbers followed the King to Cologne, where he had halted; others dispersed. On the 27th the *Moniteur Westphalien* appeared for the last time in French and German. In it was published the following proclamation, signed by Counts Wolfradt, Höne, and Marienrode :—

"Imperious circumstances of the moment oblige His Majesty to leave his realms. In quitting them temporarily His Majesty has confidence in the loyalty of his faithful subjects, that they will continue to conduct themselves with the same devotion and the same calm for which they have always been distinguished."

This was the farewell of Jerome to his king-

The End of Westphalia

dom of six years. The evacuation of Cassel was completed, and the realm of Westphalia fell apart. Little more than a week later the Elector of Hesse was dragged in his coach through the streets of his capital, and addressed a triumphant proclamation to an enthusiastic populace. In the meanwhile the late King, surrounded by the crowd of refugees at Cologne, and guarded by the remainder of his army and their French auxiliaries, found himself in great straits through want of money. After selling all the royal silver, and even the uniforms of the remaining Westphalian troops whom he dismissed, to defray daily expenses, he moved with all his retinue across the frontiers of Berg, which alone of the German states remained entirely in French hands.

The Grand Duchy was still under the administration of Beugnot. Arriving at Mulheim, the King sent a message announcing the fact to his old Minister of Finance, who hastened to see him. In his memoirs Beugnot has left a record of their meeting, with an amusing account of Jerome's state at the time. Though he was now occupying but an ordinary house instead of a palace, the King clung to all the tinsel of royalty still. Everywhere were

The Burlesque Napoleon

stationed the Westphalian Guards, in their theatrical gold-laced uniforms. Chamberlains were on the stairs, since there were no antechambers in which to wait. His Ministers of Foreign Affairs and War were with their Sovereign. All reminded Beugnot of a tragedy being played by a troupe of provincial actors. Introduced in due form by the Chief Chamberlain, he found Jerome in great agitation. He was full of reproaches against his brother for the disasters which had befallen everyone in consequence of his retreat across the Rhine. He talked of offers which the Coalition had made to him, not only to confirm him on the throne of Cassel, if he would join them, but also to increase his territories. These offers, he said, he had rejected indignantly, but he regretted it sometimes when he saw all being ruined by Napoleon's obstinacy. Beugnot complimented him on having adopted the honourable course, and urged him to go to France. Jerome thought that it would be a mistake to cross the Rhine. All might not yet be lost for France if he remained in Germany. Or he might go to Holland, if Berg were to be abandoned. Holland, replied Beugnot, would be no better protected than Berg. Finally the

The End of Westphalia

King yielded, and consented to retire to France; whereon Beugnot left him, and returned to his post at Düsseldorf.

Though he does not spare his weaknesses in this sketch of him at Mulheim, Beugnot adds a note of his judgment on Jerome, which is more favourable than might have been expected. "I had remarked in him," he writes, "through all the excesses of his youth, both loyalty and resolution of character. Better prepared, he would, I have no doubt, have sustained the burden of his name, heavy though that was." These two sentences make us regret that Beugnot did not leave in his memoirs any narrative of his term of office at Cassel, for they lead us to believe that we might have had some additional evidence of value to correct or supplement that of Reinhard.

Jerome, in abandoning Germany against his will (for he still believed that his people of Cassel wished to see him back!), contemplated proceeding to Paris. He had entrusted Catherine, who had been living at Meudon, outside Paris, since March, with the task of buying the chateau of Stains, and fitting it up for their residence. Napoleon was unwilling that he should come to the capital. As is

The Burlesque Napoleon

revealed by a letter to Reinhard from the Duke of Bassano, he "did not wish Paris or France to have the spectacle of a dethroned King, who in his misfortune had not the consolation of leaving any friends in the country which he had governed." Napoleon had no illusion about his brother's "people" at Cassel. Nor would he allow Jerome to come to him at Mayence. "The King never having been willing to follow the Emperor's advice," continues Bassano's letter, "nor to do any of the things so important to his own interest and his throne's, his interviews with His Majesty could but be painful and useless." The purchase of Stains annoyed Napoleon still more, and caused him to show coldness even to Catherine, though she was but Jerome's agent in the matter. He ordered all ideas of living there to be given up at once, and consulted Cambacérès as to whether it was not contrary to the Family Statute for any prince of the family occupying a foreign throne to acquire property in France without his consent. "I am shocked," he wrote to Cambacérès,[1] "that, when all private individuals are sacrificing themselves in their country's defence, a King who loses his throne should be so

[1] From Mayence, 6th November 1813 (Lecestre).

The End of Westphalia

tactless as to choose this moment to buy property, and to give the impression that he only thinks of his private interests."

The Family Statute, as Napoleon thought, forbade the acquisition of property by Jerome if he were to be considered occupant of a foreign throne. But Jerome resisted the Emperor's will strenuously. He would not go to Aix-la-Chapelle, which was suggested to him by Napoleon as a residence, if he wished to stay in France, and he clung to the idea of Stains. He met defiantly the remonstrances of Reinhard, still nominally Ambassador to his Court. "I know that I am in the power of a stronger. Still, it is known that I have character. I would rather risk a scandal; and the man who is sent to compel me had better be firm in his stirrups!" This was the old spirit which had made him exclaim once to de Norvins at Cassel, when some order had just reached him from Paris: "Here I too am Emperor!" Instead of going to Aix-la-Chapelle he went on a visit to his mother, and then took up his residence at Compiègne while the repairs and decorations at Stains proceeded. But in spite of the desperate struggle in which he was on the point of engaging in

The Burlesque Napoleon

January 1814, with the European hosts pouring over the Rhine, the Emperor found time to watch even so petty a matter as this. In the middle of the month he sent orders for the architect engaged by Jerome, and the latter's business man, to appear before Savary, who was to direct them to stop work at Stains instantly, and to dismiss all the workmen. Jerome himself might stay at Compiègne, but must not leave the immediate neighbourhood on any account.

In this curious contest between the two brothers, victory went to neither side completely. The younger failed, it is true, to take advantage of the elder's preoccupation in affairs which might well engage the whole attention of even a man of genius; he failed to establish himself in the comfortable chateau which he coveted, just outside Paris, although he did spend a few days there before long, on his way from Compiègne with Catherine. On the other hand, Napoleon did not succeed in driving Jerome to Aix-la-Chapelle. He was compelled to permit his residence in France, and, as will be seen, very soon consented to a move into Paris itself.

1814 AND WATERLOO

JEROME BONAPARTE.

CHAPTER XII

1814 AND WATERLOO

ALTHOUGH the question of a home in France appeared to be the matter of chief moment to him, the refugee King of Westphalia was not altogether lost to a sense of patriotism; perhaps we should rather say that hopes of military glory had not altogether abandoned him. When his first conviction that all had been lost by the Emperor's "obstinacy" in retreating from Germany after Leipzig had weakened at the sight of the splendid efforts of Napoleon in February 1814, he was spurred to offer his services once more, in spite of his rebuff the previous summer, and to ask for a command. The request passed through Joseph Bonaparte, then acting as Governor of Paris. The answer from Napoleon to Joseph was not encouraging. "These are my intentions with regard to the King of Westphalia," he wrote. "I authorise him to wear the uniform of a grenadier of my Guard, as I authorise all French princes to do." He was

The Burlesque Napoleon

to dismiss all Westphalians from his service and the Queen's; and they might move to the house of Cardinal Fesch in Paris, retaining the titles of King and Queen. This done, Jerome was to present himself at Napoleon's headquarters, whence he would be sent to Lyons in command of the department and of the troops there, "but only on condition that he promises me to be always at the outposts, to keep up no royal retinue and not more than fifteen horses, to bivouac with his men, and to let no shot be fired when he is not the first to expose himself."[1]

The commission did not appeal to Jerome's taste. He was not a coward, and he would have welcomed an order to join the Emperor himself. But he saw no glory awaiting him at Lyons, and consequently, ignoring this part of the letter to Joseph, he contented himself with taking up his residence with Catherine at the house of Cardinal Fesch. Not a long stay was made there, however. The march of the Allies on Paris scared all the family of Napoleon away. Marie-Louise and the young King of Rome had the Emperor's orders, again through

[1] Napoleon to Joseph, Nogent, 21st February 1814 (Lecestre).

a letter to Joseph,[1] not to await capture, but to fly rather to the farthest village in France. The Kings of Spain, Holland, and Westphalia fled too, creating an execrable impression; but after all not one of the three was capable of making Marmont's and Mortier's 30,000 men avail against the 150,000 of the Coalition, and their capture on the 29th March, when the two Generals capitulated, would certainly not have improved Napoleon's position when he reached Fontainebleau next day.

Jerome and Catherine remained at Blois with the Empress and her child until after the abdication at Fontainebleau. Three days after this Marie-Louise left for Orléans, accompanied by Jerome. He and Joseph had already made vigorous attempts to persuade her to leave Blois. The Bourbon partisans, naturally, only saw the worst of motives in this conduct of Napoleon's brothers; and accusations of intended robbery of the Crown jewels, and of desire to secure their own safety by holding as hostage the Emperor Francis' daughter, are amongst the mildest charges brought against them. It is reasonable to suppose that Joseph was really anxious to carry out Napoleon's wish, as expressed in the

[1] "Correspondance," xxxvii. p. 131.

The Burlesque Napoleon

letter already mentioned. Nor was it unnatural that Jerome should escort his sister-in-law and nephew while yet the fate of the family was unsettled. Catherine, leaving her husband to proceed to Orléans, went herself to Paris to appeal to the generosity of Würtemberg and of Russia on behalf of her husband and herself. She had hopes that Alexander would support Jerome in a claim for an indemnity in Italy for the loss of Westphalia, which both Russia and Prussia had guaranteed to him at Tilsit. From her father she trusted that she might at least ask a temporary shelter in his realms during the present distress of the House of Bonaparte. Her brother, the Prince Royal, was at Paris, having entered with the Würtemberg contingent of the Coalition; but when she attempted to see him he gave a striking proof of the brutality of his nature by entirely refusing an interview with her for whom he had expressed so much affection three years before. He merely wrote bluntly that Würtemberg was an impossible refuge for her and Jerome. The Minister for Würtemberg was little kinder. He offered her an asylum at her father's Court only on condition that she would abandon Jerome. The manner in which Catherine received this

1814 and Waterloo

proposition has won her universal admiration. It will be, perhaps, sufficient to quote a short passage from each of the two letters which she addressed to Frederick from Paris.

"My visit here," she wrote on the 15th April, after her interview with the Minister, "is terrible for me, who am obliged to listen to the most revolting proposals concerning my husband. The Prince Royal is exasperated against him; but what has moved and astonished me most is the suggestion which M. de Wintzingerode thought fit to make to me, to separate myself from the King. He assured me, my dear father, that it was not your idea, nor could I have ever imagined that your paternal heart dictated it, or that you could have given such an order. Look for a moment at the past. Married to a King whom I knew not, my conduct guided at the time by high political considerations, I attached myself to him, and I carry within me to-day his unborn child. He has been the cause of my happiness for seven years by his sweet and loving acts; but had he been the worst of husbands, had he made me unhappy, I should not have abandoned him in misfortune. . . . Never will I separate my interests from his. My resolution is unshakable here; it is inspired by feeling and by honour alike."

However fond may seem this testimony to Jerome's character as husband, at least its utterance in adversity is a glory to his wife. Her reward was but further trial. In unconscious answer she received next day a letter from her father in Würtemberg, which showed her that Wintzingerode had merely executed the charge of his master. Catherine none the less wrote, two days after her former letter, affirming her intention of listening only to the commands of duty and honour. "Do not look at political interests," she besought Frederick; "look at the most sacred duties of a father and those of husband and wife. Please grant at least, dear father, your blessing on the pure motives which guide me; please think that every dream of happiness is over for me, and that I can find no consolation or compensation save in the love and tenderness of my own people."

It may easily be imagined how much Frederick was likely to be induced by this appeal to neglect political interests. Catherine's efforts with Alexander were more successful. He procured her passports for herself and

1814 and Waterloo

Jerome, promised to speak in favour of an indemnity in place of Westphalia, and learning that Jerome was determined to refuse the pension of 500,000 francs which the Bourbons were to allow him by the terms of the treaty just drawn up, offered to shelter husband and wife in Russia. The Tsar's protection availed them but little in the end, except that he was able to lift them from actual want by granting a pension to his cousin. But Catherine left Paris comforted in heart, and assured that she would not be torn from Jerome. Everything else she had the strength to bear.

Catherine's brief visit to Paris involved her in a strange affair, the full details of which can never be known. Her share in it, however, is perfectly straightforward. She spent the week of her stay in the house of Cardinal Fesch, which was still as she and Jerome had left it at the end of March. Finally, her mission over, she prepared to start for Orléans to rejoin her husband. Fürstenstein and the Countess of Bockholtz still accompanied her from the old Westphalian Court, and she had a number of domestics also with her. Leaving Paris early on the 18th April, she reached Etampes the same night. Here a messenger from Jerome

The Burlesque Napoleon

met her, and directed her to make for Berne, whither he had already departed from Orléans. Accordingly she turned eastward, in the direction of Nemours. She was passed on the road by a rider whom she recognised as the Marquis of Maubreuil, ex-equerry and cavalry officer in Westphalia, whose connection with the story of Madame de Keudelstein will be remembered. She thought his movements suspicious, but paid little attention to them until she was inconvenienced at Nemours by the fact that Maubreuil had taken the only available change of horses. The delay, which lasted twenty hours, was fortunate as it happened, for it enabled her to see for the last time the brother-in-law whom she so genuinely admired. On the morning of the 20th Napoleon passed through Nemours, accompanied by the Allied commissioners and a strong escort, on his way from Fontainebleau to Elba. Catherine was resting at the inn, when she heard shouts of "*Vive l'Empereur!*" Hastening out, she was allowed to take farewell of Napoleon, who, as on the first occasion when he saw her at the Tuileries, in such different circumstances, embraced her tenderly. He then rode on at a rapid pace, while she remained until the evening.

1814 and Waterloo

Horses being at last procured, she made a start in the direction of Dijon, but was only close to Montereau early next morning when her journey abruptly stopped again. A body of horsemen—"mamelukes," she called them in her account—barred the road, at the head of whom she recognised Maubreuil again. She was riding in a six-horse coach with Fürstenstein and her Grand Mistress, having with her all her valuables and Jerome's, in eleven cases. The other carriages following contained the servants and the heavy baggage. In answer to her demand why she was stopped, Maubreuil alleged that she had stolen Crown jewels with her, pointed to a companion, who he said was M. Dasies, a police agent, and produced orders, signed by the provisional Government at Paris, and by the representatives of Russia and Prussia, which authorised him to search when he thought fit. Catherine in vain produced her own passport from the Tsar. Maubreuil and Dasies conducted her coach to a neighbouring farmhouse, took out her boxes, opened all before her, and finally took everything, including 84,000 francs in cash, and jewelry worth more than double that amount. Her prayers to Maubreuil not to take all her money

The Burlesque Napoleon

induced him at length to give her less than 1000 francs, which he already had on him. He seemed sensible, Catherine in after years told the Countess Potocka, to her reproaches against his baseness, and showed her secret instructions, "ordering the bearer to rid the world of all male members of the Bonaparte family." When the plunder had been secured Maubreuil and Dasies put Catherine, whom they had detained for six hours, with her carriages on the road to Villeneuve, leaving two men to see that she did not turn back, while they rode in the opposite direction.

Torn between her desire to join her husband at Berne and her anxiety to recover, if possible, her jewels and money, Catherine despatched a messenger at once to the Tsar at Paris, telling him of the robbery, and asking his help. Next day she wrote another and a longer letter, imploring pity in her miserable situation between the calls of duty and the threats of her father. Alexander at once sent one of his aides-de-camp to escort her to Berne, and promised that the promptest steps should be taken against the "brigands." At the end of the month she was able to write to him from Berne, thanking him for securing her safe arrival thither.

1814 and Waterloo

The remainder of the story of Maubreuil's plot need not be told here. It seems probable that the robbery of his former Queen was the scoundrel's own idea, his mission having really been, as he alleged it to be, the assassination of Napoleon.[1] He took credit to himself for refraining from this deed, and claimed also that in commissioning him Talleyrand's agent had promised him he might keep any Bonaparte property on which he might come while executing his task. At any rate, in spite of Alexander's help, Catherine never recovered either her jewelry or her money. Maubreuil and Dasies both escaped justice, though arrested, and this alone should suffice to show that there was someone more powerful at the back of the plot. Maubreuil ended by obtaining a small pension from Napoleon III.,

---

[1] The most recent writer on this affair, Mr E. A. Vizetelly, in his biography of "The Wild Marquis," is convinced that "Talleyrand and his acolytes" were at least privy to the plot to murder Napoleon, if they did not originate it; while he exculpates the Russian and Prussian Governments. Mr Vizetelly shows that Maubreuil was watching Catherine during her stay in Paris, knew beforehand the date of her departure, and followed her on the 18th April. Napoleon did not leave Fontainebleau until the early morning of the 20th, so that the meeting at Nemours was a strange coincidence.

The Burlesque Napoleon

presumably on the ground that he had not executed the commission of murdering his uncle.

Reunited at last to her husband at Berne, Catherine continued to endure the pressure brought to bear upon her by her father to induce her to quit Jerome. But the discredited and almost penniless exile was still as dear to her as ever the King of Westphalia had been. To Frederick's offers and menaces she could only return the same answers as before. "Forced by political considerations to wed the King my husband," she wrote,[1] "Fate has willed that I should find myself the happiest woman that could be. I feel for my husband love, tenderness, esteem. How can the best of fathers wish to destroy my domestic happiness—the only happiness left, I dare tell you, dear father?" Nor did she relax her appeals to Alexander to use his influence on her behalf. The Bourbon Government insisted on keeping not only such proceeds of Maubreuil's theft as they recovered, but also Jerome's property left in his recent home in Paris. In consequence, he was reduced to a very simple style of life, seeing nobody, going out seldom, and not even able to afford

[1] Catherine to Frederick of Würtemberg, 1st May 1814.

liveried servants.[1] In June he moved with Catherine to Grätz, and two months later to Trieste, where she gave birth to a son, just over seven years since her wedding day.

The feverish excitement of the Hundred Days arrived to break in upon the peaceful and constrained life of exile at Trieste. It was on the 12th March that news of the escape from Elba reached Jerome. He decided to go at once to the nearest point where he could be in touch with Bonapartist feeling—to the Court of Naples. To thwart any designs the Austrian Government had of detaining him where he was, he feigned severe illness for a few days, and then left his house in disguise with three aides-de-camp—for his poverty did not prevent him from keeping so many. Sailing in a small boat at midnight on the 24th March, he reached Neapolitan territory four days later. At Naples he found gathered his mother, Cardinal Fesch, Lucien, Louis, and his sisters. Murat had already declared war against Austria, and the situation was perilous. On a visit to Florence, Jerome was almost captured by a body of Austrian cavalry. Returning to Naples in April,

[1] Catherine to Frederick of Würtemberg, 7th December 1814.

The Burlesque Napoleon

he awaited the opportunity of escaping to France, which the English rendered as dangerous by sea as the Austrians by land. It was not until the middle of May that he, Madame Mère, and the Cardinal made a start. Then, touching at Corsica on the way, they reached on the 22nd the very spot on the French coast where Napoleon had landed two months and a half before them.

Once on French soil again Jerome cast all prudence to the winds. He was a king again, and had not to wait long for a court. Already at Lyons he was surrounded by equerries, dames-of-honour—though Catherine was far away—and uniformed servants. So at least says Barras, who met him at Lyons, and is very scornful about "His Majesty."[1] Jerome was in high spirits. "Times have altogether changed," he cried to Barras. "The Bonapartes have mended!" Lyons received him with open arms. He could not for ten hours tear himself away from the enthusiasm of the good Lyonnais, he wrote to Catherine. But he freed himself at last, and pressed on towards Paris.

The welcome given to him by Napoleon on his arrival was most cordial. At the Champ

[1] Barras, "Mémoires" iv. pp. 292 *ff.*

1814 and Waterloo

de Mai three brothers supported the Emperor—Joseph and Jerome, as kings, on his right; Lucien on his left. The scene must have recalled to many present the spectacle on the same spot on the distant *25 messidor*, after Marengo. Then also Jerome sat at his brother's side, very different from the gold-laced and satin-clad figure which he now presented. Far more different, however, was the solemnity of the Champ de Mai from the wild rejoicings of 1800. There was no time to spare for display now. Jerome himself was impressed with the gravity of the situation, and at no time in his career does he appear to better advantage. No pride prevented him from accepting a subordinate command. Imperial Highness though he was once more, he obtained but an infantry division to lead, under the orders of General Reille, and he resigned himself to ideas which would have revolted him in 1812 and 1814.

The actual share which Jerome took in the last campaign of Napoleon has become, thanks to recent writers on the Hundred Days, easier to disentangle than it would have been in the past. If the *rôle* which he played was not as heroic as his eulogists made out, nor such as to prove any talent for command, at least it was

The Burlesque Napoleon

creditable to his courage as a soldier. In Ney's attack on Quatre Bras, Jerome's division took a considerable part, and its leader was slightly wounded. By a curious coincidence it was in fighting against the second brigade of the ex-King of Westphalia that the Duke of Brunswick, hero of the march through Westphalia and Hanover to the sea, was killed. Indirectly, Jerome had first deprived the Duke of his throne, and later caused his death.

If Napoleon had listened to a report which his brother brought to him on the morning of Waterloo, that battle might never have been fought. He was at breakfast at Le Caillou, when Jerome arrived to tell him of the statement made to him by the waiter at the Roi d'Espagne Inn, where he had supped the night before. Wellington had breakfasted there on his retreat from Quatre Bras, and the waiter claimed to have overheard one of his aides-de-camp speaking of the intended junction with Blücher at the Forest of Soignès. Napoleon dismissed the report as "impossible," and the battle was fought. The duty which fell to Reille's corps herein was the demonstration against the chateau of Hougomont, on Wellington's right. That this was only intended to be

1814 and Waterloo

a demonstration, to cover the assault of Mont-Saint-Jean, is now generally agreed. It was Jerome's impetuosity which turned the movement into a serious attack. Reille entrusted the task to his 6th Division (Jerome's), which, led by the ex-King himself, and Bauduin, commander of the 1st Brigade, opened the battle by a charge into the Hougomont wood. Bauduin was killed almost instantly. The French gained the wood, however, and after an hour's fighting cleared it. It was at one o'clock that the 6th Division stood within thirty paces of the chateau itself and the walk of the park. Then, in the words of M. Henry Houssaye, "Jerome only needed to keep to the level or in the hollow behind the wood, and maintain in front of him a good line of skirmishers. But whether the order was badly explained or misunderstood, or whether the Emperor's brother would not consent to play this passive part, or whether the excited soldiers rushed on of their own accord, they dashed forward to the assault." The murderous reception at the hands of the concealed Hanoverians, Nassauers, and English heaped the French dead in front of the chateau, and drove the shattered 1st Brigade back into the wood. Jerome only brought up his 2nd Brigade to the assault, in

The Burlesque Napoleon

spite of the advice of his chief of staff, while he sent the remainder of the 1st to turn the left of the position. The Light Infantry actually penetrated to the northern side of the buildings, and broke in the door. But the assailants were shot down as they entered through the opening, and the arrival of four companies of Coldstreams to reinforce the garrison drove the French into the wood again.

Napoleon hastily called Jerome to his side, perhaps hoping to check the unnecessary fury of the attack on Hougomont. He left for La Belle Alliance; but his men could not be held back. Nearly the whole of Reille's corps was drawn into the struggle, in which so much success was attained before the end of the battle that the chateau itself and the bulk of the farm-buildings were burnt, and the garrison driven to the chapel and the gardener's cottage. The price paid for this was too heavy, and the blame must at least partly rest on the divisional commander. "The demonstration against Hougomont," M. Houssaye sums up,[1] " ordered by the Emperor degenerated through Jerome's eagerness, through the enthusiasm of

[1] "1815," III. chap. viii. 4.

1814 and Waterloo

the soldiers, through the lack of vigilance and firmness on the part of Reille, into a headlong attack, in which the lives of half the 2nd Corps were uselessly sacrificed."

In this attack on Hougomont Jerome had vindicated his courage if not his skill. In the great disaster which followed he had still a part to play. The legends of the Second Empire attributed to that part a greater prominence than was due to it. M. Martinet complains in his biography that Jerome was the victim of legend. In this case, at least, he was its beneficiary. M. Martinet himself makes the Emperor, struck by the heroism of Jerome, seize him by the hand, and exclaim: " My brother, I have known you too late!" Jerome himself, in his description to Catherine of Waterloo, merely makes the Emperor say, when he summoned him from Hougomont: " It is impossible to fight better. Now that you are reduced to two battalions, stay in order to take yourself wherever there may be danger." As for the story of Jerome, when the flight had begun, dashing to the bridle of the Emperor's horse, and crying: " Here must die all who bear the name of Bonaparte!" it has no authority at all. Jerome, in his letter to

The Burlesque Napoleon

Catherine,[1] gives the following plain and credible account of his action during the retreat:—

"At ten o'clock it was a rout," he says. "The Emperor was carried along; there was no one to give orders. I reached Avesnes next day, having been at the rear-guard all the time with one battalion and one squadron. I found here neither Emperor nor the marshals who had gone on ahead. I made unheard-of efforts to rally the remains of the army, and at length I succeeded in rallying 18,000 infantry and 3000 cavalry, with the twelve guns with which I arrived at Laon on the 21st June." The Duke of Dalmatia (Soult) being at Avesnes to take the command, Jerome continues, he made for Soissons himself, where he received a letter of thanks from the Minister of War for the efforts which he had made. He proceeded at once to Paris, to hear on his arrival of the Emperor's second abdication and the elevation of Napoleon II. to the throne.

[1] Jerome to Catherine, 15th July 1815.

EXILE, RESTORATION, AND DEATH

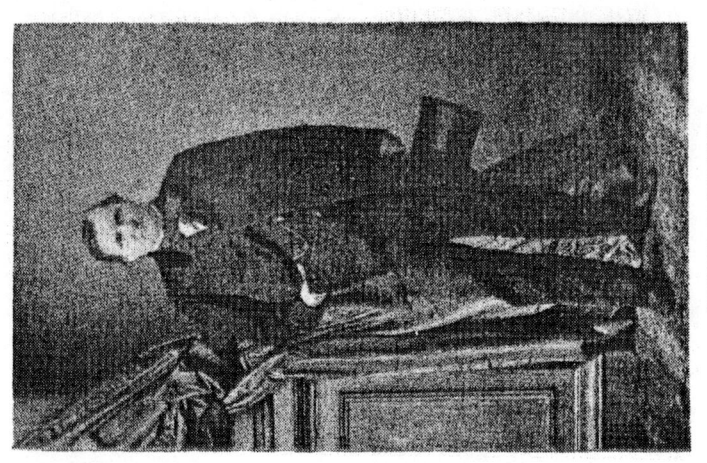

PRINCE NAPOLEON.

PRINCE JEROME

CHAPTER XIII

EXILE, RESTORATION, AND DEATH

A LONG life still remained to be lived by the youngest member of the family which fell so disastrously from empire to exile at Waterloo. Not until forty-five years later was Jerome Bonaparte destined to end his days. But although he thus lived long enough to figure, after over thirty years of obscurity, once more in the public view, a personage very close to the throne of France, the second and longer division of his life needs not nor repays such attention as his earlier years. There is not much in the protracted period of exile which demands more than passing notice; and in the story of the Bonapartist revival, culminating in the Second Empire, the subordinate political part played by Prince Jerome, as he then again became, is not counterbalanced by the supreme interest of his private career. It will perhaps, therefore, suffice in the following chapter to give a few glimpses of the man as he appeared

The Burlesque Napoleon

to contemporaries, to supplement the main outlines of his middle life and old age.

The position of Jerome in France after the final break up of the fugitive from Waterloo was extremely perilous. There was no safety in Paris, which he received orders to quit at once from the Commission acting until the return of Louis XVIII. He left on the 26th June, three days after his arrival, but returned again secretly after wandering about the country in hiding. His object was to see the representative of his father-in-law, and to ask his final terms. While waiting to interview the Ambassador he lay concealed in the house of a small Corsican shoemaker; but his presence soon became known. Louis is said to have given orders that he was to be arrested and shot. Fouché, to whom the task of capture was entrusted, had kindlier feelings towards Jerome than to any other of the Bonaparte family, and enabled him to escape not only from Paris, but also, after a mock pursuit, across the frontier into Switzerland. Jerome had gained his object. He had seen Wintzingerode, and learnt that he would be received in Würtemberg on his oath not to leave the country without the King's permission. He

Exile, Restoration, and Death

acquiesced. The terms seemed better than he could have expected; but he did not know that he was to be practically a prisoner. He started without delay for Würtemberg, and on the 22nd August was reunited to Catherine at Göppingen.

Here the unhappy wife had been bestowed by her father. When Jerome left her to go to Naples the Austrian police had immediately descended on her house at Trieste. After some delay—caused by the young Jerome's teething troubles!—they sent her to Grätz, whence she was hoping to be able to start for Naples. Suddenly a peremptory message reached her from her father, ordering her to repair to Würtemberg at once with her infant. She had an Austrian passport to enable her to proceed to Naples, but Frederick's agent threatened her with violent abduction if she did not come to Würtemberg of her own will. Helpless, she yielded, and was conveyed to Göppingen. Knowing of Waterloo, but unaware whether Jerome were alive or dead, she was not reassured except by his appearance in person. The life at Göppingen was little better than that of political prisoners, and though Jerome and Catherine were moved to Elvangen

The Burlesque Napoleon

shortly, the same restrictions hedged them round. In 1817 Frederick at last consented to give them liberty—and a title. As the Comte and Comtesse de Montfort, they left Würtemberg, and returned to Austria, where the widowed Caroline Murat had settled down already. They were permitted to make Austria their home on the understanding that they must not move beyond its boundaries.

The King of Würtemberg was brought at last to make some amends for his animosity against Jerome; or rather, he found his will powerless against the strength of his daughter's love for her husband. He agreed to allow her a pension for life, though he knew, of course, that this was equivalent to giving the pension to Jerome. Catherine also received now an annuity from her cousin the Tsar, whose conduct towards her is one of the best points in a very contradictory character. With the two allowances together there was enough to live on with ease. Nevertheless, Jerome, for all that he was apparently a faithful husband at this period of his career, contrived to spend far beyond his, or his wife's, income.[1] An

[1] Altogether, du Casse puts Jerome's income about this time at 70,000 to 80,000 francs.

Exile, Restoration, and Death

appeal to Madame Mère produced only the wise advice: "Imitate me! Retrench!"[1] Now, retrenchment, so easy and congenial a task to Letizia Bonaparte, was totally foreign to her son's disposition. Even a Count of Montfort, according to his views, must have an expensive home and keep up an expensive state. After some wanderings he moved to Trieste, where for the second time he established himself. Here his second child by Catherine, the Princess Mathilde of history, was born in 1820, and two years later the third, afterwards Prince Napoleon. In the meantime his sister Elisa, who was also residing at Trieste, died, two months after the birth of Mathilde, and in the following year fell the blow that seemed to condemn all to oblivion. Napoleon died at Saint Helena, and the whole family was plunged in the utmost grief. Not least of the sufferers was Catherine, who had already sent a brave petition to the Prince Regent on the prisoner's behalf. She asked to be allowed to

[1] "I mourn that I cannot impart my character to you," she wrote in the same letter. "It would be more honourable to struggle against adversity, and conquer, and I am convinced that Catherine is strong-minded enough to draw in as closely as possible" (Quoted by C. Tschudi, "Napoleon's Mother," p. 245).

The Burlesque Napoleon

go to Saint Helena. "I should esteem myself most happy," she wrote, "if I could by my care help to alleviate the rigour of his captivity." But she appealed in vain to the Brunswick blood which united her to the Regent. No member of his family was to be allowed at Napoleon's side in his last days.

The death of the Emperor was in some degree an advantage to his relatives, since, the fear of him removed, a greater freedom of movement was allowed to the rest. The ban which prevented Jerome from leaving the Austrian dominions was taken off, and after the birth of the young Napoleon Trieste was quitted for Italy, which became the home of most of the surviving Bonapartes. A dramatic accident now brought Jerome face to face with his past. Walking with Catherine in the gallery of the Pitti Palace at Florence, he suddenly saw before him his former wife. With an agitated whisper to Catherine as to the reason, he led her from the gallery, and they left Florence. Not a word passed between Jerome and Elizabeth, and they never saw each other again. She had procured a divorce from him in Maryland after the Empire's downfall, in order to guard herself, it was presumed, against any financial claims

Exile, Restoration, and Death

which Jerome might try to make. She did not cease, however, to take an interest in her former husband. She was well informed as to his condition at the end of 1821. He is, she writes to her father,[1] "entirely ruined, his fortune, capital, income entirely spent, and his debts so large that his family can do nothing for him if they were inclined, which they are not." This was before he had come to Italy. The truth of the reports was amply confirmed afterwards.

Though she was never to meet Jerome after the encounter in Florence, his first wife's story and his continued to touch. The connecting link was the son whom he had endeavoured to have brought to Westphalia in 1808. Elizabeth had very reasonably refused to part with her child, in spite of the offers of a career sanctioned by the great Napoleon himself. After the triumphs which she enjoyed in Europe on her second visit, she brought the young Jerome Napoleon from Baltimore, and sent him to school at Geneva, whence he joined his mother in Italy at the age of sixteen. The position was now curious. Madame Mère, Lucien, Louis, and Pauline all received the boy with affection, and recognised him as Jerome's eldest son. A

[1] To William Patterson, 28th November 1821.

The Burlesque Napoleon

project was even formed of a marriage between him and Charlotte, daughter of Joseph Bonaparte, who was living in the United States as the Comte de Survilliers. In the letter quoted above, to William Patterson, his daughter says: " Madame [Mère], knowing the state of Jerome's finances and the impossibility of his ever doing anything for anyone, wishes Joseph to provide for this child by a marriage. I have given my consent." Moreover, Pauline, whose husband, Prince Borghese, allowed her a handsome income in spite of her unfaithfulness, promised to leave 300,000 francs to the two if they married. This plan was never carried out—" Bo," as his mother called him, ultimately marrying someone else. But in 1821-23 both sides of the family cherished the idea. Jerome senior had not spoken yet, and had not even seen his eldest son when the latter went home again for three years at Harvard. The meeting came about in 1826, when Jerome and Catherine were living at Rome and Elizabeth at Florence. It was arranged that the young man should visit his father's home. He did so, and wrote to his grandfather at Baltimore: " From my father I have received the most cordial reception, and am treated with all possible kindness and affec-

Exile, Restoration, and Death

tion. . . . I have not seen mamma for two months; she is still at Florence." He was gratified, too, at the welcome given to him by his grandmother and the other Bonapartes, but, nevertheless, desired to return to America, "to whose government, manners, and customs I am so much attached." He remarked that all his relations, except his grandmother, were living beyond their means, and that there was not the least hope of any of them doing anything for him. The observation showed considerable penetration, and in the event not even his father left him anything in his will.

It was probably to his own advantage, as it certainly was to the advantage of the United States, which thereby gained a gifted family, that the young Jerome gained his wish, and returned to America. Not only his father, it is true, but also Catherine and his half-brothers and sister, treated him as one of themselves; but complications must assuredly have arisen in time, from the embarrassed state of the family, if not of the nature which afterwards arose. His marriage in 1829, though it was a great blow to his mother,[1] was made the ground of the

---

[1] She ultimately brought herself to write: "I would rather die than marry in Baltimore, but if my son does not feel as I

The Burlesque Napoleon

general congratulations of the Bonapartes, who had by then abandoned their idea of a union with Joseph's daughter. From this time the name of Prince Jerome's first wife enters no more into his history. That of their son is heard again some fifteen years later, when, coming to France with yet another Jerome, his son, he was so well received by Napoleon III. that the jealousy of his half-brother was aroused. The old Prince was induced by Prince Napoleon to protest against the legitimacy of his first-born being recognised, and desired him to leave France. He was obliged to see the son declared, by a decree of August 1854, "*reintégré dans la qualité de Français,*" and the grandson serving with honour as a French lieutenant in the Crimea. The influence of Prince Napoleon, however, after his father's death prevented the legitimacy being legally established in the French courts.

To return to the period when Jerome, as Count of Montfort, was living with his family in Italy. The life of the various Bonapartes in Rome was one marked by few incidents except the occasional deaths. We hear very little of Jerome at this time. A slight sketch of him,

do upon this subject, of course he is quite at liberty to act as he likes best." The bitterness is ill concealed.

Exile, Restoration, and Death

Catherine, and their manner of existence has been preserved by the same Countess Potocka who described the visit of the King of Westphalia to Poland in 1812. In her account[1] we see Jerome, the Legion of Honour ever prominent on his breast, living splendidly in the palace which had once belonged to Lucien. The interior was notable for much greater luxury exhibited than in any of the other Bonaparte homes. Lights and perfumes were everywhere in abundance, and the staff of servants was very numerous. Jerome insisted on a certain pomp —perhaps in honour of his wife's royal origin. He succeeded, too, to a great extent in getting himself accepted as a king still in society. Yet the Countess sums him up as "a fallen prince and superannuated lady-killer"—though he was only forty-three when she wrote, and had some thirty years of gallantry to come! Catherine is described as amiable, talking well, and free from all German stiffness of manner. She was delighted to hear her elder son Jerome noted as resembling the great Emperor. The boy was being educated at Siena, and it pleased his father that he should wear the Crown of Westphalia in his buttonhole.

[1] " Voyage d'Italie " (1826-1827), p. 69.

The Burlesque Napoleon

For amusements the exiles had the ordinary entertainments of society in Rome: dances for which Catherine did not care, but Jerome no doubt did; excursions to the country, and so on. Jerome was pleasantly and expensively engaged in building a fine villa on the Adriatic shore, whither he transported his family when it was finished. Scandal naturally connected his name with a lady in the neighbourhood, and may have been right. He was known not to have settled down permanently to the career of a good husband which he led at Elvangen and Trieste. But the intrigues may be left in their obscurity. Such had been his reputation that he was bound to be accused whether he were guilty or not. That he continued to live beyond his means is at least certain, and though he might go on appealing to his mother, his debt was a subject on which he found the old lady unsympathetic still. His position was really far from secure. The French Ambassador at the Vatican watched the refugee Bonapartes with a hostile eye, and the King of Naples with still more hatred. Finally, the pressure put on the Pope was so strong that he consented to banish the Count of Montfort from the Papal States. The villa on the Adriatic had to be sacrificed at what it would

Exile, Restoration, and Death

fetch; while its master went to Florence with his wife and children, and launched out there in further expenses, necessary, from his point of view, to his rank, but ruinous to his estate. Moreover, that estate was not his but Catherine's, as has been said, and the revenues ceased entirely with her death. The former Prince Royal of Würtemberg, who had succeeded his father on the throne, was willing to receive his nephews into his army, but he was not disposed to continue his sister's pension after her death out of love for her husband. The allowance from the Tsar Alexander stopped also when his cousin died. It so happened that both Würtemberg and Russia afterwards indirectly subsidised Jerome through his son Napoleon and his daughter, but for some years after 1834 he was without either means of support.

The death of his faithful and devoted companion was thus in every way a heavy blow to Jerome. He had accompanied her to Lausanne, whither the doctors ordered her in hopes of relieving her dropsy. She grew worse, however, and finally died, with her husband's hand to her lips and her children at her side. Her last words were recorded to be: "What I loved most in the world was you, Jerome. I wish I

The Burlesque Napoleon

could say farewell to you in France." She was fifty-one years of age, and had been married for twenty-seven years — twenty-seven years of happiness, as she would have insisted. If we consider all the facts, we cannot find in history a more remarkable marriage of convenience.

Financially the widowed husband was quite ruined now. His establishment in Florence, of course, could be kept up no longer. He retired to a country house in the neighbourhood, which was all that his credit was sufficient to support. Two years later, Madame Mère died in Rome. Jerome and Lucien were the only two sons able to be present at her death-bed. Her scrupulous division of her savings left only to her youngest-born his just proportion of the inheritance, and a share in her golden table service. She knew too well that she could do little to relieve the wants of one who so persistently neglected her advice, and who showed so little of her own character. More years of struggle followed, until at last, in 1840, six years after Catherine's death had reduced him so low, two marriages raised Jerome again from his abasement. His daughter Mathilde wedded a Russian noble, Prince Demidoff, and he himself contracted his third union with a

Exile, Restoration, and Death

Florentine widow, the Marchesa Bartolini-Badelli. Of the three wives of Jerome Bonaparte the third was destined to suffer the hardest fate. She was rich, well born, and possessed of good looks; du Casse, who saw her nine years after her marriage, describes her as still beautiful—she was then forty-nine—and distinguished. She was, moreover, according to him, sweet, charitable, and "the best of creatures," but, unhappily, very indolent and languid in her ways. Jerome had his debts, and whatever was his mysterious attraction, to offer her; but he could not agree to anything more than a morganatic marriage. Although fifteen years his junior, and able with her fortune to pay off all his debts, she accepted the terms, and established him once more in Florence in a life of ease. She hoped, no doubt, to win him to recognise her full rights as his wife, but he insisted to the end of their life together that she should be styled "Madame la Marquise," and addressed her so himself.

Jerome's chief hopes now centred in a return to France. For this reason he looked with extreme disfavour on the attempts of his nephew, Louis Napoleon, against the Government of Louis Philippe, and thenceforward

The Burlesque Napoleon

conceived a bitterness against him whom he had formerly desired to see wed his daughter Mathilde. It was, as can well be imagined, from no kindly feelings for the Bourbons that he condemned the intrigues against them. The Royalist Government yielded at last to the representations of the exile, who found an able advocate in Victor Hugo. At the end of September 1847 he was authorised to return to France with Napoleon, now his only son, the elder having died the previous year. At the age of sixty-three Jerome was once more on the soil from which he had been thirty-two years banished.

The pain — to which, however, he had reconciled himself—of dwelling under the rule of a dynasty that had destroyed the fortunes of his house was not his for long, and when the provisional Government was established, he and his son were among the most ardent Republicans. Jerome's proclamation of adhesion to the Republic is quite a masterpiece of patriotism. "Gentlemen," it ran, "the nation has at length torn up the treaties of 1815. The old soldier of Waterloo, the last brother of Napoleon, returns at this moment to the bosom of the great family. The time for

Exile, Restoration, and Death

dynasties has passed for France. The law of proscription which struck me down has gone with the last of the Bourbons. I ask that the Government of the Republic shall pass a decree that my proscription was injurious to France, and that it has disappeared with all that strangers have imposed on us. Pray receive, Members of the Provisional Government, my expressions of respect and devotion. JEROME BONAPARTE."[1] Equally enthusiastic was his son Napoleon. He, unfortunately, carried his fervour so far as to write to his uncle of Würtemberg, signing himself "Citizen Bonaparte," whereon the King cut off a pension of 30,000 francs a year which he had allowed him for his services in the Würtemberg army. So good a Republican, he said, could not take a pension from a tyrant like himself.

There was no question of financial distress, however, for the remaining years of Jerome's life. The Marquise Bartolini's money had relieved him from that, and the Republic rewarded the "old soldier of Waterloo" with the post of Governor of the Hotel des Invalides, to which an annual salary of 45,000 francs was attached. The triumphant elevation of his

[1] Declaration of the 26th February 1847.

The Burlesque Napoleon

nephew Louis Napoleon to the Presidency was followed by his restoration to the rank of General, with another 12,000 francs a year. Fortune was making amends rapidly now for the humiliations to which she had so long subjected him. Once more he was a personage about whom the pens of memoirists found much to write. At this period arose the connection of Baron du Casse with Jerome, to which we owe the chief materials for his history. In the last of his three books dealing with his patron[1] du Casse presents what seems to be a fair picture of the old man and his household, less malicious than some other accounts—such as that of General Ricard, for instance, who joined Jerome as aide-de-camp at the beginning of the Second Empire. Du Casse does not conceal the faults of those whom he describes in his personal recollections, but at the same time he does justice to their merits.

In 1849, the year when his future biographer entered his service Jerome was living at the Invalides with his third wife and his son Napoleon. Generous and wasteful as ever, the ex-King still found his chief amusement in the society of the opposite sex. He was devoted

[1] "Souvenirs d'un Aide-de-camp du Roi Jérôme." Paris, 1890.

Exile, Restoration, and Death

to the theatre too, and du Casse records his infantile joy when, Napoleon dining on occasions away from home, he was able to send his aide-de-camp to order dinner at a restaurant, and take seats for some performance afterwards. Nor was it the leading houses which amused him most. He took du Casse once to a play acted by dogs and monkeys, sitting for a whole act in the front row, but, to the aide-de-camp's great relief, not being recognised by the crowd. On another visit, described by the same writer, to the Port Saint-Martin Theatre, he was condemned to see himself on the stage, in the play of "Napoleon at Schönbrunn." The public recognised the real Jerome sitting in a box; but he was the first to laugh at the spectacle of himself listening to the reproaches of his justly indignant brother.

His son was much annoyed at these escapades of his father, but he had, nevertheless, a deep love and respect for the old man. Du Casse's estimate of Prince Napoleon is that he was "the most prodigiously intelligent and prodigiously vicious man that ever lived." Only very violent enemies have ever denied his great ability. Unfortunately, his faults are as generally admitted. Low tastes, habitually coarse language, and an intri-

The Burlesque Napoleon

guing jealousy of nature, left him few friends even among the admirers of his talents. His physical resemblance to the great Napoleon was as striking as that of Jerome's other legitimate sons. To the Third Napoleon he was an ungenerous foe, and his cousin's forbearance towards him was remarkable. The fact that Louis Napoleon alone stood between them and the throne of France was, no doubt, the main explanation of the attitude of Jerome and his son to him. The amiable nature of the Emperor did not allow him to resent their malice. Only one bitter remark has been attributed to him with regard to them. Jerome had sneered at him for having nothing of Napoleon about him. "Pardon me," replied the Emperor, "I have his family." The retort was not unmerited; and there was no one, least of all among themselves, entitled to complain of the manner in which Napoleon III. treated the inconvenient relatives whom his uncle had left to him.

The luckless Marquise Bartolini was of little account in the household of the Invalides. Her efforts to be recognised as Jerome's full wife had been unsuccessful in exile, and were not likely to succeed now that the husband was once more a high dignitary of the State. Her indolence

Exile, Restoration, and Death

and lack of will left her a nonentity. Her stepson hated her, and his influence over his father was greater as the years went on. The story of the manner in which she was at last driven from the home is pitiful and revolting. Jerome was, for all his sixty odd years, constantly unfaithful to her, and he fell at length a victim to the wiles of a woman who ruled him for the last eight or nine years of his life. There seems to have been little reason for Jerome's infatuation with the tall, red-haired creature that she is described as being, yet he not only behaved atrociously to the Marquise, but also for this woman's sake took under his protection her husband, a ruined gambler and debauchee, whose function it became to act as buffoon and fool to his patron. Already Prince Napoleon and his *âme damnée*, as du Casse calls him, Jerome's Corsican steward, had engineered a plot against the Marquise, accusing her of an intrigue with Jerome David, a young man whom Jerome owned as his son by the daughter of David the artist. Old Jerome had at least the decency not to credit this story, and to dismiss Pietra-Santa, the steward. But in 1853, when he had been created once more a Prince of the Empire, being

The Burlesque Napoleon

still more than ever under the dominion of his red-haired enchantress, he suffered the abominable story to be revived, and the Marquise was driven away to Florence, broken-hearted. There can be no possible mitigation for the chief actors in this horrible drama.[1] Jerome, however, repaid the Marquise her money which he had spent in Florence, and took a palazzo by the Arno for her. Napoleon III. allowed her a pension after his uncle's death, and even Prince Napoleon made a slight atonement by continuing to pay for the rent of her house. The poor victim meekly accepted her fate. She wept in reply to the odious charges brought against her; she was hurried away from Paris in tears; and she lived to weep over the death of him who wronged her so.

But for this revelation of the inner life of Jerome we might have been led to imagine that he had settled down to be an amiable old gentleman in his declining years. We see him from time to time, in the pages of various writers, most pleasantly pictured. A profile like that of

---

[1] The outlines above are taken according to du Casse. The more highly-coloured version of the anti-Bonapartist partisans may be found in M. J. Turquan's "Le Roi Jérôme," where the details are distinctly unpleasant.

Exile, Restoration, and Death

his great brother, locks turning grey, a quick eye, a benevolent and charming smile; a gentle voice, a graceful and often witty manner of speech; dressed always in black, with the Legion of Honour, the Iron Crown, and his own Crown of Westphalia in his buttonhole, with trousers strapped under his patent boots, and white gloves—such are the main items of his personal appearance as described by Hugo, for instance. To the end of his life he was looked on as a pattern of manners. In the year before his death we hear of the old Prince, seventy-four years of age, giving a fête at the Palais-Royal in honour of the Empress Eugenie, and "leading her round the rooms, giving her not his arm, but his hand, after the custom of his youth, and preceding her slightly, with an antiquated but most chivalrous grace."[1] It is sad to think how belied this appearance of courteous and venerable age was by the domestic life of the old man, even if we reject the most malicious tales of his enemies.

[1] Madame Carette, "Souvenirs Intimes de la Cour des Tuileries." So Miss A. L. Bicknell, in her recollections of the Second Empire in *The Century Magazine* for September 1895, recalls the "courteous old man, very like his illustrious brother, with old-fashioned manners, holding ladies at arm's-length by the tips of their fingers."

The Burlesque Napoleon

Little more remains to be told. The metamorphosis of Louis Napoleon from President to Emperor in December 1852 had secured to his uncle tranquillity and high honours for the remainder of his days. The Presidency of the Senate was followed by the gift of the Marshal's baton, and the rank of Prince Imperial established him and his son on the very steps of the throne. Only his inveterate habit of spending more than his income, whatever its size, and certain family discords, remained to trouble him. With his daughter Mathilde he was for some time not on speaking terms. She had been in the habit of allowing him 40,000 francs a year out of the pension of 200,000 francs granted her by the Tsar as wife of Prince Demidoff. When, as Marshal of France, Prince Jerome received an annual salary of 30,000 francs, the Princess saw no necessity to pay him 40,000 francs from her pension. At the end of 1854, however, a reconciliation was effected, and the Princess had even to force herself to countenance the woman who had driven out the poor Marquise a year before. Difficulties occurred with Prince Napoleon, who showed much jealousy of certain other sons whose paternity his father admitted, and whom the old man

Exile, Restoration, and Death

wished to help. Jerome David he succeeded in involving in the ruin of his stepmother. He had far more serious dread of the American son and grandson. He perverted his father's mind against them successfully, but it took all his powerful influence to prevent the Emperor from recognising the justice of their claim to legitimacy by French law. He triumphed in this unrighteous campaign against the Patterson-Bonapartes when the Cour Impèriale rejected the appeal of the American branch in 1861, the year after Prince Jerome's death, and so secured to his own descendants the headship of the Bonapartes when the young Prince Imperial fell in Zululand.

The death of Jerome took place in the summer of 1860, in the seventy-fifth year of his age. Scandal made his mistress watch over him nearly to the last. He retired by the advice of his doctors to his chateau of Villegenis, and on the 24th June the end came. After receiving the sacraments of the Church he died peacefully, with both Napoleon and Mathilde at his bedside. A State funeral was accorded to him, and the Bishop of Troyes pronounced the oration on "the brother of Napoleon, faithful to the flag of France, who performed prodigies

The Burlesque Napoleon

at Waterloo." "If so much valour could not save the Empire, if all was lost save honour," declared the panegyrist, "the Prince at least has shown by his unvarying constancy in adverse fortune that outside the field of battle there remain sufficient great victories and glorious triumphs to be won!" The malicious did not hesitate, on their part, to connect with the closing of this long and wasted life numerous ridiculous tales to counterbalance the adulation of the Imperial flatterers.[1] But, on the whole, it may be said that Jerome Bonaparte received in death more true honour than he had any right to expect from his life. It was a very real mourner who followed his bier, wrapped in a huge black cloak, drawing the attention of all the crowd by the Napoleonic features that matched so well his name. And the last scene of all was a woman kneeling at his tomb, to weep and pray. It was the Marquise Bartolini, monstrously accused and cruelly cast off by him, yet unable to forget him now that he was dead.

[1] As, for instance, the story of the telegram received by the Emperor on the night before his uncle died. Tearing it open, Napoleon III., to his astonishment, read the words "*Le vieux persiste.*" An indignant inquiry elicited at length the explanation that what he had taken for *vieux* was really *mieux*, and that the message was intended to reassure him.

INDEX

ABRANTÈS, DUCHESS OF. *See* Junot, Madame
Alexander of Russia, 338, 342
Allix, General, 322
Augusta of Brunswick, 145

BARNEY, 57 *ff.*
Bartolini, Marquise, 369, 375, 380
Beauharnais, Eugène, 16, 19
Beauharnais, Hortense, 16, 19
Bercagny, 225, 256
Bernterode, Countess, 225
Beugnot, 187, 199, 325
Bonaparte, Jerome (Patterson), 104, 361 *ff.*
Bonaparte, Joseph, 13, 120, 335
Bonaparte, Letizia (Madame Mère) in Corsica, 4 *ff.*; in France, 11 *ff.*; and Jerome's first marriage, 77, 92; visit to Westphalia, 281; advice to Jerome, 359; and Jerome's eldest son, 361; death, 368
Bonaparte, Princess Mathilde, 359, 378
Bonaparte, Prince Napoleon, 359, 371 *ff.*, 380
Bourrienne, 45, 256
Brunswick, Duke of, 249, 348
Bülow, Baron von, 199, 209, 256, 284

CAMPAN, MADAME, 15
Carrega, Blanche, 107, 268 *ff.*
Catherine of Westphalia, 143; birth and family, 145; at Raincy, 152; appearance, 153; marriage with Jerome, 157; influence on him, 211;

Catherine of Westphalia—*continued*
blindness to his unfaithfulness, 262, 275; regent of Westphalia, 294; leaves Cassel, 318; appeals to her father, 336; refuses to leave Jerome, 337 *ff.*; robbed by Maubreuil, 341; in the Hundred Days, 357; at Rome, 364; death, 367
Catherine of Russia, 145

D'ALBIGNAC, GENERAL, 234, 281
Daru, 167 *ff.*
Davoust, Marshal, 285
Decrès, 79
Du Casse, Baron, 372, etc.
Du Coudras (Count Bernterode), 224

EBLÉ, GENERAL, 255, 281

FESCH, CARDINAL, 9, 26
Frederick II. of Würtemberg, 145 *ff.*, 337, 358
Fürstenstein. *See* Le Camus

GANTEAUME, ADMIRAL, 32

JEROME, KING OF WESTPHALIA, birth and childhood, 3 *ff.*; leaves Corsica, 11; at the Collège Irlandais, 15; at Juilly, 19; early debts, 23; his duel, 27; sent to sea, 32; on San Domingo expedition, 36 *ff.*; attack on British merchantman, 47; resigns command of his ship, 49; lands in Virginia, 55; meets Elizabeth Patterson, 65; first marriage, 74; attempts to leave America, 86 *ff.*; returns to Europe, 92; yields to

Index

Jerome, King of Westphalia—*continued*
Napoleon, 99; letters to Elizabeth, 108; mission to Algiers, 116; commands the *Vétéran*, 122; adventure at Concarneau, 126; made Rear-Admiral, 127; campaign in Silesia, 130 *ff.*; made King, 138; second marriage, 157; enters Westphalia, 164; struggle with Jollivet, 193, 258; at Erfurt, 200; threatened by plots, 228; Saxon campaign, 233; resistance to Continental System, 253; desires to resign, 254; creates Westphalian Order, 260; at Compiègne, 267; and Hanover, 283; and the Polish throne, 295; described by Countess Potocka, 298, 365; his blunder in 1812, 301 *ff.*; last year in Westphalia, 311 *ff.*; flight from Cassel, 322-24; in France, 329; at Blois, 335; during the Hundred Days, 345 *ff.*; at Waterloo, 348; in exile, 355 *ff.*; loses Catherine, 367; third marriage, 369; return to France, 370; in old age, 377; death, 379; levity of character, 22, 101, etc.; extravagance, 120, 175 *ff.*, 224, 255, 313, etc.; gallantries, 135, 179, 215 *ff.*, etc.; military ambitions, 27, 129, 292; attitude to his subjects, 199, 231

Jollivet, Count, 178, 190, 258, etc.
Josephine, Empress, 16 *ff.*
Junot, Marshal (Duke of Abrantès), 95, 235
Junot, Madame, 18, 95, 152 *ff.*

KEUDELSTEIN. *See* Carrega *and* La Flèche

LA FLÈCHE (Baron Keudelstein), 269, 277
Le Camus, Alexandre (Count of Fürstenstein), 55; Madame Junot's impressions of, 97; character and manners, 176; Minister of Foreign Affairs, 177; marriage, 232; interview with Reinhard, 243; Reinhard's view of, 244 *n.*
Leclerc, General, 37 *ff.*, 45
Löwenstein, Baroness, 276, 312

MACDERMOT, 15
Malchus, 285
Marie-Louise, Empress, 297 *n.*, 335
Maubreuil, Marquis of, 270 *ff.*, 339 *ff.*
Meyronnet (Count Wellingerode), 55, 85, 220
Morio, General, 130, 268, 290
Müller, Johann von, 188

NAPOLEON I., EMPEROR, and his family's education, 5; his choice of schools, 16; early lenience to Jerome, 23; naval ideas, 31, 118; and San Domingo, 36; severe letter to Jerome, 49, 194, 235; attitude over Jerome's American marriage, 77 *ff.*, 109; designs for Jerome, 128, 137, 150; creates Westphalia, 138; and the Westphalian Constitution, 161; exactions from Westphalia, 167, 181, 286; sends Reinhard to Cassel, 201; anger over Saxon campaign, 241; enforces Continental System in Westphalia, 253, 283; cedes Hanover to Jerome, 259; takes it back, 282; and Poland, 295 *ff.*; conduct to Jerome in 1812, 304; refuses interview, 315; and Jerome in France, 327 *ff.*; last meeting with Catherine, 340; in the Hundred Days, 346 *ff.*; effect of his death on the family, 369
Napoleon III., Emperor, 369, 374
Norvins, J. de, 37, 187, 255, etc.

Index

PAOLI, 6 *ff.*
Pascault, Henrietta (Madame Rewbell), 65, 251
Patterson, Elizabeth (Madame Jerome Bonaparte), her family and education, 62 *ff.*; determination to marry Jerome, 67; married, 74; at Washington, 83; wrecked on the *Philadelphia*, 89; at Lisbon, 95; goes to Holland and England, 103; return to United States, 105; refuses Jerome's offers, 111; her belief in Jerome's love, 112; last meeting with him, 360
Patterson, William, senior, 62 *ff.*
Perman, Madame, 18, 25
Perman, Laure. *See* Junot, Madame
Pichon, 56 *ff.*, 189, 287
Pius VII., Pope, 109

Potocka, Countess, 297 *ff.*

REINHARD, COUNT, 201, 242, 291, etc.
Rewbell, 55, 250

SALHA (Count Höne), 127, 281
Siméon, 187, 261

TRUCHSESS - WALDBURG, COUNTESS OF, 217 *ff.*

VANDAMME, GENERAL, 130 *ff.*
Villeneuve, Admiral, 39 *ff.*

WILLAUMEZ, ADMIRAL, 72, 118 *ff.*
Würtemberg, Prince Royal of, 274, 336
Würtemberg, King of. *See* Frederick II.